William Hart. Boyd

The queen cook book

William Hart. Boyd
The queen cook book
ISBN/EAN: 9783744786027

Printed in Europe, USA, Canada, Australia, Japan

Cover: Foto ©Lupo / pixelio.de

More available books at **www.hansebooks.com**

THE
QUEEN COOK BOOK.

A Careful Compilation of Recipes and Practical Information for Cooking and Other Household Requirements.

BY

MRS. WILLIAM HART BOYD.

FLEMING H. REVELL COMPANY,
CHICAGO,   NEW YORK,   TORONTO.

To My Daughter,

AT WHOSE EARNEST REQUEST
THE WORK WAS COMMENCED,
I MOST AFFECTIONATELY DEDICATE
THIS VOLUME.

THOUGHTS BY THE WAY.

"The world is ever as we take it,
And life, dear friend, is what we make it."

'A desire for useful knowledge is a laudable ambition."

Persistent training tends to efficiency.

"Live so that thy life some others may bless."

"For the burden borne in patience,
Joy will crown the endless years."

"This is but 'Gold Dust,'
This but the thought,
The real block of gold
Is the deed well wrought."
—I. P. B.

"If ye abide in me, and my words abide in you, ye shall ask what ye will, and it shall be done unto you." John xv: 7.

"Give us this day our daily bread." Matt. vi: 11.

"Be of good courage and he shall strengthen your heart, all ye that hope in the Lord." Ps. xxxi: 24.

PREFACE.

When any woman of the royal families of Europe has in prospect the sharing of the throne with the king of a nation, or of ruling alone as its sovereign, she is especially prepared to fill the position in a manner befitting a queen, that she may rule her subjects well. The royal girls of European nations are very carefully educated and why should not the girls of our beloved America, or of any country, who are royal only as their characters are such, be well educated and fitted to preside over homes which sooner or later may be theirs. Every wife and mother should be queen of her own home, if she is fortunate enough to possess one, and she can not fill her position in its full meaning without a knowledge of cooking and all domestic economy. Even if she does not cook as a rule herself, she will find many annoyances, embarrassments and perhaps an absolute stand-still in household affairs, if she has not as much or more knowledge of the kitchen arts than her cook. Then too, hired cooks are as uncertain as April weather and when they say farewell and no one is at hand to take the vacated place, that housekeeper is in a sad plight, who is ignorant of how to cook and without experience. We advise all girls and women, if they have already grown to womanhood without a knowledge of cooking to learn this indispensable art while mother, sister or friend is with them, to help and give information in the more difficult parts. There are so many nice little points to know, that are learned only by practice, which are too numerous to put in print, and are scarcely thought of, perhaps, till one is in the midst of the work. It seems to be one sad lack to-day that mothers so generally neglect to train their daughters in the many practical methods connected with housekeeping. They can be learned only by degrees, and must largely be acquired when the opportunity offers, not waiting for a stated time.

> "Knowledge is gold to him who can discern,
> That he who loves to know must love to learn."

A cook book lying on the shelf does not make a good cook, but study is absolutely necessary, and must be joined with carefulness and good judgment. As the public is already supplied with many books of this kind, (still, this is one by itself) it is with some misgivings that this volume is presented.

It is the fruit of a life-long experience in housekeeping and the writer trusts it will prove both helpful and instructive to the numerous home-makers and render their lives easier, brighter and better.

INTRODUCTION.

HOME.

> "'Tis home where'er the heart is,
> Where'er its loved ones dwell."

There is a charm in a well ordered home which commends itself to every observer. A man's and woman's home is their earthly paradise. The true home feeling is a matter of quality, and is not dependent upon the things which can be bought. It is found in the absence of the artificial, and in the presence of the natural and the real. Here, as elsewhere, it is the spirit that giveth life. I believe there is as much or more true home feeling in homes which are exceedingly plain and simple, homes in which the strife for maintenance is a constant struggle, as in those possessing every luxury wealth and taste can contribute. It is free alike to all; it is largely independent of outward conditions because it depends upon the spirit of the individuals that compose the home circle. Love, gentleness, truthfulness, unselfishness, patience, self control, courtesy, considerateness and self adaptation are jewels that never shine more brightly than in the home. As the atmosphere depends upon the united heads of the family, it should be their constant study to make it so attractive (without any "family jars") that of all other spots, they and the children leave that with the most regret, and turn to it from the outside world with the most delight.

> "A few sunny pictures in simple frames shrined,
> A few precious volumes. the wealth of the mind;
> And here and there treasured some rare gem of art,
> To kindle the fancy or soften the heart."

> "Home is not merely roof and room;
>   It needs nothing to endure it;
> Home is where the heart can bloom,
>   Where there's some kind lip to cheer it!
>
> What is home with none to meet?
>   None to welcome, none to greet us?
> Home is sweet, and only sweet,
>   Where there's one we love to meet us."

THE QUEEN COOK BOOK.

Wheat Bread and Biscuit.

1 pint and three table-spoons milk
2 quarts flour
2 even teaspoons salt
½ tea cup yeast

Take out one pint of flour for kneading next morning, make a hollow in center of flour, put all the ingredients in, stir together, then stir in the flour to a thick batter (not dough). Use a tin pan with a good fitting cover, then wrap in double flannel and set it on two warm bricks in a warm room over night. (It is a good plan to keep two bricks in the oven.) Take it out early next morning, soon as you can get it warmed through. Work in the largest half of your reserved flour and knead ten minutes, by doubling the hand and pressing the knuckles in the dough, lifting one fist up, as you put the other down, with some force. Then flour the board and knead on that for ten minutes more with the palm of the hand, using the rest of the flour or more, having the dough as soft as possible to manage well. At first the soft dough will seem to stick and trouble the inexperienced cook, but she will soon learn to manage it, to her great relief. The dough must not get cold. Butter your pan before making out the bread. Set it in heater and keep warm. If good it will be light in one hour. Raise up the edge of loaf; if it looks light and foamy (not stringy) it is light for baking. Bake three-fourths of an hour, if oven is hot enough. If you can hold hand in oven till you can count twenty only, it is right heat, or if a teaspoon of flour on a tin browns in five minutes. Bread should be in the oven fifteen minutes before it begins to brown. When baked through take it out of pan and stand it on end; lean it against something, so as to let the air circulate around it, to give a dry crust. When perfectly cold, put it in a sweet clean jar, cover with paper and plate. Do not wrap a cloth around it, as our mothers used to, as the cloth absorbs the moisture of the bread. If you wet the bread with water you can put one rounded teaspoon of butter in water. Milk or water should always be warm. This receipt is for bottled yeast and makes one large loaf. If you use dried yeast, take one-fourth of a cake for a loaf and a half cup more wetting, and you can knead it and raise it twice after the sponge. To make good bread it is best to know how to select good flour. When pressed tightly, it adheres to the hand, remains in shape and shows the imprint of the lines on the hand. It has a yellowish white tinge and when made into a paste with water, and well worked, is tough and elastic. Use one kind of flour for bread, pastry and cake. After selecting the flour, the next important thing is to have good strong, sweet yeast. The compressed yeast cakes are very good and convenient. In large cities you can obtain the soft yeast cakes done up in tin foil. They are very nice, but must be fresh. I much prefer the flavor of bread made from bottled yeast. I have been thus minute in describing the process of bread making for the sake of the inexperienced, while it may seem unneccessary to the practical housekeeper. Always use a tin pan to raise the dough in. Wooden bowls are not good.

BOTTLED YEAST.

6 medium-sized potatoes ½ cup sugar
2½ quarts water ½ cup salt
1 handful good hops ½ pint yeast or ½ of a cake

Boil the six potatoes in the two and a half quarts of water; when just done skim them into a gallon crock, mash fine, and stir light with a fork. Put hops in a thin bag and boil five minutes in the potato water, then squeeze dry and pour the hop water on to the potatoes, sugar and salt. When cool enough to hold the finger in it, put in the yeast. Make it about 3 o'clock in the afternoon. Stir it well every hour till bedtime. Keep it warm and covered all night. Bottle it the first thing in the morning in pint bottles. If good it will sparkle and foam when stirred. Put your corks in loosely until they stop popping out, say three hours. Then tie them down as beer bottles are tied. One-half cup of this yeast makes a large loaf, ten inches long, six inches wide, and three or four inches high—a good size for sandwiches cut in three pieces. For a large family make twice the quantity, which would be one gallon. It will keep six weeks in cool weather, and four in hot weather. Keep it in cellar. This yeast simply foams, never rises any higher.

SALT-RISING BREAD.

Stir into one pint of warm milk one teaspoon of salt, flour enough to make quite a thick batter, beating it well. Set the dish in hot water till light, then put it in the center of flour in bread pan, and add warm milk and salt according to desired quantity. Make it up (without sponging) and put into pans the same as other bread. The yeast will rise in about six hours. You can take a part of the yeast and make a small tin of biscuit for tea.

Bread for the Sea.

Bread on sea, on account of constant moisture, seldom has crispness as on shore. If you are yachting, it is wise to have tight tin boxes to keep your bread in, wrapped in thick white paper. Bob, the sea cook, says: "I buy my yeast of the brewer, and take a board two feet square and cover it with white blotting paper. I pour my yeast on the paper and stand it in the sun. When it is dry I break up the yeast cake in small pieces and put it in a ground-glass-stoppered bottle. This yeast will be good for two months. One heaping tablespoon of this dried yeast is sufficient for three pints of wetting, which will make three large loaves. For making the bread, sponge and raise it the same as other bread." When the bread is being made, he says: "Now comes real work, and go for it. Mash her and knead her all you can." I think this is good for all bread. Let rise, and bake as other bread. When bread or cake cleaves from the pan it is done, and it also has a hollow sound when you knock on the bottom of loaf. Do not open the oven door when the bread or cake is just boiling hot, for it is almost in a liquid state and the least cold air will make it fall in the center.

Rye and Indian Bread.

3 cups sour milk
2 cups rye meal
1½ cups corn meal

½ cup molasses
1½ teaspoon soda
2 teaspoons salt

Put one teaspoon soda in milk and the half spoon in the molasses. If you use sweet milk use three teaspoons of baking powder. Beat well together as soft as loaf cake. Steam three hours, or bake one hour and a half. I prefer sweet milk and three teaspoons of baking powder.

RYE BREAD, BAKED.

Make a sponge of half wheat and half rye, the same as for other bread. Double the quantity of salt. In the morning add sufficient rye flour to make a soft dough. Knead lightly; when light bake in a moderate oven one hour or more.

GRAHAM BREAD, BAKED.

Make a sponge the same as rye only using the graham flour, adding one-half cup molasses and two teaspoons salt. One-half teaspoon soda in molasses.

BOSTON BROWN BREAD.

2 large cups corn meal
1 large cup rye meal
½ cup yeast
½ cup molasses
1 teaspoon soda
2 teaspoons salt

Make a pint of sponge early in the morning, with your yeast, of wheat flour. Scald your meal stiff with boiling water, when cool and sponge is light, stir all the ingredients well together as stiff as cake only. It should be ready to bake in an hour, or steam, just which you prefer. Steam three hours or bake in slow oven one hour and a half.

BOSTON BROWN BREAD.

1 pint corn meal
1 pint graham flour
½ cup yeast
½ cup molasses
½ teaspoon soda
2 teaspoons salt

Scald the meal with boiling milk. When cool enough add all the ingredients and the cool milk enough to make a sponge batter, stir in the rest of the flour next morning, beat well, let rise. Can steam it three hours and bake one-half hour, or bake it one hour and a half.

GRAHAM BREAD, WITHOUT YEAST, BAKED.

3½ cups graham flour   1 heaping teaspoon salt
¾ cup of molasses   2 teaspoons soda

Equal parts of sour and sweet milk to make a batter as thick as pound cake. Put half of soda in the milk and half in molasses, beat to a foam and add to the batter. Bake one and a half hours in a moderate oven. This has the merit of being more quickly made than others when you discover there is not bread enough for the next meal. It is nicest when just cold. You can add one-half pint of hot oat meal gruel to any of these brown breads if you choose.

BOSTON BROWN BREAD, STEAMED.

2 cups graham flour   1 cup milk
1 cup white flour   1 cup molasses
1 teaspoon soda   2 teaspoons (even) salt

Steam three hours and bake twenty minutes.

OLD SCHOOL YEAST.

Boil two liberal handfuls of good hops in three quarts of water in a thin bag, squeeze dry. When cool stir in one quart of flour, one small cup of sugar, and one small cup of salt. Cover this in a stone jar and stand three days in a warm place stirring it occasionally. On the fourth day add one quart of nicely mashed potatoes. Let it stand until the day following, when it will be ready for use. A small half tea cup is enough for two good sized loaves of bread. If kept in a cool place, will keep six weeks in summer, and three months in winter. This yeast does not foam. You may think it worthless; try it and you will not doubt. *Messenger.*

POTATO YEAST.

Take ten potatoes from the dinner pot; wet a pint of flour with a pint of the potato water. Two tablespoons each of white sugar and salt. A yeast cake dissolved. Let it rise till next morning then cover tight or bottle. This will keep two weeks. Three-fourths of a cup will raise two loaves. Sponge and raise again.

PARKER HOUSE ROLLS.

1 pint boiled milk	1 large tablespoon butter
2 quarts flour	1 teaspoon salt
½ cup yeast	1 heaping tablespoon sugar

Beat all well together for ten minutes in soft sponge for over night, then knead well in the morning, roll out thin and soft, cut with a roll cutter or cut with a pint pail cover. Rub it over with a little melted butter and lap over like a turnover, let rise, bake twenty minutes. Heat over carefully for supper or lunch. These are splendid and never fail if directions are followed. Keep warm. Knead fifteen minutes.

You can use this same recipe using the yeast cake, making the dough stiff enough to knead fifteen minutes at night instead of sponge, then knead it fifteen minutes more in the morning. Let stand till 3 P. M., knead fifteen minutes more, make in rolls, when light bake for tea.

FRENCH BREAKFAST ROLLS.

Take of good bread dough that is kneaded ready for its last rising what would make a half loaf of bread, more or less, as you need, in quantity. Cut from this pieces of dough about the size of a biscuit (after working in two tablespoons of butter and one of sugar if you like it). Then roll the pieces of dough under the hand till it is round. Flatten it a little and then let it stand on the molding board till the last of the rolls are finished. Then let them remain five minutes covered to prove if light. Have a saucer of melted butter in which dip the ball of your hand and press the whole weight of the ball of your hand across the center of each roll so as to dent it almost through. Then fold them over and place in a baking pan so they do not touch. Let rise till very light. It will most likely take twice as long as bread. They should bake in twelve minutes. If you wish these rolls for tea or for the next morning breakfast set them in the refrigerator. They are very delicious when thus treated.

BAKING-POWDER BISCUIT.

1 quart flour
3 heaping tablespoons butter
1½ cup milk
2 heaping teaspoons baking-powder
1 teaspoon salt

The first thing is to see if the oven is very hot. Have everything ready to work with, then sift the baking-powder, salt and flour together twice; then rub the butter in well. Mix with the milk as soft and as little as you can handle it. Roll from half to three-quarters of an inch thick and bake in a quick oven. Some set them ten minutes in the cold. Let all the ingredients be right cold. Success depends largely on speed and the hot oven. All biscuits, rusks or rolls when nearly baked can be washed over on top either with milk or the sweetened white of egg.

CREAM BISCUIT.

Cream biscuit and cream short cake are made the same as baking powder biscuit, using cream (or if very rich use half cream and milk) in place of milk and butter.

RUSKS.

1 cup sugar
1 cup butter
2 eggs
2 cups milk
½ cup yeast
1 teaspoon salt

Stir butter and sugar to a cream; add the eggs beaten separately, then the milk warm, and yeast, with flour enough to make a sponge; let this stand in a warm place till light, then knead in flour enough to make soft biscuits; cut with cutter and put in baking pan, let them stand three hours; bake forty minutes in a moderate oven. It is always best to set the sponge at night, then it is ready to bake the next morning. If they are desired warm for tea, they can be set early in the morning.

GALETTES.

1 quart flour
½ pint sweet milk
½ cup butter
⅓ cup yeast
1 even teaspoon salt
1 tablespoon sugar
3 eggs

Use what flour yo need for the sponge, set to rise, keep warm, when light work in the rest of flour, roll out, cut round, handling the dough as lightly as possible. Set to rise; when light bake fifteen minutes in a hot oven. Brush the top with egg. These are most delicious. Eat hot, or when cold split and toast.

SALLY LUNN, RAISED.

3 pints flour
1 pint milk
½ cup yeast
1 tablespoon sugar
3 eggs beaten separately
1 teaspoon salt
Butter the size of an egg

Warm the milk, and soften the butter. Mix it in morning if wanted for tea. This must be stirred, let rise, when light, stir down and pour into dripping pans, let Sally take another rise. Bake from three-fourths to one hour. This is broken up.

SALLY LUNN WITH BAKING-POWDER.

1 quart flour
1 pint sweet milk
2 teaspoons baking-powder
1 cup butter
2 eggs, 1 teaspoon salt
1 tablespoon sugar

Bake twenty minutes in a quick oven, in cups.

TEA BISCUIT, RAISED.

1 pint milk
3 or more pints flour
2 heaping tablespoons butter
2 eggs
½ cup yeast
1 teaspoon sugar
1 teaspoon salt

Scald the milk, add butter, salt and sugar, when cool enough add the yeast and flour enough for sponge, beat light for six minutes. Let rise over night. Then beat eggs well, and add sufficient flour for a soft dough. Roll out about one-half inch thick, cut into biscuits, let rise and bake in quick oven. If made with care, these are very fine. You can add four mashed potatoes, rubbed through a colander, if preferred.

MUFFINS AND GEMS.

Graham Muffins.

1½ cups graham flour
1 full cup milk, take out two tablespoons
1 heaping teaspoon salt
3 tablespoons brown sugar
3 tablespoons melted butter
2 teaspoons baking-powder
1 egg

Beat the egg, stir all well together, bake in gem pans one-half hour, a steady bake, do not burn them. This quantity makes eight gems. Fill each pan only one-half full. Very fine for breakfast or tea.

Corn Meal Muffins.

1 cup corn meal
¾ cup white flour
1 cup sweet milk
1 heaping teaspoon salt
2 tablespoons melted butter
2 tablespoons white sugar
2 teaspoons baking powder
2 eggs

This quantity makes eight muffins. Corn meal always requires slower bake than flour. Fill the gem pans only half full; or bake in one loaf.

Corn Bread.

1 cup corn meal
½ cup sugar
½ cup milk
½ cup cream
1 cup flour
2 eggs
1 teaspoon salt
2 teaspoons baking-powder

Bake in two loaves.

Flour Muffins.

8 tablespoons, heaping, of flour
1 teaspoon butter
1 teaspoon salt
½ cup milk
The whites of two eggs
1 heaping teaspoon baking-powder

Measure the spoonsful all heaping, beat light and

bake in twenty minutes, either in cups or gem pans, heating very hot and butter them before filling. If liked add a spoon of white sugar and brush the top with sweetened egg—the whites.

OAT MEAL GEMS.

1 cup sweet milk
1 cup oat meal fine
4 tablespoons melted butter
2 teaspoons, rounded, of baking-powder.
1½ cups flour
1 egg
2 teaspoons salt
3 tablespoons sugar

Fill gem pans half full, bake thirty-five minutes in moderate oven. Make thin enough to pour. This fills eight pans. One can easily double any of these recipes for a large family.

RAISED MUFFINS.

1 pint milk
3 cups flour
2 eggs
2 tablespoons butter
½ cup yeast
1 teaspoon salt

Scald the milk, add the butter, when cool enough add the salt and flour, beat well and let sponge over night. Then add the eggs beaten separately, beat well, put in buttered gem pans, let stand fifteen or twenty minutes, till light, bake in moderate oven.

CRUMPETS.

1 pint milk
3 cups flour
4 tablespoons butter
½ cup yeast
1 teaspoon salt

Scald the milk; when cool enough stir all together, beat vigorously ten minutes, stand in a warm place till light, about five hours. Butter the muffin rings and place on hot greased griddle. Fill each ring half full of the batter; bake brown, then turn with cake turner till brown on the other side, till well cooked in center. When ready to use them, split open, toast and butter them nicely, and serve quickly while hot.

BREAD BISCUITS.

Take one pound of bread dough, more or less, as needed. When it is being molded for the pans, work into it two tablespoons of butter, at first chopping it in with a knife. Sprinkle flour on the board and knead for eight minutes, then form into small biscuits, place in your pan, keep warm till light, perhaps two hours, and bake.

WHEAT AND INDIAN BREAD.

2 quarts Indian meal
1 quart wheat flour
2 teaspoons salt
1 cup good hop yeast

Scald the meal with boiling water till as thin as mush; when cool, so as not to kill the yeast, stir all together, knead it as soft as possible, and put it in baking pan to rise; when it cracks open and looks light, bake two hours in stove oven with paper over it, to keep from getting too hard, leaving it in warm oven, not hot, all night. It must bake moderately. A brick oven is the best for leaving in all night. If liked, add two tablespoons of molasses, with a little soda in it.

CORN BREAD FOR BREAKFAST.

3 cups white corn meal or yellow corn meal
2 cups wheat flour
2 heaping teaspoons baking-powder
1 teacup white sugar
1 heaping tablespoon butter
2 eggs
Milk as needed

This is for teacup measure. Mix it soft so as to

pour out into baking pan, have it an inch thick, corn meal swells very much. Bake three-fourths of an hour. Cut in pieces like cake.

CORN BREAD.

2 cups corn meal
1 cup flour
3 eggs
2 teaspoons baking-powder

2½ cups sweet milk
2 tablespoons butter
2 tablespoons sugar
2 teaspoons salt

BREAKFAST PUFFS.

1 cup milk
2 eggs—salt

1 cup flour
2 tablespoons cream

Have the cups or gem pans hot and only half full.

WAFFLES.

1 pint sour cream having one-half milk

1 heaping pint flour
1 even teaspoon soda

3 eggs—salt

To be baked in waffle irons at just the right heat to be brown when done. Eat with butter and powdered sugar or maple syrup. Very nice for tea. Beat eggs light.

BUCKWHEAT CAKES.

Get buckwheat free from grit. It is also adulterated with rye. Into one pint warm water put one teaspoon of salt, two cups of buckwheat flour, and one-half cup yeast. Beat well and stand in a warm place twenty-four hours. Dissolve one-half teaspoon, or less at first, of saleratus, in water enough to make the batter as thin as you can turn them, and bake brown and dry. Beat thoroughly, bake on a hot griddle. Leave a cup of this batter in jar to start the next with. I bake every other morning, stirring up over night. After the first time, they will need a full teaspoon of saleratus to make sufficiently sweet. Stir up entirely new ones with new yeast every three weeks.

BREAD GRIDDLE CAKES.

One pint bread crumbs soaked in milk over night. Rub through a colander, add two well beaten eggs, a teaspoon salt, a cup of flour, with just milk enough to make a thin batter. Teaspoon baking-powder sifted in flour.

RICE GRIDDLE CAKES.

These are made the same way as the bread griddle cakes, using the rice boiled to a jell and hot, instead of bread. Or use rice flour.

SWEET CORN GRIDDLE CAKES.

1 pint grated corn	1 teaspoon salt
1 cup flour	Milk enough to mix well
1 tablespoon melted butter	1 teaspoon baking-powder
4 eggs	

FLOUR GRIDDLE CAKES.

Sift two teaspoons of baking powder into one pint of flour. Stir in one cup of sweet cream, and milk enough to make a thin batter with two beaten eggs. One teaspoon of salt. I think all griddle cakes are more tender wet with sour milk or sour cream and soda. Half cream and half milk. A great deal depends upon the right heat of griddle.

CREAM SHORT CAKE.

1 quart flour	1 teaspoon salt
2 cups sour or sweet cream	1 even teaspoon soda

If sweet cream is used, use two teaspoons of baking

powder instead of soda. If one has no cream, can use two cups sweet milk and two tablespoons of butter cut with a knife into the flour, with salt and baking powder. Whenever baking powder is used it should be sifted twice through the flour with the salt. Roll out long and bake in long tin; cross the top with three tined fork. Some prefer to cut them into biscuit, I think they are better.

ORANGE SHORT CAKE.

1 quart flour
1 cup and three tablespoons milk
1 tablespoon white sugar
1 egg
1 teaspoon salt
2 heaping teaspoons baking-powder
3 tablespoons butter

This quantity makes two short cakes

Sift baking powder and salt through flour twice; then chop the butter in flour, then rub it in. Mix the whole together as quickly and with as little handling as possible. Roll into three sheets, long as your tin, each about half an inch thick. Bake, laying one sheet on top of the other, butter the under sheets lightly. Slice the oranges while it is baking, pour off the juice, sprinkle well with granulated sugar. As quick as baked, separate the sheet, spread with butter and put a thick layer of oranges between the two layers. Set it in oven four minutes. The oranges should be cut from around the core in small pieces, taking out all the seeds. This is delicious. This is the best kind of crust for strawberry shortcake.

MARYLAND BISCUIT.

1 quart flour
½ pint milk and water each
2 tablespoons butter
1 teaspoon salt

Rub the salt and butter well in the flour, add the

wetting gradually to the flour, stirring and kneading all the while—add just enough to moisten the flour, the dough must be very stiff; knead five minutes; and beat with the back of an ax thirty minutes. Then form into small round biscuits, stick with a fork three times, each one, bake in a moderately quick oven about twenty-five minutes. Brown on top and bottom.

EGG BISCUIT.

1 quart flour	5 tablespoons butter
5 tablespoons sugar	2 teaspoons baking-powder
5 eggs well beaten	1 teaspoon salt

Sift the flour, salt, sugar and baking-powder together twice, then rub the butter in, and add the eggs; knead until light and elastic, cover with a damp cloth, let stand fifteen minutes. Roll out into a sheet a quarter of an inch thick, cut with round cutter. Drop a few at a time into boiling water, till edges curl, then into cold water for a minute, place in buttered pans, bake in moderate oven to a light brown.

CORN MEAL MUSH.

To three pints of boiling water add one pint of corn meal, a heaping teaspoon salt; wet the meal with one pint of this water before heating; then when the two pints boil, stir in the wet meal; keep it where it will just boil good and not burn for a full hour or more, stirring often; use a hard wood paddle, two feet long, with a blade two inches wide and seven inches long to stir with. The secret of good mush is its thorough cooking, which gives it the relish. It needs to be stiff enough to slice when cold. You can double or treble this quantity according to size of family.

Fried Mush.

An acceptable breakfast dish is made by slicing cold mush thin and frying in half butter and half lard. Can dip in beaten egg and cracker crumbs if you like it.

Oat Meal, Cracked Wheat, Hominy, Rice.

For one even *tea* cup full of oat meal washed in three waters, pour on one good pint and a half of good sweet milk, one teaspoon of salt. Put it in double boiler; let it swell for one hour at the boiling point, stirring four times; then let it just boil for another hour. If you have no milk use water, but it is not so good. Cook cracked wheat, hominy and rice the same way. Wash each till there are no black specks in the water. I have washed one cup of hominy in ten waters, before I stopped looking for black specks. Keep the water in motion as you pour it off, so the specks will rise. Hominy is the white southern corn. If you wish either of these for breakfast put a little water on it the night before; it will swell over night.

Plain Fritters.

1 cup milk   2 eggs
1½ cups flour   1 teaspoon salt
        1 teaspoon baking-powder

Sift flour and baking powder together twice, beat the eggs to a froth, then beat all thoroughly together, stiff enough to cut soft with a spoon to drop into boiling lard; when brown on one side turn and brown on the other; a wire skimmer is best to take them out with; then sprinkle fine sugar over them while hot, and cinnamon if you like. If fat gets too hot drop in two or three slices of raw potatoes or a bit of dry bread, which furnishes something for the heat to act upon. Test the heat also by dropping in a little bit of batter. If the heat is right it will quickly rise in a light ball with a splutter, and soon brown; serve hot.

Pork fritters are made by dropping bits of fried breakfast bacon in the batter. Fruit fritters by dipping quarters or halves in batter, having one piece in each fritter. Moisten the flour with milk an hour before using, that the flour may swell and thus be lighter. Do not put a fork in them; lay them on brown paper to drain a minute.

Sweet Corn Oyster Fritters.

2 finely floured crackers, 1 pint grated sweet corn
   or more if needed   2 eggs
           Salt and pepper

Must hold together well.

Beat well together; have ready in spider your hot lard (half of it beef drippings is better, they will not soak fat so much) but not scorching hot, drop in little cakes about the size of an oyster, when brown turn and fry on the other side, watching constantly for fear of burning. If fat is just right heat, the corn fritter will be light and delicious; if not, soggy. Beat the whites of eggs to a stiff froth just before frying. Serve hot to eat with meats; have them cooking while the table is being served.

Japanese Fritters.

Cut stale bread into slices a half inch thick, then cut the slices in pieces about two inches square. Soak these squares in fritter batter, about one minute and fry in boiling fat, turning them as they brown; when done skim out with wire skimmer, lay on brown paper, serve hot. Serve with fairy sauce, or maple syrup.

French Fritters.

1 tumbler water	½ cup butter
1 teaspoon sugar	1 teaspoon salt

Put all together in stew pan on the stove, and when well heated so that the butter is thoroughly melted, stir in rapidly one heaping pint of flour. Take it from the fire and break in one egg, blend it and break in another, and then another, till five have been broken in; then in very hot lard and butter drop spoonfuls of this mixture and cook as fritters. When you take them out roll them in sugar and cinnamon, or eat with fairy butter, as you like.

From a French Chef in Heidelberg.

Fried Cakes.

1 cup milk	1 tablespoon butter
1 cup fine sugar	2 teaspoons baking-powder
1 teaspoon salt	1 egg

Sift the baking powder into flour enough to make a soft dough, say one quart or more of flour. Roll out one-half inch thick or less, then cut in strips and twist, or cut with cutter, then with smaller cutter cut a hole in center and fry in fat.

Queen of Doughnuts.

1 cup butter	1½ cups sugar
1 small cup yeast	1½ pints milk
5 eggs	1 teaspoon salt

Stir all well together in stiff sponge over night, after you have stirred butter and sugar to a cream, and beaten the eggs separately, have the milk warm and add the yeast. Make them stiff enough in the morning after kneading well to roll out; pinch off pieces as large as a walnut, roll into balls, let rise, roll out some, and cut in rings, or whatever form you like, sprinkle a clean napkin (which lay on the board) or two slightly with flour, lay the cakes on napkins on board, cover lightly, let rise; roll about one-half inch thick, keep warm, after they are cut out, let stand from thirty to fifty minutes, then have ready a spider of boiling fat (suet is best); put the cakes into this fat upside down, that is, the side that was top on the napkin, should be the under side in the fat, because the crust which forms on top prevents them from rising. As soon as they rise and are brown on the under side slip the fork under the cake and turn. Cook them done through. Drain on brown paper. If you prefer it sift together powdered sugar, cinnamon or nutmeg, and sift it on cakes while hot.

VERY NICE RAISED DOUGHNUTS.

1 quart raised dough	1 tablespoon butter
1 cup sugar	1 egg, 1 teaspoon salt

Work thoroughly together, roll one-half inch thick, cut in what shape you like and let rise thirty or fifty minutes, then fry in hot fat as other cakes.

DRINKS.

TEA.

The tea plant in its mild state is a bushy shrub, and sometimes a small tree, but in cultivation is kept dwarfed. Like other plants long in cultivation, the cultivation has produced several varieties. The original country of tea is not known. It was found in a wild state in Assam. It only grows in very warm climates. The Portuguese are said to have been the first to import tea into Europe, and were acquainted with it as early as the sixteenth century. In 1664 it is recorded that the English East India Company made the Queen of England what was considered the brilliant present of two pounds of tea. Previous to this, and at this time it was the custom among European nations to make tea of hot infusions of various kinds of leaves, notably those of the sage (salvia), which at one time had a high reputation, and was regarded as a sort of panacea. Indeed, it is a good hot drink, for one who has just taken a cold. Its dried leaves were taken to China by the Dutch East India Company to be exchanged for tea. Teas are classed as black and green, distinctions not due to the production of different species, but to the age of the leaf when gathered, and the methods of preparation. It is raised in abundance in China, Japan, East Indies, and now some in California. The quality of the tea depends largely upon the age of the leaves at the time of picking. The younger the leaves the more delicate their flavor. There are four different pickings through the season. Teas of the cheaper kind are very much adulterated. Never buy the powdered tea. The best quality of black teas is the pekoa. The best green teas are the best Japan, and the gunpowder, (which are the first gatherings), are the best. Excessive use of tea produces wakefulness and increased mental and bodily activity, which is followed by a reaction that brings exhaustion and a corresponding depression. Most of the unpleasant effects of tea are ascribed to the volatile oil. The long continued breathing of air impregnated with this oil, produces illness in the packers of tea, who press it down with their bare feet; and the tea tasters at the tea marts in China, who are ever careful not to swallow the infusion, are obliged in a few years to give up their lucrative positions, with shattered constitutions. The Chinese, who drink tea at all times, are careful to use none less than a year old, as in that time the oil either evaporates or is so modified that it ceases to be injurious. Is it not safer not to drink tea at all, and healthier and more nourishing to drink milk either hot or cold (but do not boil) for supper or have a cup of hot cocoa, or chocolate made of milk? The best way to steep all kinds of tea is, take one even teaspoon of green tea for two cups of boiling water, after you have brought it just to a quick boil with two tablespoons of water. Black tea is coarser, take a heaping teaspoon for two cups and steep it the same way. The old custom of boiling black tea twenty minutes makes it blacker, but not a refreshing cup of tea. Wash and dry the tea steeper, tea pot, coffee boiler and coffee pot, every time they are used, as much as you do your silver; and scald them well before using. Do not use a metal tea pot. Green teas are an astringent.

Cocoa.

Cocoa or chocolate nuts are the seeds of Theobroma cacao, a handsome tree from fifteen to twenty feet in heighth growing in Mexico, the West Indies and South America. These seeds are roasted and ground and the oil partly extracted. These seeds make our cocoa. To make good cocoa allow one teaspoon to every cup of milk. Put the quantity of milk according to the number of persons to drink it in a double boiler. When it boils wet the cocoa, work it fine, put it in the hot milk and boil ten minutes and let it settle.

CHOCOLATE.

Chocolate is the cocoa nut pounded to a paste in a hot mortar; mixed with sugar, starch, cinnamon and vanilla it forms the chocolate of commerce. To make good chocolate take one tablespoon of the sweetened grated chocolate to each cup of milk. Put the required quantity of milk in double boiler; when it is hot wet the powder fine, put it in and boil fifteen minutes. Serve with sweetened whipped cream, two tablespoons on top of each cup.

COFFEE.

Coffee is the seed of the coffee tree which grows wild in southern Abyssinia and western Africa in great profusion, and there it has been in use from very remote times. It attains the height of eight to twenty and sometimes thirty feet. To increase its productiveness and for convenience of gathering in cultivation it is kept as low as five feet. Its trunk is covered with a grayish bark, and its white blossoms growing from the angles of the leaf stalk, three to four in number, resembling in form the jasmine blossoms, often suddenly appear scattered among the dark leaves like flakes of snow. The plant being an evergreen, the foliage is always fresh. Like the orange, it has blossoms and green and ripe fruit of every grade at the same time, so the ripe coffee may be gathered at various seasons, but the real harvests are usually two. The fruit when ripe becomes red and finally dark purple. It resembles a cherry. Each berry contains two seeds, their flat sides are opposed to each other in the center of the pulp. In the West Indies the fruit is picked by hand, but in Arabia, where no rains prevail to beat it from the trees, it is allowed to remain till ready to fall, and is then shaken off upon cloths spread upon the ground. Its perfect ripeness may be one reason of its superior quality. The cultivation of coffee is widely diffused throughout the tropics. Coffee should only be scorched thoroughly through to a light brown, not a dark chestnut brown. A slight excess of heat injures the quality of the coffee. Brown it in a sheet iron pan in the oven, stirring it often and watch it closely, about one pound at a time, As soon as browned empty in a tight box.

Brown only enough at a time to last one week for your family. If you buy your coffee roasted do so in small quantities. Keep it in a tightly covered fruit jar, and grind just before using; grind fine, not floured, as it is quicker settled Mocha coffee, which is known by its small, roundish grains, agreeable odor and flavor, is preferred to all others. The Java, a large, flat grain, is next in quality. Some like it mixed three-fourths Java, one-fourth Mocha, or one-half each. The Brazilian coffees are between the two in size and inferior to both in flavor. It is preferable to purchase coffee unroasted, as the roasted and ground are mostly adulterated. The darker the coffee is roasted the more injurious its effects. Some people can not drink it at all; some can only drink it in the morning. Some people of a full habit can not use it because it produces dizziness, on others it produces nervousness and others wakefulness.

To Make Coffee.

Measure one heaping tablespoonful of the berry for each cup, grind it fine but not like flour, then for four or six, stir in one-fourth of an egg, and one-half pint of cold water in a bowl, beat it well with a fork, put it in coffee boiler and add one cup of boiling water for each spoonful of coffee, and let it boil slowly five minutes. If there are six persons or more, add one cup of water extra for waste.

To Make Coffee Without Boiling.

An infusion made just below boiling point is thought by some to be much better than a decoction made by boiling. Purchase a coffee pot for table made with a cloth strainer to put your coffee in without egg, pour the water boiling hot upon it just as you are ready for breakfast. It will be ready in ten minutes. Always put the sugar and cream into the cup before pouring the coffee, the scalding of the sugar and cream enriches the coffee.

Another Way of Making Coffee.

Mix it with egg and cold water then put it in coffee pot, with boiling water on it, let soak for fifteen minutes and then just come to a boil. In browning coffee it must be a light brown, not dark brown, or burnt. It should be ground fine, but not to a flour.

SOUPS.

Soups should be made nutritious, healthful and palatable, with flavoring so commingled, or delicately blended that no one can be detected. As every good cook knows the right way to use salt and pepper is to not have the food taste of either, but simply to give it strength or body. How insipid any soup would be without salt and pepper however rich the broth. Mrs. Rorer says, " The most important point in making good soup is to have the best of materials. To make our soup a perfect food we must change the solid meat into a liquid form; to do this, we must first soften the fibrin, so as to draw out the juices and blood, consisting of albumen and fat; the gelatine, which exists in the bone, cartilages, membranes and skin, which is nitrogenous matter, but not nutritious, and the osmazome, that substance which gives odor and flavor. As a low degree of heat changes the albumen into a solid form, we at once see the necessity of using cold, soft water. Soft water because it makes its way into the tissues more readily than hard water, thereby softening the texture of the meat and allowing the juices to escape more easily; and we also see the importance of not boiling the soup, as the albumen on the surface of the meat immediately coagulates and prevents the gelatine, fat and osmazome from dissolving and being drawn out into the water. Have a granite iron soup kettle with a close cover. Why? Because the juices of the meat are always acid and will act upon a metallic kettle, thereby giving the soup an inky bitter taste. A close cover to keep in the steam and prevent evaporation." A good soup-maker (as well as a good cook) should be a skillful taster; keep a spoon on purpose for it. To make a nourishing soup one must have meat as well as bone. The best stock for soup is beef, mutton, lamb and chicken; some like a bit of ham added, for a change. The legs of all meats are rich in gelatine. Any meat soup is poor that does not jelly when cold. If one wishes light colored stock use light colored meats, such as veal or chicken. Make your soup stock the day before you wish to use it; let it stand over night, then take off all the fat (which simmer and cleanse for browning mush and potatoes), when it is ready to flavor, thicken and serve, unless you wish a bouillon. It is a good plan to make stock enough at one time for two or three days in cool weather, using it every other day. It gives variety and economizes labor. Always use fresh meats.

Dash a dipper of cold water over the meat to cleanse it from specks or hairs; it takes the juices out to lay it in water.

To every pound of meat and bones allow one quart of water, which will just about cover it nicely. Some authors say cut the meat in small pieces two inches square, keeping it at just simmering heat, but not boil, from four to five hours (try it), but I have always had good, nourishing soups by keeping it just at a boiling point from three to four hours, putting the salt in when it is first put over, it will not bear enough to season the meat, but just for the water; skim it before it boils, and wipe the scum off that clings to the kettle. The goodness is all out when the meat is juiceless. If you wish to use the best pieces of the meat cold, sliced off for supper, or for a stew for breakfast, take out the best pieces for it in two hours and let the rest boil longer. Keep a tea kettle of hot water to add to it if needed; and also tightly covered. Nice additions to soups are rice, vermicelli, macaroni, parsley, celery, celery seeds and all kinds of vegetables; the first three, require one-half a tea cupfull to three quarts of stock. Some prefer only one kind at a time. All vegetables should be boiled by themselves, throw the water away and put the vegetables through a seive. For thickening it takes two tablespoons of flour for each quart of soup. As nice a soup as one needs to eat is made of beef stock, thickened, parsley and celery tied together, with croutons in the tureen. If you wish clear soup you can clarify it with the white of an egg, and strain it, making a perfectly clear soup, but stimulating rather than nutritious; as the boiling and straining takes away its albumen and fibrin; as we can not have a very clear, and a very nutritious soup at the same time. In a family of six or more, the bones and trimmings from two or more steaks, and from the roast beef of the day before, boiled three hours, will make a tolerable soup. Flavor with celery and parsley; thicken and pour onto croutons, or rolled crackers.

CROUTONS.

Cut a slice of stale bread twice as thick as for table use, spread the top lightly with butter, then cut into dice, toast in oven on tin plate.

BROWNING FOR SOUPS.

Put three tablespoons of brown sugar and one heaping tablespoon of butter in an iron spider over the fire; stir all the time so it will not really burn, until it is of a bright brown color, and gives forth a burning smell, add a half pint of hot water, boil and skim, when cold bottle for use; use as needed.

TO MAKE CARAMEL.

Brown one cup of granulated sugar until it melts and burns, add one cup of boiling water, boil one minute. Bottle, cork tight. This is used for coloring soups.

CREAM OF CELERY SOUP.

Boil twelve stalks of celery, cut in small pieces, in three pints of water for half an hour till tender. Add half an onion and two blades of mace, and pass through a sieve. Mix one tablespoon of flour and a heaping tablespoon of butter; add to the soup one pint of cream, salt and pepper to taste.

Tomato Soup (Queen of Soups).

1 pint cooked tomatoes
2 quarts soft water
1 pint cream
1 teaspoon soda
Salt and pepper
½ pint milk

Gently boil the tomatoes and water one hour covered tight, then strain. Add one even teaspoon salt, then the soda a part at a time, so it will not foam over, then the cream, milk and pepper, and pour it, after it comes to a boil, on four tablespoons of finely rolled cracker. The cream is indispensable in this soup.

Tomato Soup (Very Nice).

1 quart beef stock
1 quart strained tomatoes
4 tablespoons butter
1 quart milk
Salt and pepper
4 tablespoons flour

Heat the strained tomatoes boiling hot and put in soda enough to take out the acid (should say about two even teaspoons), stir the butter and flour to a cream, then add all together and boil three minutes to cook the flour, stirring all the time.

Green Pea Soup.

1 quart green peas
1 quart soft water
Yolks of 2 eggs
1 tablespoon flour
1 tablespoon butter
Salt and pepper to taste

First wash your pea pods before shelling, and souse them well, to get the dust and sand off. Do not wash the peas after they are shelled as you loose the sweet juice that is in the inside of the pod. Shell them and put them into the cold water, with salt, boil about twenty minutes till fit for eating, according to age. Rub through a sieve, return to soup kettle with a pint or more of milk or cream. Stir butter and flour together smoothly then stir it in boiling soup, boil five minutes to cook the flour. Beat the yolks well, add two tablespoons of milk to thin them and stir it in the soup; season.

GREEN CORN SOUP.

1 pint grated corn
1 quart of water, or mutton stock
1 quart milk
2 tablespoons butter
1 tablespoon flour
Salt and pepper

Put the corn in the water cold, boil five minutes, scrape the milk from cob, rub flour and butter together, put in your milk; if you have cream, use one pint cream, and one pint milk; when hot stir in the worked butter, salt and pepper, boil to cook the flour three minutes.

ASPARAGUS SOUP.

Wash the asparagus, using only the top about three inches long, tie in bunches of six or eight stalks each, boil in water enough to cover, with a little salt (asparagus bears less salt than any other vegetable). Boil six minutes and throw away the water; then put on the cup of water and boil till tender, then rub through a colander, stir the butter and flour together, put all together with pepper and salt, boil to cook the flour. If preferred use veal stock instead of milk, with the cup of cream. Early asparagus boils tender very quickly.

HARICOT (HARAKO) SOUP.

One and a half pints of good small white beans, wash and soak over night in luke-warm water. In the morning drain off this water, cover with fresh cold soft water, bring slowly to a boil for thirty minutes, drain off this water. Take three pounds of beef or a good sized shin-bone and put the beans and beef in four quarts of cold water, bring to a boil slowly, skimming often. Keep hot water to add as fast as it boils away. Slice and fry an onion and put it in with salt, six cloves, a dozen peppers and some parsley. Boil for three hours till the meat will fall from the bones. Stir from bottom often, and boil slowly; when cooked take out the meat, strain the soup, which should be four quarts, through a colander, mashing the beans, let no skins go through. If you wish it to be superfine, you can slice two or three hard boiled eggs and put in the tureen with croutons hot. Boil the eggs twelve minutes, then drop into cold water before peeling to prevent the discoloring of outside of yolk.

Bob, the Sea Cook.

Plain Bean Soup.

Prepare the beans the same as in the preceding with salt, and boil in soft water, one pint of beans to two quarts of water, boil till they all burst open very soft, then strain through a soup sieve; return to the kettle, add a little butter and pepper and boil up. For a change you can boil with beans two bunches of parsley and one of celery, and pour on croutons, and two hard boiled eggs sliced, and one lemon sliced, if liked.

For a good beef stock for any soup or bouillon choose a piece of round of beef of about four pounds; have also three or four pounds of beef leg and bones. Put the leg of beef and bones in a pot with four quarts of cold water. Let it just boil for three hours. Then cut into two pieces the round of beef and put in, let boil altogether for three hours more; remove the piece of round of beef and eat plain, and dished up in some of the bouillon; thicken for a breakfast dish. Strain the bouillon and it is ready for any kind of soup you wish to make. Keep water hot to add to it as it boils out. I should think this would make six quarts of rich stock, which will keep well in cold weather. The reason why the round is put in last, is because it would be overdone and tasteless if cooked the six hours.

BOUILLON.

Bouillon is rich stock, made from beef with only pepper and salt. Use stock like the above, or buy soup bones, have them cracked, with meat enough on them for the desired quantity. To each pound of meat and bones put one quart and one pint of water. Allow one hour's boiling for each pound. Cover tight; only just boil, skimming as it rises. When the meat is separated from the bones and looks juiceless, take it up, strain, set in a cool place, cover; next day skim off the fat. If it is a jellied mass, it is rich enough. Bouillon is served in cups half full, and must be very hot, at fashionable lunches and at evening entertainments; it may be used to form a dinner soup by boiling celery and parsley in it, thickening it, and adding vermicelli well washed. Or make vegetable soup by boiling vegetables in water by themselves, mashing through a sieve or cutting them up as preferred.

CONSOMME.

2 pounds lean beef	Stalks celery
2 pounds veal	Sprigs parsley
1 onion	1 bay leaf
4 quarts cold water	2 tablespoons butter

The under part of the round of beef, and the knuckle of veal are the best for this soup. Cut all the meat into pieces about an inch square. Put the butter in the soup kettle and let it brown. Add to it the meat and stir over the fire about five minutes, or until the meat is a n e rown. Now, cover the kettle and let it simmer fo thirty minutes. Add the water and let simmer for four hours. Now add the vegetables and bay leaf and simmer one hour longer. Strain through a soup strainer and put in a cool place to cool. When cold remove the fat and it is ready to use. Thicken a little and pour onto croutons. (It can be clarified with white of egg and browned with caramel the same as bouillon.)

Julienne Soup.

2 quarts stock
2 carrots
1 turnip
1 head celery

2 onions or 6 young leeks
1 head cauliflower
1 head lettuce
½ a gill green peas

1 pint asparagus heads

Pare and cut up all the vegetables, cut the celery into bits, the head of cauliflower into flowerets. Put them into a kettle, cover with boiling water, boil fifteen minutes, then drain them in a colander. Melt the stock and bring it to a boil; put the vegetables from the colander into it, simmer half an hour. Put the peas and asparagus heads into boiling water and simmer them for twenty minutes; then drain and add to the boiling soup, then the lettuce, cut into pieces (or chopped) the lettuce should cook about ten minutes; add salt and pepper, serve at once.

Vermicelli or Noodle Soup.

Two quarts of beef stock, two ounces vermicelli, washed and cut up; season to taste; boil fifteen minutes. Macaroni soup is made just the same way, using the macaroni instead of vermicelli.

Vegetable Soup Without Meat.

2 tablespoons rice
2 quarts water
1 head celery
1 onion, salt
2 white potatoes
2 tablespoons butter
1 tablespoon flour
1 parsnip
1 sweet potato
1 head parsley

Cook the rice perfectly soft; cook all the vegetables, throw away the water; put them through a colander; salt them just right for eating. Beat the butter and flour to cream, first browning the butter with one teaspoon of sugar; add one cup of sweet cream if you have it. Do not let the vegetables get cold, but stir gradually on them the two quarts of boiling water till well commingled. Then boil fifteen minutes, take out the bunch of parsley, then add your cream and thickening and boil five minutes, and it is ready for the table.

Dumpling Soup.

Take four pounds of good lean meat, either veal or mutton, and only *just* boil in five quarts of cold water for three hours. Peel, slice and brown in one tablespoon of butter, and boil the last hour in the soup, six small onions. Wash and cut in half-inch pieces three small heads of celery and put in at same time. When it is done, beat well one egg, take one tablespoon of milk, and thicken with flour till stiff, then cut off bullet-like pieces and drop in the soup; let soak fifteen minutes, then boil five minutes; if not the right thickness add flour to make it creamy thickness. A little salt in the dumplings. Salt and pepper to taste.

Mutton Soup.

Six pounds of neck, four quarts of cold water, one-half cup of rice, parsley; salt and pepper to taste. Prepare the same as other soups. Thicken.

Clam Soup.

30 clams	4 tablespoons butter
3 quarts water	3 fresh eggs
4 tablespoons flour	1 pint milk or cream

Pepper and salt

Add the native liquor to the water; bring to a boil and skim it. Chop up the clams very fine and stir in with butter and flour worked together, and boil just three minutes; if much boiled they will be tough; add three fresh eggs well beaten; stir well. Pour on croutons if you like. Very delicious.

Jenny Lind Soup.

1½ pounds lean veal	1 quart chicken broth
3 pints water	2 cups cream
½ cup rice	4 yolks of eggs

Pepper and salt

Chop the lean veal fine and put into the water cold with salt, and simmer for two hours, or to cook the veal tender; do not boil. Boil the rice tender in a pint of water. Strain the veal broth through a soup strainer; add your chicken broth, rice, salt and pepper, and one cup of cream; beat the yolks well; add the other cup of cream to them. Pour on to rolled cracker.

Ox Tail Soup.

2 ox tails	1 onion, 1 turnip
2 quarts cold water or stock	1 bay leaf, 1 carrot
2 tablespoons butter	4 cloves, salt, pepper

Wash and wipe the ox tails. Cut them in pieces about the fourth of an inch long. Put the butter into a frying-pan; when hot, throw in the ox tails and stir until they turn brown, then skim them out and brown the onion; then put all the ingredients in the soup kettle and simmer about two hours or till the tails are tender, removing the vegetables; season right.

OYSTER SOUP.   (Have good oysters.)

50 oysters or 1 quart
1 cup hot water
4 tablespoons sifted rolled cracker
2 heaping tablespoons butter
½ pint each of milk and cream
Salt and pepper

Pour the oysters into a colander, pour on slowly the cup of hot water, stirring with the hand, to take out the shells, and wash off all the liquor. Put the liquor in the soup kettle, heat slowly to let the scum rise; when it is near boiling skim it well, taking off every speck, then put in milk and cream; bring to a boil; put in butter; put salt and pepper on the oysters; set the kettle out of stove, where it will not boil, and pour the oysters in the kettle and stir lightly for ten minutes, till hot through, tasting to see if *seasoned* right, as on this depends their beauty with the *cream*. If you can not get cream, use milk and one tablespoon of corn starch, which must be cooked in the milk before adding the oysters. As soon as they begin to shrink pour it all slowly in the tureen, stirring the cracker, so it will not be lumpy. Oysters must not be allowed to boil, as it makes them tough and tasteless. Be equally careful that the oysters are heated through, as an uncooked oyster in a hot soup is unacceptable; serve immediately. Delicious.

CHICKEN SOUP.

For one chicken cut up, put two quarts of cold water; let it simmer for five hours. When half done add two tablespoons boiled rice, salt and pepper;

a spoonful of flour and butter when done. If one likes onions or parsley in, put them in, but I prefer the relishable chicken flavor. Remember to skim it well. Put croutons in the tureen.

Perfect Mock Turtle Soup.

Endeavor to have the head and the stock-meat ready for the soup, the day before it is to be eaten. It will take eight hours to prepare it properly.

Cleaning and soaking the head	1 hour.
To parboil it to cut up	1 "
Cooling nearly	1 "
Making the broth and finishing the soup	5 "
	8 "

Get a fresh calf's head; have it skinned. Clean out the eye and ear sockets, take out the brains, cut off the entire jaw, wash the head in several waters, let it soak for about an hour in soft water, then lay it in a stew pan, and cover it with cold water and add two quarts over; as it becomes warm a great deal of scum will rise, which remove as fast as it rises, let it boil gently for one hour, take it up, and when almost cold, cut the meat into pieces about an inch and a half by an inch and a quarter, and the tongue into mouthfuls, or rather make a side dish of the tongue and brains. When the head is taken out, put in the stock meat about five pounds of knuckle of veal, and the same of beef; add to the stock all the trimmings and bones of the head, skim it well, then cover it close and let it simmer five hours (reserve a couple of quarts of this for gravy stock of other meats); then strain it off and let it stand till next morning; take off the fat, set a large stewpan on the fire with half a pound of good fresh butter, two ounces of sliced onions, and one-fourth ounce of green sage; chop fine; let these simmer one hour, then rub in half a pound of browned flour, by degrees add the broth till it is the thickness of cream: season it with a quarter of an ounce of finely ground allspice, half an ounce of black pepper very fine. (Salt it when you first put it over.) The rind of one lemon pealed very thin; let it simmer gently for one hour and a half, then strain it through a soup sieve, do not rub it through, but have it thin enough to shake through; put it in a clean stewpan with the head and season it by adding to each gallon of soup four tablespoons of vinegar and four tablespoons of lemon juice, let it simmer gently till the meat is tender; this may take from half an hour to an hour; take care that it is not over done; stir it frequently to prevent the meat from sticking to the bottom of the kettle. When the meat is quite tender the soup is ready. A head weighing twenty pounds with the ten pounds of stock meat, will make ten quarts of excellent soup, besides the two quarts of stock, you have put by for gravies. You can add the yolks of four hard boiled eggs if you like. If there is more meat on the head than you wish to put in the soup, save it, it will make an excellent ragout or meat pie. If there is a good deal of meat left from the soup put with a cup of the stock thickened as for gravy, and make a crust the same as for chicken pie, and you have a good mock turtle pie.

Obs.—This is a delicious soup, within the reach of every one. The lover of good eating will only wish for more when he is through. *Home Messenger*.

MEATS.

For boiled meats, all fresh meats should be put in hot water with salt, and skimmed as often as any scum rises, letting it just boil and no more, covered tightly; have a tea kettle of boiling water to add to it as it boils down. When you can pierce it easily with a fork it is cooked enough. For soups, put the meat in cold water, as you need the juices of the meat in the water. When you have skimmed it well, put in a little cold water which will throw up the rest of the scum. Never boil meats or soups *furiously*, or *fry* or *roast* in that way; it destroys both the flavor and all that is nutritious in anything. In roasting have your oven quite hot when you put it in, afterward roast more gently; in that way the outside pores are closed, and the juices of the meat will not be lost.

A good roast is juicy in the middle and brown on the outside. Most people like beef and mutton underdone, while veal, lamb and pork should be well done. All meats are more tender and have a better flavor to be a few days old after killing, according to the weather, and the means of keeping it. A chicken is never quite as good the day it is killed. It is more tender to be from twenty-four to forty-eight hours killed, according to weather.

For boiled meats do not let the water boil for the first forty minutes. If the water boils much sooner, the meat will be hardened, and shrink, the slower it boils the more tender it will be. Count the time from its first coming to a boil, allowing twenty minutes to a pound, if gently simmered. Fresh killed meats will take somewhat longer time, than that which has been kept till what the butchers call ripe; if it be fresh killed it will be tough and hard if stewed ever so long or gently. Have the meat just covered with water. Beef and mutton a little underdone is not a great fault, but lamb, pork, veal, and chicken are uneatable and truly unwholesome if not thoroughly boiled. The liquor of boiled meats will make nutritious soups.

To Bake Meats Etc.

This is one of the cheapest and most convenient ways of dressing a dinner in small families. With regard to the time necessary for baking or roasting various meats, it will vary according to the different kinds of meat and its age. Everything should be salted when first put over to cook, except broiled beef steak. In selecting beef it should be of a clear, red color, of a fine grain, the fat firm and of a yellowish white. The best pieces for roasting are the ribs, sirloin and pin bone. Always examine a piece of meat to be sure there is nothing foreign on it, such as specks of dirt, hairs, etc. Do not wash it if you can help it, but wipe it with a damp cloth.

To Roast Beef.

Rub the salt well in the roast; pepper, and sprinkle well with flour with your seive. Put it on the rack in the bottom of a sheet iron baking pan, the skin side up, do not turn it over, but turn your pan around. When it begins to brown, put a cup of water in the pan. Baste your meat with the drippings (that is, take a spoon and dip the gravy on the meat) every fifteen minutes. Have the oven quite hot at first and then more moderate, but have it boiling hot, adding water if it boils dry; do not let it burn. It must always be rare inside and a bright red (not whitish) when sufficiently cooked and well browned and crisped on the outside. A roast of two ribs will cook in one hour, if oven is right heat. A rack is made of sheet iron to fit loosely in the pan, the two sides bent down three-fourths of an inch, to stand on, to hold the meat up from the juices, and full of holes the size of a penny. Put only a little water in at a time, so as not to steam the roast, which will make the meat whitish. Take it up when cooked to your liking, the gravy being browned, pour off the excess of fat, if there is too much fat, and add water according to the quantity of meat; salt and thicken with flour as thick as thick cream. One great beauty of all meats is to have the right proportion of salt, and not have it taste of salt. To be a good cook you must taste and see. Beef roasted in front of an old-fashioned fire-place has a finer flavor than in a oven.

Yorkshire Pudding.

1 quart sweet milk
8 even tablespoons flour, sifted twice
Salt, even teaspoon
6 eggs

This pudding is to be cooked and eaten with this previous roast. Beat the eggs very light separately, stir the yolks and salt in the milk, then stir the milk gradually in the flour beating it eight minutes. Then add the beaten whites. Thirty minutes before the roast is done take it out of pan, and the rack out, pour the gravy out, and pour the pudding in the meat pan, lay wires three or four across the top of pan on which place the meat. Do this as quickly as possible and place in quite hot oven again for twenty-five or thirty minutes. In the meantime prepare your meat-gravy for table, as everything else must be ready for table when the pudding is baked. Take up the meat and slide the pudding out on a platter, cut it in squares when helping. Keep it hot till after carving is done. This is enough for eight or ten persons. If there are only four or five persons, make half of it.

Fillet of Beef.

The fillet is the tenderloin of beef. They are of various sizes, and weigh from three to eight pounds.

Make gashes in it and insert several finger strips of nice fat salt pork; cut off the rind. Take off the thick sinewy skin from the tenderloin. Salt, pepper and flour it, put a little suet and a few strips of pork in bottom of pan and a small cup of stock, or hot water to baste it with. It will bake in three-fourths of an hour; serve with any sauce or catsup you have, with Saratoga or Julien potatoes.

BEEF ALA MODE.

Take a slice about four inches thick from the round of beef, it may weigh seven or eight pounds, remove the bone, have ready finger strip, of nice fat salt pork, and some nice turkey dressing (stuffing of bread) cut deep gashes into the meat, but be careful not to cut through, rub on the salt. Mix a half teaspoon of black pepper, same of cinnamon, quarter of a teaspoon of mace, the same of cloves, and rub them into the meat on both sides, sprinkling a little in each gash. Put one piece of pork and as much of the dressing, as it will hold when rolled up. (Add onion and parsley to the dressing if you like and vinegar.) Mix three tablespoons of vinegar with three of butter and moisten well both sides of the meat, then roll it together and fasten around it a piece of sheer muslin, sewing up the ends. Let stand over night. Then put two large tablespoons of butter into a pan, and when melted and hot, add one onion, one carrot and one turnip cut into slices; stir the whole until lightly browned, then add two tablespoons of vinegar, two bay leaves, a sprig of parsley, and two quarts of boiling water or stock; let the whole boil two minutes; then put in the beef and one knuckle of veal well cracked. Put on the cover to keep in the steam, and put in the oven and bake slowly for six hours, oven quite hot. When done take out the meat and stand away to cool. Strain the liquor, add salt and pepper to taste, and turn into a square dish to harden. This will make a jelly of a bright amber color. Serve the meat cold with squares of the jelly around it. Garnish with parsley. Serve with any meat sauce or mayonnaise sauce. In winter this will keep at least two weeks in a cold place, covered.

Broiled Beef Steak

The cuts for broiling are porterhouse, sirloin, tenderloin, and rump or round. First, plan to have good hot coals; heat the gridiron made of wire; rub it with suet. Have your steak thick, from three-fourths to an inch thick; you can not make a juicy steak out of a thin one. Pound it with a large hammer to make it tender, put no salt on it; lay it on the gridiron and cover with a tight fitting sheet iron cover (that is, fits the opening of the hearth), warm the platter, take it up every three minutes (being careful not to lose its juices on the coals, but in the platter (by running two knives under); double it on the warm platter, press a few times with your knife, turn it every time you take it up, and so on for three or four times; it will cook in ten or twelve minutes. It must be rare inside. Lay it on platter, salt, butter and pepper both sides, just enough to give it a flavor. Set it in the oven for half a minute, and serve. Some prefer not to pound it, but there are but few steaks that are tender without it. It must be eaten immediately to be at its best. The family had better wait a few minutes for the steak, than to have the steak wait for them. If you burn coal use a folding gridiron.

To Fry a Round or Tough Steak.

Heat the spider hot, pound the steak well, salt both sides, lay it in spider, cover tight, turn every half minute (watch it closely that it does not burn), but cook fast; it will cook rare in five or seven minutes; butter it both sides and pepper; take it up, put in water enough to make a gravy and pour over it. Always see that your gravies are nicely seasoned.

Beef Croquettes.

Take one pound of cold beef left from roast or steak, cut off all gristle or skin, hash it fine enough to adhere. Add the same quantity of fine rolled cracker, or grated bread crumbs; gravy or milk to moisten, two eggs, season to taste with butter, salt and pepper; lemon and onion if you like. Let stand till it swells, then make up in oblong flat rolls; brown in spider with half butter and half suet, as you would brown potato balls. Do not dry them up, as then they are cooked too much.

A Flank of Beef.

The flank of beef is a part generally unknown to housekeepers, but if properly cooked and seasoned it makes an exceedingly good dish. The flank is the part between the ribs and the hip. Have about four pounds of the flank cut in a strip twice as long as it is wide, wipe with a wet cloth, trim off the gristle, season with salt and pepper, spread it with a layer of turkey dressing as thick as it will roll, roll it compactly and tie it tightly in shape with cord; brown it in a saucepan with sufficient hot drippings of suet and butter to keep it from sticking. When it is brown all over cover it with boiling water. Add salt and pepper a little as the water will boil down; keep covered all the time from first to last, boiling slowly for about three hours till tender, or just gravy enough for the meat; thicken and serve. Boiled rice is nice served with it, or boiled onions. Serve with tomato pickle or chow chow.

STUFFED ROAST BEEF:

For a change have a piece of the ribs boned by the butcher. Prepare a nice turkey dressing. Unroll the beef; spread the dressing as thick as it will admit; roll it up, tie it firmly and roast as other roast beef. A joint of beef boned can be prepared the same way. This requires more gravy than a usual roast. Slice it around, not lengthwise. This can be boiled if you like.

SCALLOPED MEAT.

Lamb, mutton or chicken make nice dishes scalloped. Chop nicely, taking out all refuse bits; season to taste. Have half as much rolled cracker or grated bread crumbs as meat. Put in your baking dish (already buttered) a layer of meat, then a layer of crumbs, little bits of butter, a few spoonsful of gravy to moisten the crumbs. Alternate the layers till dish is full, putting a thick layer on top. Sprinkle the top well with milk. Bake one-half hour, browning the top.

BEEF LOAF.

Three pounds of raw chopped beef, two cupfuls of rolled cracker or grated bread (which is prepared by slicing and drying in the oven till it will grate nicely), sufficient sweet milk to moisten and cling together, four well beaten eggs, salt and pepper to taste. Let stand an hour or more to swell, then press in your pan and bake an hour. Eat cold, sliced thin, veal or lamb is prepared in the same way and is better.

BOILED MEAT WITH ROBERT SAUCE.

Take any meat which has been previously used for soup, cut into fillets or bits, and warm up well in the following: Robert sauce, slice a large onion and brown in a large tablespoonful of butter, add soup stock and season as you need for the meat, and simmer for five minutes. The soup meat for this should not have all its goodness boiled out of it.

SPICED BEEF.

Take ten pounds of beef from the fore quarter. Take one pint of salt, one cup brown sugar, one tablespoon ground cloves, allspice and pepper, and two tablespoons of powdered saltpeter; rub thoroughly with the mixture. Turn and rub each side twice a day for one week. Then wash off the spices, put it in boiling water, and only just boil on the back of the stove for five hours. Add more water as it needs. Press under a heavy weight (in the liquor) till cold, and you will never desire to try corned beef of the butcher again. Your pickle will do for another ten pounds of beef; first rubbing into it a handful of salt. It can be renewed and a piece kept in preparation every week. This is good to pickle tongues also.

MEAT PIE.

Cold scraps of mutton, lamb or veal, cut in small bits, cooked in a gravy seasoned ready for eating, line the sides and bottom of pan with pie crust or biscuit dough, then put in the meat, cover the top with dough one-third of an inch thick, having the under crust twice as thick as for a pie. As soon as the crust is cooked through it is ready to eat.

Corned Beef Hash.

Boil the beef just tender, let get cold, save fat that rises on the liquor when cold. You can not make good hash out of tough, or poor corned beef, nor over-boiled potatoes. To each cup of hashed corned beef, add what would make two cups of hashed cold boiled potatoes, and chop in the meat, put in the spider with a little of the fat, and water enough to moisten, adding as it boils out; season as needed. Let it slowly boil for half an hour or more, not stirring but scraping it up often till it is somewhat glutinous, then let brown on the bottom. Dish it and sprinkle pepper on top. Corn beef hash rightly made is a nice winter breakfast dish with the relish of gooseberry catsup, and nicely cooked buckwheat cakes.

Fresh Meat Hashes.

The poor ends of steaks fried, or any bits of meat can be hashed and cooked a little in a gravy and put on bread or buttered toast, is another breakfast dish. Mutton, lamb or veal can be used in the same way. Fresh meats are not as good eating to have potatoes hashed with them.

Dried Beef Cooked—Tea Dish.

Take one-half pound of thin sliced dried beef (the grocer will slice it for you) pull it into smaller pieces, put it in stew pan with nearly a quart of milk and one-half cup of cream, or one spoon of butter, when boiling hot thicken with flour, and only let it boil enough to cook the flour; if it boils longer it will be tough. Lay as many half slices or slices of bread on your platter as you desire and pour the beef on the bread; sprinkle top with pepper.

BEEF TEA FOR INVALIDS.

To one pound of lean beef (the sirloin is best) cut in little finger strips, put one coffee cup of cold water, a very little salt; set your dish in hot water; as soon as it is warm (wash your hands) and squeeze the meat with the right hand till the meat is perfectly white through, then take it out, and strain it through a coarse sieve. It is ready for use when you heat it quite hot, by setting the cup in hot water for a few minutes, a little more than blood heat, for any higher temperature would destroy all the nourishment; so do not let the blood congeal.

ANOTHER BEEF TEA.

Though I have not found it so good. Take sirloin of beef, cut it in two inch pieces, a little salt; put it on gridiron over hot coals, just to let the heat strike through it but not cook it. Then squeeze out the juice till white with a lemon squeezer.

SCRAPED BEEF SANDWICHES.

Take a thick piece of beef scrape with a sharp knife the required quantity, season with pepper and salt, stir with a fork, slice the bread thin and spread the beef thin between, cut into dainty bits of different shapes and serve on a tiny napkin. Some invalids prefer the taste of toasted bread. In that case slice the bread a trifle thicker, and when the sandwiches are made, toast the outsides quickly and lightly.

Beef Balls.

The beef is prepared and seasoned as for sandwiches, rolled between the hands into balls the size of marbles; heat a tin plate hissing hot, rub it with salt, then shake off the salt, place on the balls and toss until lightly seared.

Raw Beef Cakes.

Make the scraped seasoned beef into little cakes about half an inch thick, grease the broiler slightly, and broil the cakes until they begin to change color.

Cold Pressed Beef.

Take four or more pounds of a brisket of beef (a brisket of beef is that part of the breast that lies next to the ribs) fresh or salt, if fresh rub with salt and flour, after removing the bones (the butcher will do this) tie it tightly in a cloth, then put it in a kettle of boiling hot water, a little salt in the water as needed. Simmer gently for four or five hours; when done place it between two plates, put a heavy weight upon it over night, when it will be ready for thin slicing. Always remember the skimming of boiled meat. If this is fresh meat, the broth is good for soup.

A Nice Brine to Pickle Beef.

For 100 pounds beef   6 quarts common salt
4 pounds brown sugar   4 ounces saltpetre

Powder the saltpetre in a mortar at the druggists, then mix all well together, then rub the mixture all over each piece of beef; let it lie over night, then pack close in jars or a good beef barrel, a layer of mixture and a layer of beef alternately. Put a board and

and a heavy weight on top; cover closely. Shake the barrel every day for a week, then once a week. If it does not make brine enough of its own juices in a few days to cover the meat, pour on water that has been boiled (when cold) to cover the meat, then pour the brine all off, stir well and pour it back. If any scum rises skim it all off before shaking. The pieces for drying will be salt enough in three and a half weeks, and for eating. When purchasing a quarter of beef for corning for winter use, be careful to select a tender beef of the right age, about 7 or more years old. A young beef is always tough. November is the best month to salt beef. Follow directions for selections of beef for table, under the the head of baked meats. Beef should be killed three or four days before salting, according to weather.

MUTTON AND LAMB.

To roast a leg of either lamb or mutton, it is prepared the same as beef, only it is improved by making incisions and placing within finger strips of salt pork; baste every fifteen minutes. Roast twelve minutes for every pound of lamb, and fifteen for every pound of mutton. The outside must be brown and crisp. Make a gravy; serve with green peas, pickles and currant jelly.

A BOILED LEG OF MUTTON.

Put it in boiling water just enough to cover it, boil slowly fifteen minutes for every pound. When done, have just water enough to make the drawn butter of. Serve with spiced pickles and jam.

FORE QUARTER OF LAMB, ROASTED.

Have the butcher take out the leg bone and shoulder blade (which you can take home toward a soup) stuff the cavity with turkey dressing, tie it up, seasoning right. Bake twelve minutes to the pound. Place it on the frame and have only a little water in pan, so as to let the gravy brown when it is baked, then add water and make the gravy.

Fore Quarter Lamb, Broiled.

This is the most delicious method of cooking lamb. Choose a young and tender, but small fore quarter; have it well nicked by the butcher; and forty minutes before dinner place it on the gridiron over bright coals, but not too hot; every ten minutes baste it on both sides with a bit of butter and turn on the gridiron; send it to table just off the fire and well buttered; it will make its own gravy; it should be done thoroughly, that is, past the pink color demanded by French cooks, but not enough to dry the natural juices of the meat. *Home Messenger.*

Lamb Chops.

Lamb chops can be fried or broiled, not cooked hard, but browned, salted, peppered and buttered. Can make a gravy for the fried chops.

Roast Leg of Veal.

Prepared the same as lamb, only it requires longer and more thorough cooking and is always better to lay bits of salt pork in bottom of pan, or gash it in. Make a gravy of the brown drippings.

Veal Cutlets.

For veal cutlets it should be cut one-half inch thick from the leg, cut in right sizes for helping, have a spoonful of lard and butter each in a hot spider; lay in the veal and cook well, brown on both sides, salt and pepper the veal first, then dip in beaten egg and rolled cracker; lay it in spider and brown again. Make a gravy.

PICKLED TONGUE BOILED.

Wash it and put it in a kettle of cold water, boil gently three or four hours, till when you pierce it with a fork it is tender; then take out and skin it, trimming off the roots. Do not let the water boil out. When cold slice it thin, place it on platter, the pieces overlapping each other all around the platter; put in the center nasturtium flowers or seeds, and parsley around the edge. A nice supper dish. It is also nice warmed up in milk gravy.

JELLIED TONGUE.

Boil until tender a pickled beef tongue. When cooked throw into cold water for a few minutes, then peel. Save a pint of the liquor which the tongue was boiled in. When the tongue is perfectly cold slice thin as for the table and half hash it. Dissolve two ounces of gelatine in one pint cold water. Plan to cook a piece of veal the same day or day before, so as to have the gravy. Take one teacup of the gravy, two tablespoons of light brown sugar, add to the gravy three tablespoons of vinegar or juice of one lemon, one pint of liquor the tongue was cooked in, the dissolved gelatine and a pint of boiling water. Strain through a fine sieve and set in cold water till it begins to thicken. Take a jelly mold and put in a layer of jelly, then a layer of tongue and then of jelly, and so on till all is in. Set it on ice over night to get solid. When you are ready to use it, dip the mould in hot water quickly and turn out on platter. Garnish with parsley or any soft fine green. This makes a handsome dish for lunch or tea. Cut it with a sharp knife.

JELLIED CHICKEN.

Take one or two chickens according to number of persons; cut up as for fricassee chicken; cook slowly with just water enough to cover, till very tender; season as for eating; take up the chicken; boil the liquor till it will jelly thick when cold. Pick the meat to pieces; cut in small pieces; season with salt, pepper and a little butter while hot, and then put a layer of each in the mold alternately when just cool; then set it in the cold to harden. To use on table cut in slices with sharp knife.

GLAZED PIGEONS.

Pluck, singe, draw, and wash lightly (do not lay them in water, but rinse off) rub in the salt, and brown both sides in a hot spider, with half butter and half suet for a few minutes, then put them in your kettle with the browned butter, add enough hot water to cover them, season just right and cook gently until tender, one or more hours, according to age, tightly covered; when cooked remove the cover and let boil rapidly (taking the birds out, being careful not to break them) till the broth is rich enough to jell when cold. Add a little cream and thicken. Serve the pigeons on a platter, pour the sauce over them. Serve with the ordinary sour orange now so abundant and cheap, cut in pieces (not slices) around the core, after peeling, and take out the seeds, sprinkle well with sugar or any salad dressing you like. They are nice to serve with any game or poultry.

BAKED PIGEONS.

Clean the birds as directed before, season, stuff with a nice turkey dressing adding a little fine chopped salt pork, place them compactly in your baking pan, with thin slices of salt pork on top, three, say, to season, dredge with flour and nearly cover with hot water, cover tight and place in a moderately hot oven till tender. If the birds are old and tough, this is the best way to cook them, but it will take two or three hours. Add cream to gravy and thicken. Add water while baking as needed.

To Dress Turkey and Chicken.

Take your fowls from the roost at night, without frightening or injuring them. Take them by the feet, place the neck on a stick of wood and with an ax cut off the head with one blow. Hang it up by the feet till it stops bleeding. It is best killed three or four days before using, in winter, and twenty-four hours or more in summer, according to your convenience for keeping it. If one has ice, it is a great help.

Thorough bleeding renders the meat of fowls whiter. I have often wondered why some chickens purchased at market were so dark. They probably killed them without bleeding. Scald them well by dipping them twice in a pail of boiling hot water and giving them a shake in it quickly. Be careful not to scald too much so as to set the feathers, as then it will tear the skin. Place the fowl on a board taking hold of its head, pulling the feathers in the direction they naturally lie. Remove all the pin feathers with a knife run under and your thumb on top. Singe the hairs but do not smoke over a blazing paper. Cut off the legs a little below the knee; remove the oil bag above the tail which is small and yellow; take out the crop by making a little slit in front, being careful to remove the gullet and wind pipe. Cut out the vent and cut a place or slit long enough to put in your two fingers of the right hand, and detach all the intestines and lights, being careful not to break the gall sack which is attached to the liver, situated near the upper part of the breast bone. If this breaks you must not cook anything it touches, and you must throw the liver away.

Now wash the inside well and quickly; rub inside and out with salt and it is ready for the dressing.

Turkey Dressing.

Take as many slices of stale bread as you need to fill your turkey (according to size). For a turkey of eight pounds perhaps six large slices, cut thicker than for table, or eight of baker's loaves, cut off all crusts and spread with good butter as you would for eating; cut it into strips and chop it fine with a chopping knife. Season with a little salt, pepper and sage. Dry the sage in the tin on the stove slowly, rub it very fine and sift it on the bread, enough to give it a good flavor; beat two eggs and stir in with just hot water or milk enough to moisten so it will cling together somewhat. If in the season of oysters, it improves it very much to add a large pint lightly chopped, taking out the hard lobes. Stir well together and make good use of your tasting powers. Stuff the body lightly full, do not pack it. It must have room to swell, or it will be heavy. To have good dressing you must use light bread. Stale baker's bread sliced and dried in the oven and grated on a coarse grater makes the nicest and lightest dressing, then stir in two tablespoons of butter with the other ingredients. By stale bread I mean two or more days old. You can use onion or sage or any other flavoring you like for the dressing.

To Roast a Turkey.

The dressing adds very much to the flavor of the turkey as well as keeping it plump. Stuff the body then the crop and sew it up with a coarse thread; then truss it by turning the tips of the wings under the shoulder (they will stay themselves); then tie the legs down to the rump with cord, tight. Of course you have rubbed it inside and out with salt before stuffing. Put it on the rack in your dripping pan on its back, after you have rubbed the outside with butter. Put water in pan, not enough to cover rack or you will have a par-boiled turkey, a little salt in water, and baste it every fifteen minutes. Do not burn it, but it it may get brown a little in three-fourths of an hour. Then make a stiff dough of flour and water, a little salt, and roll out the dough one-half inch thick, large enough to cover the top and sides of turkey; leave it on till about done, then lift it off and baste again, and have the top and sides a nice crisp brown. Keep hot water in tea kettle to replenish as the water boils out. If too fat dip it off of gravy and thicken with flour, making the quantity according to size of turkey. An eight or nine pound turkey will roast in two hours. A fourteen-pound will take three or more hours. If you like you can boil the giblets (that is, the liver, heart and gizzard) till tender, hash fine and add to gravy. Allow twenty minutes' time for every pound of turkey and twenty minutes longer. A young hen turkey is the best for roasting. It should be plump and fat, the legs black, the skin white and short neck. If old the legs will be reddish and rough. A gobbler, if young, will have black legs and short spurs. They are much larger than a hen at same age. The flesh of an old gobbler is strong and tough, legs reddish and long spurs, and the grizzly end of breast bone will be hard and sharp, the same as in an old chicken. You can not give it the flavor of a young turkey. Serve with cranberry sauce, pickles, sweet potatoes and fried oysters. Fry the oysters while the turkey is being carved, as a cold oyster is not relishable.

To Boil a Turkey, or Steam It.

Dress and prepare it the same as for roasting. Rub it with lemon, sprinkle with flour, tie it up in a sheer cloth with cord; put it into boiling hot water, after stirring up two tablespoons of flour in a little milk, adding one quart of milk and the flour to the water, salt also; let it simmer, not boil hard, till tender. Stir the water four times as the flour settles. This preserves the juices of the fowl, which makes it more nourishing. Make a drawn butter of the liquor.

Cold Roast Turkey.

Is nice sliced off for tea, or warmed in the gravy for breakfast, or made in croquettes.

To Prepare Giblets.

Cut the gall bladder (being careful not to break it) from the liver and throw it in the fire or bury it. Cut the heart open, remove the clotted blood. Cut the gizzard open to the inner lining, but do not cut it, drawing the meat from it. Wash and they are ready to boil till tender, salt.

Chickens.

Chickens, ducks, geese, pigeons and all birds, are cleaned, dressed and trussed in the same manner as turkeys, according as you wish to broil, fry, or roast.

Select a chicken with firm flesh, yellow skin and legs. If young, the cock will have short spurs, and cock and hen will both have soft smooth legs, and tender skin. The small end of breast bone will be gristly and not a sharp bone. A chicken not full grown has not a good flavor. A chicken six months or more old is best for broiling. They should be drawn or emptied as soon as killed and hung in the coolest place, if cold weather, two or three days.

Roast Chicken.

Prepare it for roasting in the same way as a turkey, allowing fifteen minutes to every pound, basting every fifteen minutes. Fifteen minutes before it is done, rub it with butter, sprinkle with flour, let brown, make a gravy, adding a cup of cream, using the giblets if you like.

Boiled or Steamed Chicken.

Prepare it and boil it the same way as a turkey to eat with boiled rice.

To Broil Spring Chicken.

Singe and clean the outside taking off the head and feet, split the chicken down the back, taking out the internals. Break the breast bone, so it will lie flat. Rub both sides with butter and salt. Rub the gridiron with suet, lay the chicken on; the inside down, and have a close sheet iron cover, and not very hot coals, renewing them twice. When it is over half done turn it and let it brown. It will take from thirty to forty-five minutes to broil, with a steady heat. It must not burn. Take it up, rub a little butter on it and sprinkle with pepper. Serve immediately.

CHICKEN WITH CREAM.

Take a spring chicken and prepare it the same as for broiling, place it skin side up, on the rack of roasting pan, with a little water salted, and covered. When just done, brush it over with beaten egg and sprinkle with rolled cracker, and let it brown; make a cream gravy and put in gravy boat.

FRIED CHICKEN.

You can cut it up as for fricassee chicken and fry, or butter it and put in oven in dripping pan to bake and brown, or cut it up and cook it the same as chicken with cream, only put the cream, on the chicken platter.

FRICASSEE CHICKEN, WHITE.

Singe and dress the chicken as directed, first disjoint the legs at each joint, then the two wings making six pieces. Cut through the ribs on both sides breaking off the lower back. Disjoint the neck and upper back from the breast, cut the breast in half lengthwise, smoothly in two pieces, make two pieces of lower back. Salt and put in kettle and cover with boiling water, and just boil only till tender, an hour or more according to age. When the chicken is done, there should be nearly water enough for gravy by the addition of a cup of milk, or a half cup of cream, and a little butter if the chicken is not fat. Pepper. You can put on bread or biscuit split if you like. Some like finger strips of salt pork cooked with it. Serve with boiled rice.

FRICASSEE CHICKEN, BROWN.

Prepare the same as the above only brown your flour and butter for the gravy, and brown the chicken in the butter and put it back in kettle and thicken with the brown flour.

Chicken Pot Pie.

Prepare and cook the chickens the same as for fricassee ready for table, only have more broth for gravy. When the chicken is within twenty-five minutes of being done, stir up stiff enough to cut off with spoon, baking powder biscuit, what you need; drop in steamer on top of chicken. Steam thirty minutes; take up, thicken gravy, pour some on platter over the chicken, put the rest in gravy dish.

Baked Chicken Pie.

Make a fricassee of two chickens and thicken, cook and season all ready for table. Then line the sides and bottom of your baking pan (all in one piece of crust), with a good pie crust one-fourth of an inch thick. Put in the chicken hot, with part gravy and cover with crust a little thicker. As soon as the crust is baked it is done. Put it on table in same dish. Have some gravy in gravy dish, for crust at table. This is always nice to have with roast turkey on Thanksgiving day, and if a large table it helps the turkey to go farther. Remember, the right seasoning with pepper and salt is the beauty of meats.

Chicken Salad.

Cut up two tender chickens, salt as for eating, and put in boiling water, enough to hardly cover, cook till tender, take all the bones out while hot, let get cold, then cut in small bits like large peas and the celery the same with a silver knife. Have one-half as much celery as chicken, in measure, that is, to one quart of chicken, one pint of celery. Mix them together and cover tight to exclude all the air. You can prepare this and the salad dressing in the fore part of the day for the evening. The broth that is left will make a nice little soup.

Salad Dressing.

Boil six eggs eight minutes, then drop them one minute into cold water (which prevents the outside of yolk from turning green). Rub the mealy yolks smooth with a silver spoon and in an earthen dish, add gradually, beating well, one even teaspoon of salt the last thing, six tablespoons of softened butter; two even teaspoons of mustard, twelve tablespoons of vinegar. Melt more butter than you need, so as not to use the froth and settlings. This will thicken as you stir in or drop in the vinegar; if too thick stir in more vinegar and butter. When nearly ready to use it, mix carefully with a silver fork; this dressing, with the salad, arrange nicely in a salad bowl, garnished with parsley.

Chicken Croquettes.

Cook one four pound chicken tender as for eating; take out all the bones, skin and gristle. When cold chop fine, add one fourth as much rolled cracker, or bread crumbs as you have meat by measure; one-half pint of cream or milk, boiling hot, or the hot broth of chicken, enough to make it just moist, to cling together nicely and swell the crumbs, a heaping tablespoon of butter, two well-beaten eggs; season. Stir well together, and make up in cone-shaped balls, flatten a little, then dip in beaten egg, and then in rolled cracker, and fry a light brown on both sides in spider, with half butter and half suet. Do not dry them up by cooking too fast, as this destroys the nourishing juices of any thing. Most recipes say cook them in boiling lard, but they are not so healthy. It might do in boiling hot suet. Serve with a napkin on platter, and garnish with parsley or celery tops and half quarters of lemon.

Chicken and Oyster Croquettes.

These are made the same way with the addition of one pint of oysters to every pint of chicken. Wash the oysters in as little hot water as possible, which scald with the oyster broth, and skim, then use it to moisten the croquettes instead of milk or cream, as far as it will go. Take out the hard lobes of the oyster, season with salt and pepper, chop raw, lightly, then mix with the chicken.

Meat Croquettes.

Cold roast chicken, turkey, lamb, or beef, can be prepared in the same manner, taking out all the hard bits, for meat croquettes.

Tender Chicken.

"After a fowl is killed by cutting off its head, hang it in a cool place until it becomes cold; keep it one, two or three days, according to weather; it is then as tender as it ever will be, and the flavor will never be better; no further keeping will ever improve it. This advice should be heeded by those housewives who precipitate a chicken from the hen-coop to the dinner-pot when company comes unexpectedly and then wonder why the chicken is so tough, or lacking in the best flavor." Those who keep chickens can try it.

Pork.

Pork is considered more indigestible than any other meat, and should not be eaten by persons of weak digestion or by young children. It is particularly injurious to any one that is liable to any skin disease. It is best used in cold weather, and should be thoroughly cooked. In healthy pork the lean is of a fine grain and pale red color, the fat white and the skin smooth. If the flesh is soft, the fat of a yellowish white with small kernels, it is diseased pork, do not eat it under any circumstances. It is the way the pig and hog is fed that causes diseased pork. Many people think any slops they can pick up round town is good enough for a pig, no matter how old it may be. No wonder there is trichina in pork. Feed them as if you were a rational being appointed to care for them and keep their pens clean, take the same forethought and care of them as one ought of his chickens or cow, and you will be rewarded accordingly.

ROAST LEG OF FRESH PORK.

Wash and scrape the rind, salt and sprinkle with flour if you like; first take out the bone and fill the cavity with turkey dressing. Gash the rind in half inch squares. Roast in hot oven from three to four hours, according to size. Dip off the fat, add water and make the gravy. Serve with onions and apple sauce.

ROAST LOIN OF PORK.

Roast a loin the same way, with or without dressing. Bake twenty minutes to the pound and twenty minutes longer. Serve with apple fritters.

ROAST SPARE RIB.

Crack the ribs across the middle, double together, fill in with turkey dressing, rub with salt, sprinkle with pepper and flour, sew it up, put it on the rack of dripping pan, when one side is brown turn it and brown the other, pour off the fat and make a gravy; or roast plain.

Pork Tenderloins.

Split them in two or three slices for they swell very much in cooking, salt and pepper and fry brown in drippings, cook thoroughly and make a gravy.

Pork Steaks and Chops.

This is simply to salt and fry in the spider, thoroughly cooking till a nice brown on both sides; take out the meat, add water, salt and pepper; thicken with flour.

Fried Salt Pork.

Cut slices one-third of an inch thick (freshen if too salt), fry brown, pour off if too fat, make a milk gravy.

Boiled Ham.

First soak it over night in just warm water. Wash and scrape it, place over a slow fire, not to boil, for two hours, with plenty of water, then place it on the stove where it will just boil till a fork goes in easily. If it is a whole ham it will take six or seven hours, according to size; let it stand till cold in liquor. Then take up and peal off the skin, rub over it beaten egg and sprinkle fine rolled cracker all over it and place in oven till it browns nicely. Then stick the top with cloves. Make a paper ruffle for the shank bone. A large porcelain kettle is the best to boil it in. Letting it stand in its own liquor till cold, with cover off, renders it more tender, juicy and of fine flavor, if it was good to begin with.

Cold Boiled Ham.

It can be used in other ways, besides slicing off cold. Slices can be dipped in egg batter and fried, or the scraps can be hashed and stirred into an egg omelet, or scrambled eggs; or hash some and season right (not too much as they do at restaurants), with mustard, salt, and pepper for ham sandwiches.

Fried Ham and Eggs.

I do not think it very eatable; it is so hard, but the eggs are very relishable fried in the ham fat. This is one way, cut the slices not quite one-half of an inch thick, trim off the rind and all that is discolored. Heat the spider hot and lay in the slices of ham. As they brown on one side turn and brown the other side, then pour over the ham a few tablespoonfuls of boiling water, how many will depend on the quantity of ham. Cover the spider closely, and set where the heat is slow for fifteen minutes. The water by that time should all be absorbed and the ham delicious.

To Bake a Ham.

Many persons have never thought of baking a ham. This is the way they do it down in old Virginia. Soak it over night in warm water. Scrape it clean, wipe it dry. Make a stiff dough of water and flour, roll it out one-fourth of an inch thick, the size of ham and lay it on the ham with the rind up. Put it in deep pan on muffin rings to keep it out of drippings. A good sized ham will take from five to seven hours. When it is tender take off the crust and peel off the skin, cut off all the discolored places, glaze it all over with the yolks of two well beaten eggs, and sprinkle fine rolled cracker on, and put it in oven again to brown.

Another Way.

Prepare it as for boiled ham, and boil till nearly tender, three or four hours, according to size, remove the skin, put it in on the rings in pan, rub over it the juice of two large lemons, then cover with brown sugar, place in oven until nicely browned. Cover with a large tin pan, press with a heavy weight over night. Some like grape or currant jell well rubbed into the ham while hot, instead of lemon or egg.

Virginia-Cured Hams.

From the American Agriculturist.

In Virginia we pride ourselves on our knack of curing hams, and the fact that Virginia-cured hams are greatly prized and sought after by outsiders proves that our pretentions are not altogether groundless. There is, in fact, a delicacy of flavor in a ham cured after the old Virginia method that is not found in bacon raised and cured elsewhere. This is partly due to the feeding of the hog. The hogs of Western pork-raisers are fed with a view to producing a great mass of flesh, for every pound adds to the profit of the pork dealer; but in Virginia, where we are merely raising for our own households, we aim for quality rather than quantity. We do not aim to have enormously large, fat hogs, knowing that they will not be delicately flavored, but are satisfied to have them weigh about one hundred and fifty pounds. We let them run out in the pastures and graze, or range the woods and live on mast until about six weeks before killing time, when we put them up and fatten them on corn.

After the hogs have been killed and cut up, we cure the hams as follows: First, rub a teaspoonful of pulverized saltpeter on each ham, to give it a red color, then rub it thoroughly with salt, and lastly with a mixture of molasses, brown sugar, and black pepper. The same flavoring may also be applied to jowls if desired. Pack the hams away, with the skin side down, leaving them in the bulk from four to six weeks, according to the weather, as it takes the saltpeter a longer time to strike in when the weather is cold. In old times when they were unpacked the hams were always put in the smokehouse and smoked about six weeks by a slow, smoldering fire made of green hickory chips. About April first, the smoking was completed, and then there were two ways of proceeding; either to leave the meat hanging or to pack it away again in hickory ashes carefully saved during the process of smoking. The latter plan was doubtless the best and safest. When it was pursued there never was any complaint of skippers or other vermin in the meat. This was the method pursued by the Massie family, in Virginia, whose hams commanded an extra price from their superior excellence. The early spring is the time these insects first appear, and as the smoking goes on then, it serves to keep them at bay. But of late years Virginians have almost given up smoking their meat. We kill hogs on so much smaller a scale than in slavery times that we can keep the meat in our storerooms without the need of a smokehouse. Some housekeepers congratulate themselves on having cut loose from the old, troublesome method of curing meat, and they say it is just as well flavored without smoking. Possibly it may be; but I have noticed that skippers and other insects have increased enormously since we discontinued smoking our meat, and many a ham that ought to have furnished the family with choice cuts finds its way into the soap fat. I am, therefore, convinced that the old plan is the best and safest. If, however, this is inconvenient, try to protect the meat from insects by means of bags. As soon as they have dried out, after being unpacked from the bulk, rub them thoroughly with black pepper, and put them in sacks of stout cotton, tied above the hock. Do this by the middle, or at latest by the last, of February, as any delay might occasion the loss or serious damage of the meat.

The mode of boiling a ham has a great effect on its flavor. A ham should be soaked twelve hours before it is cooked. Then it should be scraped and sunned the previous day, unless it is very fresh. It should be put on in cold water, and cooked slowly and gradually. Then leave it in the pot until it is cold, as it will thus re-absorb a considerable portion of the juices it has given out in boiling. Then skin it, and brown it slightly in the oven, sprinkling it first with grated crackers and a little black pepper. Serve it in a dish garnished with parsley, and you will find it " a dainty dish to set before a king.

HAM FORCEMEAT.

1 pint cold cooked ham chopped fine
1 pint new milk
½ pint dried bread crumbs or cracker
½ teaspoon salt
⅛ teaspoon cayenne pepper
1 teaspoon, even, mustard
Yolks of three eggs
2 tablespoons chopped parsley

Put the bread in the milk on to boil, stir until it thickens, take from the fire, stir in the eggs, add the other ingredients, set away to cool. This may be sliced off cold or used as stuffing for game or meats, or made into croquet shape, dipped in egg and bread crumbs, fried or browned in hot fat.

Chicken Forcemeat.

This is made the same way, only using a four pound chicken instead of ham.

Pickle for Curing Hams.

To six gallons of water add nine pounds of salt, half coarse, half fine, three ounces of saltpeter, three pounds of brown sugar, one pint of molasses, one heaping tablespoon saleratus. Boil all together and skim; let it stand till cold, then pour over the hams, which have been rubbed with a little fine salt and pack in a barrel. Let them lie in the brine five or six weeks, after which drain and smoke for three days. You must make enough to cover the hams. Put a weight on top. The same preparation is used for pickling beef. A pork barrel will answer for pickling beef, but after being once used for beef must never again be used for pork. Many losses occur from ignorance of this fact.

Pig's Head Cheese.

Split open a pig's head, singe off the hair; cut off the whole mouth, nostrils, ears and dig out the eyes, brain and everything but the meat. Wash it clean, soak it over night in warm water with two even teaspoons of soda in it. Next morning scrape the skin well and wash in two waters. Rub it well with salt and put over to boil with water enough to cover it. Skim it as often as it rises. When cooked so the flesh leaves the bones take it up with the help of a skimmer. Then take out all the bones; be careful to get all the small ones. Chop it fine. Season to taste with salt, pepper and dried sifted sage; stir it in. Lay a thin cloth over a colander, put in the meat, fold the cloth tightly over it, cover with a plate the right size and lay a heavy weight on it over night to press. Some add the pig's feet with it dressed as for souse. It makes a nice dish sliced off for tea. Can put vinegar on it as you eat it. A good change for breakfast with soft-boiled eggs and milk toast. A good winter dish.

PIGS' FEET SOUSE.

Take the legs and feet of two pigs about eight inches long from the toes up, cut them in two about four inches long each, cut off the entire foot, singe off the hairs, soak them over night in warm water, putting in two even teaspoons of soda as a cleanser. In the morning scrape them well, dipping them in hot lye, then wash them in two more waters. They must be scraped and soaked till they look white. Then put over to boil for one-half hour, throw off that water and put on another with salt. Skim often; let boil till the bones will easily pull out, but do not pull them out, but put them in a jar with half vinegar and half the liquor they were boiled in. To prepare for table for any meal you wish, though best for supper, season, add more vinegar and boil for five minutes. Serve hot.

FISH.

Fish is not considered so nutritious as meat, but we can eat more of it, as it is more easily digested. There is not much doubt but that it would be better for us, if we ate more fish than we do. It is very healthy and by some considered brain food. I notice in most recipes for cooking fish, that lemon, onion and vinegar are recommended. Use them if you like, but we prefer the delicate flavor of the fish. Lemon or vinegar may be a relish on frogs or shrimps.

BAKED FISH.

The fish should always be very carefully and thoroughly cleaned, scraped outside and washed well. All fish should be thoroughly cooked. Wipe it with a dry cloth, rub in the salt, on both sides, and fill with turkey dressing; sew it up carefully, do not pack it, as it will swell. If you leave the head on clean it well. I take it off. Lay it on the rack of roasting pan after rubbing it with softened butter, put in pan a little water and baste three times. It will take an hour or more according to size. It is served with drawn butter, Hollandaise, or oyster sauce. When fish is well cooked it will cleave from the bones easily.

STEAMED FISH OR BOILED

Fish to make turbot is better steamed than boiled. Dress it nicely, rub with salt, and wrap it in a sheer cloth, that you may take it out without breaking. It can be steamed and stuffed with turkey dressing for dinner and served with drawn butter. To boil fresh fish of any kind, clean the fish, wipe dry, rub with salt both sides, roll firmly in a thin white cloth, wind a cord around the fish in several places, put in a large kettle of hot water salted. If the fish weighs ten pounds allow one and a half hours or less in proportion. When done take out and drain, take off the cord and cloth, peel the skin off, taste to see if it is salt enough. Serve with Hollandaise sauce or drawn butter.

FRIED FISH.

Fish to be fried, after being well cleaned, wipe with a dry cloth, rub with salt, dredge lightly with flour, place in hot spider with drippings and butter. Turn carefully without breaking, when brown. Brown both sides, but do not burn. Cut the pieces three inches wide for frying. All fish should be freshly caught.

CREAMED FISH.

A nice breakfast dish. The day before you wish to use it, prepare a fish the size you need, rub salt on it, wrap in cheese cloth, either steam or boil it slowly for thirty minutes; skin it and take out the bones while hot, and when cool take a silver fork and pick it into flakes. Be careful not to muss it. In the morning put over the fire one pint of milk, braid together two tablespoons of butter and one of flour until smooth; when milk is hot stir in some of it gradually on the paste until it is boiled enough to cook the flour, pour on the fish; a sprinkle of pepper and salt.

TURBOT A LA CREME.

Steam until tender one white fish, first rubbing it with salt, after nicely cleaning. Then take off the skin, pick out all the bones; pick the fish up. For dressing: One pint of milk, boiled; braid together two teaspoons of flour, four tablespoons of butter and stir in milk with white pepper and salt as you like. Cook five minutes, stirring all the time. When cool add two well beaten eggs. Put in the baking dish a layer of fish then a layer of dressing, and so on, till the dish is full; a sprinkle of rolled cracker crumbs on top and sprinkle this with milk enough to moisten them. Bake one-half hour in moderate oven, browning the top. Serve in same dish, which should be a pudding dish. A nice supper dish, with hot biscuit and saratoga potatoes. The dressing must always be only as thick as cream.

FISH SOUFFLE TO BAKE IN SHELLS.

Prepared the same as for turbot, only you mix fish and dressing (after cooking) with one small cup of fine rolled cracker, with a fork. Fill the shells or cups (butter them first) with the fish; sprinkle top with cracker, dampen with sprinkle of milk. Set them in dripping pan of hot water, bake twenty minutes, brown the top. Serve hot for lunches.

CREAMED SALMON.

Drain the liquor from a can of salmon and chop fine. Then proceed the same way as for other fresh fish to make a turbot or soufflé. If you use fresh salmon you must boil it first. Season.

CANNED SALMON.

Canned salmon is cooked before canning. If you prefer it heated, set the can in steamer, or boiling water. Open, drain off all the liquid, then remove to a platter, taking out any skin or poor pieces. Garnish with parsley.

POTTED SHAD OR ANY FRESH FISH.

Make use of it the day it is caught if possible. For five pounds of fish rub in two even tablespoons of salt. Cut the fish in pieces about an inch wide and four inches long. Make a mixture of spices, of one even teaspoon of white pepper, two teaspoons each of cinnamon, cloves and allspice, mix thoroughly. Put a layer of fish in a stone jar and sprinkle each layer with the mixed spice, sprinkle flour and bits of butter on each layer, repeating till done. Fill jar with equal parts of vinegar and water. Tie on top a stiff writing paper and lay on top of that a stiff dough of flour and water. Bake from four to six hours. When cold slice.

A Supper Dish.

Select a three-pound fish, dress, salt and wrap in a thin cloth and boil or put in steamer, salt the water, cook thirty minutes. While this is boiling (if you wish it), boil four eggs hard, say eight minutes, drop them into cold water for one minute, so the yolk outside will not turn green. When cold separate the yolk and whites and chop each separately. Remove the fish to the center of a large platter. Place about four inches of the yolks and then four inches of the chopped whites alternately till you have encircled the fish. Wash and chop fine parsley enough to sprinkle over the whole. Cut lemons in two lengthwise, then cut each half in four pieces and lay around the fish, serving it with it, either hot or cold. Serve with creamed potatoes and spiced pickles.

Broiled Fish.

When fish are to be broiled they should be split down the back, leaving head and tail on. Wash and wipe dry, salt, grease the whole broiler with suet; place the fish flesh side down, which should always be cooked first and longer, on medium hot coals. When half cooked turn platter on, then turn platter and broiler over together, unless you have a double wire broiler; the skin side needs careful attention, as it burns easily. When done loosen carefully, so as not to break it, and slide onto platter inside up. Serve with pepper and butter.

SALT BOILED MACKEREL.

Soak in tepid water twelve hours, changing the water once or twice according to saltness. Clean, wipe dry with a cloth. Wrap the fish in a cloth and boil slowly fifteen minutes. Drain from the water, pepper and butter it, set in oven three minutes, serve with baked potatoes.

BROILED SALT MACKEREL.

Is prepared in the same way, only broiled instead of boiling.

HALIBUT STEAK.

Take a piece halibut an inch or more thick, rub in salt, butter the bottom of dripping pan, pepper it. Sprinkle with one tablespoon of lemon juice, cut in bits one tablespoon of butter and put on it; bake thirty minutes. Serve this with Hollandaise sauce which may be prepared, all but cooking, several hours before needed.

HOLLANDAISE SAUCE.

Measure one-half cup butter and cream it, add the yolks of two raw unbeaten eggs. When nearly ready to serve, add the juice of one lemon, one-half of a cupful of boiling water slowly beating until it thickens like soft custard, cooking in double boiler.

CREAMED COD FISH.

For four persons, pick up a bowl full of cod fish fine, picking out all the bones. Freshening by squeezing it with hand in a quart of cold water from three to five minutes, leaving salt enough in it to salt the cream or milk it is cooked in. Put it in a pint of milk or half cream, squeeze all the water out. If you use milk one tablespoon of good butter, if cream, no butter. Thicken with a tablespoon of flour, one beaten egg, and boil four minutes, just enough to cook the flour, do not boil the fish any more as it makes it hard; you can put it on as many half slices of bread as persons to eat. Sprinkle the top with white pepper, slice hard boiled eggs, as many as there are persons, laying them on top. For a weak stomach cook it in water, let them sip the thin broth. The beauty of this depends upon not freshening too much or not enough, this requires some experience. Soaking or scalding cod fish to freshen it takes all the cod fish flavor out of it, and no amount of seasoning can put it back.

COD FISH BALLS.

Freshen the fish the same as for creamed fish, squeeze dry, to one cup of cod fish put two cups of seasoned mashed potatoes, two beaten eggs, mix well with a fork, with cream enough to moisten and a little butter. Make into balls one-half inch thick, nearly three inches across, allowing two for a person. Dip in beaten egg and then in flour. Brown in butter and drippings. These are very nice. Do not cook too fast. In cool weather you can prepare enough for two meals. They are good for supper or breakfast, with boiled eggs or poached eggs on toast.

Boiled Cod Fish.

Boil a piece of cod fish according to size of family, boil thirty minutes slowly. Serve with mashed potatoes and drawn butter for dinner.

Fried Frogs.

The hind legs are the only parts that are used. In the markets you buy them ready skinned. Wash them in strong salt water, then pour on boiling hot water, let stand on them five minutes, then rub them with lemon juice after wiping them dry, then rub with salt, boil three minutes, wipe dry, dip in beaten egg and then in flour or fine rolled cracker, then fry in hot spider with half butter and half drippings and brown them. Can prepare them in same way and broil them; dress as broiled chicken.

Lobsters.

Lobsters when freshly caught, have some muscular action in their claws which may be excited by pressing the eyes. The heaviest lobsters for their size are the best. A four-pound one is good size. The male is thought to have the highest flavor, the flesh is firmer and the shell has a brighter red, and is considered best during fall and spring. It may be readily distinguished from the female, as the tail is narrower and the two uppermost fins within the tail are stiff and hard; those of the female are soft and the tail broader.

Never buy a dead lobster. They should be perfectly fresh and very lively. The male lobster is preferred for eating and the female for making sauces and soups. The female has a broader tail and fewer claws than the male. If possible always boil the lobster at home, but in some localities where it is a necessity to buy them boiled, see that the tail is stiff and elastic, so that when you bend it out, it springs back immediately, otherwise they were dead before boiling. Lobsters boiled when dead are watery and soft; they are poisonous.

TO BOIL AND OPEN A LOBSTER.

Fill a kettle with warm water (not boiling); put in the lobster, head downward; add a tablespoon of salt; cover the kettle and stand it over a very quick fire. They suffer less by being put into warm than in boiling water. In the latter they are killed by heat; in warm water they are smothered. A medium-sized lobster should boil half an hour; a larger one three-quarters. Cooking them too long makes them tough, and the meat will stick to the shell. When done and cool separate the tail from the body and twist off all the claws; shake out carefully the tom-allez (this is the liver of the lobster and may be known by its greenish color), also the coral. Then draw the body from the shell, remove the stomach (sometimes called the lady), which is found immediately under the head, and throw this away. Now split the body through the center and pick the meat from the cells; cut the under side of the tail shell, loosen the meat and take it out in one solid piece. Now split the meat of the tail, open and you will discover a little vein running its entire length —this remove. The vein is not always the same color; sometimes it is red, sometimes black and sometimes white; but in all cases it must be carefully taken out and thrown away. The stomach or lady, the vein, and the spongy fingers between the body and the shell, are the only parts not eatable. Crack the claws and take out the meat. To serve plain boiled lobster, arrange the meat thus: taken out in the center of a cold dish, garnishing with the claws, sprigs of fresh parsley, hard boiled eggs cut into quarters and pickled beets cut into fancy shapes. Let each person season to suit one's self.

LOBSTER TURBOT

Is made the same as fish turbot, or scalloped, as some call it.

STURGEON.

Sturgeon fish are only good fried or baked. For frying, boil it slowly for fifteen minutes to take out the strong taste. If it is not already skinned, skin it, and cut in two-inch pieces and fry as other fish, only longer, till well done. It is a large fish and used to be called Albany beef. It is indeed as large as a large calf, being from four to six feet long. In a large family one can use a piece large enough to stuff or fill with turkey dressing, and bake, sew it up, putting slices of ham on it and under. Parboil it first.

TO PICKLE SALMON.

12 pounds salmon	1 red pepper
3 quarts vinegar	15 pepper corns
1 pint boiling water	3 bay leaves
2 onions sliced	3 tablespoons whole mustard
20 cloves	
3 sticks mace	3 tablespoons brown sugar

Clean nicely, rub it well with salt, using a tablespoonful, cover with boiling water, and boil fifteen minutes to every pound. When done, drain off the water, roll the fish tight in dry cloth, to dry it, then skin it and cut it up. Tie all the spices in thin muslin and boil in the vinegar and water fifteen minutes till you get the strength out. Then put in the salmon and boil five minutes. Have your air tight glass jars in boiling water, empty and set in the hot water as you fill them with the salmon full, then fill up all the places well between with the boiling liquor; screw tight and keep in a dark, cool, dry place. You can pickle halibut and sturgeon in the same way.

EELS, STEWED OR FRIED.

They should not be eaten in the hot months, and be eaten the day they are caught. Skin and clean the eels, cut off their heads and take out all that is stringy, cut into pieces about three inches long; parboil them about ten minutes, drain off that water, then put on one pint of veal soup stock, season with salt, butter and pepper, boil slowly about twenty-five minutes, then thicken with flour and pour over them. Use parsley or onion if you like. Fry eels the same as fish, after parboiling.

FRIED SMELTS.

Cut off the fins, wipe dry, beat two eggs and put a melted teaspoon of butter in the eggs, dip the smelts in the egg, then in the rolled cracker and fry like fish in half butter and half lard, till they are a rich brown.

STEWED OYSTERS.

50 oysters
½ pint cream
½ pint milk
½ cup rolled cracker
½ half cup hot water
Salt and pepper to taste
2 tablespoons butter

Empty the can of oysters and broth in dish, pour

on the one-half cup of hot water, take the hand (after washing) and stir to rinse off the broth, and take out the oysters with the hand (feeling for any bits of shell); drain well; put this broth in stew kettle; let come to a simmer; skim every particle of scum, then add the cream and milk; let come to a boil. After putting butter, salt and pepper on top of the oysters, set kettle where it will not boil, pour the oysters in and let stand, stirring a little, say eight minutes. As soon as they begin to shrink take them off and pour onto the rolled cracker in hot tureen, strirring so it will not be lumpy. Serve immediately. If the oysters boil up even once they become hardened. The pure flavor of an oyster is better than anything you can flavor it with. It needs nothing.

Oysters on Toast.

This may be quickly prepared after everything and all the family are ready for tea. Have coals ready for the toast. Toast as many slices of bread as there are members of family. Take as many oysters as you need and scald the pure broth and skim, add butter, pepper, salt, a little cream, and flour enough to make it as thick as cream, and boil a minute to cook the flour, then put in the oysters and let them get boiling hot through without boiling. A half-warmed oyster is not acceptable. Lay buttered toast on platter and pour on oysters and broth. If more broth put it in gravy tureen. Be careful not to have too much broth on toast, or it will be soaked. The toast must be toasted brown, not white nor black. I prepare this myself while the maid toasts the bread, then it is all served hot and seasoned desirable.

Fried Oysters.

Take the largest oysters, pour on a half cup of hot water and stir to take off the liquor; drain well; lay on dry cloth, then pepper and salt them and dip in 1 eaten egg, then in fine rolled cracker and fry on griddle or spider. Serve hot.

Fried Oysters.

Another way is to prepare them in same way and fry them in boiling hot fat—half suet and half lard. They will cook a golden brown in three minutes.

Oyster Fritters.

Select the largest oysters, drain well, lay on dry cloth, salt and pepper them; take the liquor, boil and skim, add salt, one cup of milk, three beaten eggs, sift with six tablespoons of flour, one teaspoon of baking powder, beat all well together. Have a spider of hot fat as for fried cakes—half suet and half lard. Put oysters in batter and drop one by one in the boiling hot fat. First drop a small bit of bread in to test the heat; if it browns quickly it is hot enough. Turn them when half done. Cook them a golden brown. It will take about four minutes. Serve hot.

Baked Oysters.

Take large, fresh oysters; scrub the shells till perfectly clean, then place in baking pan in a quick oven, and bake till they open themselves. Take off the top shell, leaving the oyster in lower shell. Season with a little butter, salt and pepper. Only those who live near oyster beds can enjoy these in their freshness.

BROILED OYSTERS.

Wipe your oysters (select large ones) in a dry napkin. Season with salt and pepper; dip in raw beaten egg and then in fine rolled cracker or fine bread crumbs. Take a fine new wire, double in form of a hairpin, say two of them. String the oysters on them and lay on fine gridiron, or fasten the wires on a long stick or cane, and hold them in front of a hot fire. Grease the gridiron with salt pork or butter. Bread crumbs are prepared by drying slices in the oven and then grating. Serve oysters on hot dishes and hot plates always.

OYSTER PATTIES.

Prepare a puff paste (see index), roll thin, cut out with a cutter three or more inches in diameter. Leave the bottom layer whole, cut out the center of two other layers, leaving the rings one-half the width of circle, place the two rings on the whole one. Make as many as you need and bake on tins just a little golden tinge, as they will brown a little more when filled. You can make these the day before you use them, in winter two or three days, and fill them thirty minutes before eating. If you live in a city you can purchase these of a caterer and fill them yourself. Prepare the oysters the same as stewed oysters, only make less broth. Fill the patties with the oysters, say three or four, a little of the dressing; bake till boiling hot through. Serve hot with rolls for one course. Or you can line plain pattie pans with nice pie crust (or puff paste), filling with the same and cover with a top crust. Bake the same way. The first are delicious. Will bake in twenty-five minutes.

Scalloped Oysters.

For two quarts of oysters have two cups of fine rolled cracker. Boil and skim the broth. Sprinkle the bottom of dish with cracker then a thick layer of oysters. Season with salt, pepper, and bits of butter, then sprinkle cracker not one-fourth of an inch thick; then sprinkle with the scalded broth enough to moisten the cracker, remembering the oysters will moisten some when heated; then another layer of oysters, and so on, till the dish is full—having the crackers on top, and sprinkle the top with one-third of a cup of milk. It will take one cup of the broth and two heaping tablespoons of butter.

Raw Oysters.

There are now regular oyster plates to serve six oysters on, but if you have none, you can get six oysters to each person in shells; wash and wipe nicely, open them, leaving the oysters on the under shell. Put six on a plate with one-fourth of a lemon in the center, or you can put them on a tea-plate. Each one will season for himself.

Drawn Butter.

One pint of milk boiled, braid together two tablespoons of flour, four of butter and stir in milk; season with white pepper and salt; boil five minutes, stirring all the time, when cool add two well beaten eggs. This is really the foundation for all fish and chicken sauces, or lobster, by adding onion juice or lemon, celery juice, vinegar, mushrooms or capers, you have all kind of sauces.

HOLLANDAISE SAUCE.

Measure one-half cup of butter and cream, add the yolks of two raw unbeaten eggs. When nearly ready to serve, add one-half cup of boiling water, the juice of one lemon, slowly beating till it thickens like soft custard cooking in double boiler.

MAYONNAISE SAUCE.

Yolks of 3 raw eggs
1 teaspoon mustard
¼ cup vinegar
A pinch of cayenne

1 tablespoon sugar
1 pint olive oil
1 cup whipped cream
1 teaspoon salt

Juice of half a lemon

Beat the yolks and dry ingredients until they are very light and thick (I always find better success to beat eggs with a knife on a flat plate) set the eggs where they will be cold before breaking; add a few drops of oil at a time until the dressing becomes very thick and rather hard, when the oil can be added more rapidly; when it gets so that it stirs hard, add a little vinegar; when the last of the oil and vinegar has been added it should be very thick; now add the lemon juice and whipped cream, and place on ice for a few hours, or in a cold place. The cream may be omitted without injury. To set this on ice during the beating is better.

BOILED SALAD DRESSING.

3 raw eggs
1 tablespoon olive oil
  or butter
1 cup vinegar

3 tablespoon sugar
1 teaspoon mustard
1 cup milk
1 even teaspoon salt

Stir oil, salt, mustard and sugar in a dish until perfectly smooth; add the well beaten eggs and beat together, then the vinegar and finally the milk. Place in double boiler and stir from eight to ten minutes, keeping the water boiling, till it thickens like cream.

MAYONNAISE DRESSING No. 1.

I give this recipe to show how much a Mayonnaise depends upon the right mixing.

2 yolks raw eggs
½ teaspoon of mustard
1 teaspoon of lemon juice or vinegar
½ pint good olive oil or butter
A pinch of cayenne
½ teaspoon salt

Place the oil and eggs on ice if you have it, if not, in the coldest place, for an hour. Beat your eggs well with a knife, then stir in salt, pepper, and mustard; work these well together, and then add drop by drop the oil. Stir rapidly and steadily while adding the oil, always stirring the same way. After adding one-half the oil (or butter) alternate occasionally with a few drops of lemon juice or vinegar. The more oil you use the thicker the dressing. If it becomes too thick, add a little more vinegar. More or less oil may be added according to the quantity of dressing desired. With care a quart bottle of oil may be stirred into the yolks of two eggs alternating with the vinegar, after adding the first gill of oil. In case the dressing should curdle, that is, the oil and egg separate, which makes the dressing oily and liquid, take at once two new eggs on another plate, after beating well, add by teaspoonfuls the curdled mayonnaise, stirring rapidly and steadily as before, and then finish by adding more oil as directed. This dressing if covered tightly in a glass jar, will keep in a cold place three or four days. You can add whipped cream as you use it, or more vinegar.

Salad Dressing Without Oil No. 1.

1 half pint milk
Yolks 3 eggs
2 even tablespoons corn starch
1 tablespoon butter
1 teaspoon salt
2 tablespoon vinegar
1 salt spoon white pepper

Put the milk on to boil, moisten the corn starch with cold milk and stir it in boiling milk till it thickens and is cooked with the salt. Then add the beaten yolks, pepper, butter and vinegar. Cook one minute and let cool.

Cream Salad Dressing.

Yolks of three hard boiled eggs
1 tablespoon softened butter
2 tablespoons vinegar
½ pint thick cream
Yolk of 1 raw egg
¼ teaspoon white pepper
½ teaspoon salt

Mash the hard boiled eggs or yolks until fine, then add the raw yolks and work to a perfectly smooth paste; then add the melted butter, then by degrees the cream, working and stirring all the while, now add the vinegar, mix well, and it is finished. Keep cold.

Lobster Salad No. 1.

2 lobsters
2 heads lettuce
½ pint mayonnaise

Prepare, cook and dress two lobsters (weighing four or five pounds) as directed (see lobster). Cut the meat into dice size with a silver knife, put it in a cold place till wanted. Make the mayonnaise. Clean the two tail shells and one back in cold water, and with scissors remove the thin shell from the under side of tail. Wash and dry the lettuce leaves; put them around the salad dish in two or three layers. Join the shells together in the form of a boat, the body shell in the center; put them in the salad dish. Mix the mayonnaise and lobster lightly together, place it in this boat. If there is any coral wash it fine and sprinkle it over the top. Garnish with a chain of the whites of hard boiled eggs cut into slices and lapped or linked together.

LOBSTER SALAD No. 2.

Cut up and season the lobster the same as chicken; break the leaves from a head of lettuce, wash them well and singly; put them in a pan of ice water for about ten minutes, then shake the water off; place in ice chest till time of serving; when ready to serve put two or three leaves together in the form of a shell, and arrange these shells on a flat dish; mix half of the mayonnaise dressing with the lobster; put a teaspoonful of this in each shell of leaves; finish with a teaspoon of dressing on top; this is an inviting dish.

A PLAIN DRESSING.

2 cups vinegar
3 raw eggs
½ teaspoon dry mustard
1 even teaspoon salt
½ cup cream or milk
A sprinkle of white pepper
½ cup butter

Stir into your milk the well beaten eggs, add the seasoning, stir in the softened butter, beating thoroughly. Then in this pour the vinegar boiling hot (do not heat it in tin), but cook it all in a double granite boiler, stirring continually and briskly so it will not curdle. Return all to the granite pan, put over the fire and keep stirring till it boils lively for one minute, then remove to a cool place, then place on ice to stiffen; put all these ingredients gradually together; add sugar if you like. Plain lettuce and pealed sliced tomatoes with a liberal covering of mayonnaise sauce, is liked by many, or simply with sugar and vinegar on.

CRAB SALAD, FISH OR SHRIMPS.

This is made by simply boiling 1 dozen crabs thirty minutes, when cold pick out the meat and when ready to serve mix the crabs with the mayonnaise the same as lobsters. Fish or shrimps are used in the same way after being dressed and cooked. One can double any of these recipes, or make only half of it as they need, or use butter in place of olive oil. It is very uncertain whether you can obtain pure oil in small towns or not, as there is such a small demand it does not pay the grocerymen to keep it. Some do not think it as relishable as butter nor as digestible. The experience of one lady was, when she had a table of ten guests, she had mayonnaise dressing on the chicken salad made with pure olive oil. There were but three dishes that were much more than tasted of. Another time she had a company of about twenty-five; the mayonnaise was made of sweet butter for chicken salad, and the salad dishes were empty. Both companies were well acquainted with salads.

MAYONNAISE DRESSING NO. 2. (In bottle)

Yolks of 4 raw eggs   2 even teaspoons salt
1 quart bottle salad oil   2 even teaspoons mustard
8 tablespoons vinegar   1 quart cream

These ingredients are mixed the same way as mayonnaise No. 1. Mixing the eggs and oil or butter first, then add the seasoning. Then add by degrees the quart of cream and bottle air tight for use. If well made, this will keep for six months. If one has occasion to use this frequently, it is well to have it on hand.

SAUCE TARTARE.

1 teaspoon mustard
½ salt spoon pepper
Yolks 2 raw eggs
6 tablespoons vinegar

12 drops onion juice
½ cup butter
1 tablespoon chopped parsley
1 salt spoon salt

Mix as directed in mayonnaise.

SALAD DRESSING WITHOUT OIL NO. 2.

4 raw eggs
1½ pints vinegar
½ cup sugar
1 even teaspoon mustard

1 cup butter
1 cup cream
1 teaspoon salt
1 even salt spoon red pepper

Stir all together as directed in mayonnaise except the vinegar, beating it all the time, place it in double boiler till it boils; then remove and beat in slowly the vinegar. This will keep for weeks, corked tight, in cool place.

FRUIT SALAD.

6 oranges
6 bananas

½ pineapple
½ cocoanut

Cut and slice the oranges (after peeling them) across the grain, leaving the core out, peel and slice the bananas in rounds in a separate dish. Peel and dig out the eyes of the pineapple and then grate it. Take the dish that you are to serve it in, and lay in alternate layers of fruit and sugar, till all are in, then on the top pile fresh grated cocoanut. This can be prepared two or more hours before you wish to use it.

CHICKEN SANDWICHES.

Sandwiches of all kinds are made by spreading two slices of bread with butter and placing them together with meat between them. Bread should be twenty-four hours old, must be moist and light; cut quite thin slices with a very sharp knife; spread them thinly with nice fresh butter, then with your hashed or sliced meat. After the chicken is cooked, chop it fine, when cold, to almost a paste, then moisten this sufficiently so it will spread easily, with softened butter, a little cream, salt, pepper, and a little mustard if you like, but it must be very little. Spread and put two slices together but do not press much; when ready to serve cut in fancy shapes, diamond, oblong, etc. Cover with damp napkin till ready to use.

VEAL SANDWICHES.

Chop the nice, small pieces that are left from a veal roast, and moisten with the veal gravy.

LAMB SANDWICHES.

Are made the same way as veal, moistened with the gravy and seasoned to taste. The meats to all, must be perfectly smooth and spread evenly.

TONGUE SANDWICHES.

Boil the tongue the day before you wish to use it, let it cool in its own liquor, take out, peel. Next day slice, chop fine, add enough sweet cream, softened butter, and seasoning of salt, pepper, or mustard. The tongue should have been in brine three or more weeks. A fresh tongue has no relish. It should be a beef's tongue.

HAM SANDWICHES.

To a coffee cup of lean ham finely chopped, add three tablespoons of butter, the yolk of one beaten egg, season as needed with salt, pepper and a very little mustard. Just let it get boiling hot, then perfectly cold before spreading your buttered bread. Another way is to mix the ham with mayonnaise dressing to a soft paste, and spread between your buttered thin slices of bread. Sardines, tongue, chicken, or lobster, may be mixed this way in place of ham.

CHICKEN SALAD No. 2.

Boil two chickens tender, salted as for table, take out skin and bone and all discoloring. Cut in strips, and then in bits the size of large peas; put chicken and celery on ice. For dressing; the yolks of four fresh eggs, with the yolks of two hard boiled eggs. Rub these smoothly. A good measure of butter or oil is a tablespoon to each yolk of fresh egg. All the art consists in introducing the butter or oil and vinegar by degrees. It takes time to make a good salad. When the oil is well mixed put in two teaspoons of salt, one small even teaspoon of white pepper, two tablespoons of vinegar. When ready to serve mix celery and chicken well, then with a silver fork stir in the dressing, mixing thoroughly. This salad to be crisp must be made the day it is used. The best salad for health is simply crisp lettuce with sugar and vinegar on it. These mixtures do for a treat.

CABBAGE DRESSING.

This is very nice when one can not obtain celery for a dressing for a chicken salad, made in the same way as the chicken salad on page 101, substituting the cabbage for celery, shave it very fine and chop it a little.

Egg Salad.

Boil six eggs hard; chop the whites fine, and rub the yolks smooth with a silver spoon. Sprinkle in a little salt, pepper and chopped celery. Mix in mayonnaise dressing, put this on lettuce leaves with a cup of chopped chicken or of ham mixed in it, or use it for a lettuce salad.

Cream Dressing.

Five eggs beaten separately; two teaspoons of mixed mustard, butter the size of an egg, two teaspoons of salt, one-half teaspoon of red pepper, three tablespoons of the finest table oil, one pint of thick cream. Scald the cream, stir in the yolks and continue to stir until it begins to thicken, then add the seasoning and two or three teaspoons of vinegar, then cool and add the beaten whites. Stir in oil when cold.

EGGS.

Eggs are almost invaluable, particularly in the spring of the year, when we can obtain them so fresh and plentiful. Baron Liebig says: " There is more nutriment in an egg than in anything of equal bulk that exists in nature, or that chemistry can produce." To prove whether eggs are good or bad, place a few at a time in a deep dish of cold water. The fresher the egg the sooner it will fall to the bottom on its side; if it falls on the end reject it; if it swims, it is bad thoroughly. To preserve eggs for winter use, after testing them, put in the bottom of a one or two gallon wooden tub or keg with a flat cover, so they can stand on either end when you turn the vessel once a week, so as to keep the yolks from settling. The time to pack is the latest fall eggs you can obtain, packing them as fast as you can obtain them. You make more sure of keeping them if you stop the pores of the shell by dipping the eggs in a thin solution of gum Arabic and let dry. I knew of one lady that kept them from the first of November to the second week in April, simply packing in salt. It was a very cold winter and kept them in the cellar. Keep cool and be sure they are all fresh eggs. An egg six weeks old will not hatch. If you would like your hens to lay in winter, save all the meat bones, dry them, and have them pulverized in some way and mix a little in their food; as much as you think they would eat of gravel and sand in summer. Give them bones dried to peck at.

Hard boiled eggs should be put directly on taking out into a dish of cold water for a minute or so, to protect the outside of yolks from turning dark.

BOILED EGGS.

Dip the eggs first in cold water to prevent their cracking. Then put them in water simmering hot and let boil slowly three and a half minutes. This just cooks the whites and heats the yolks hot. Another. Place the eggs in boiling hot water, move the dish to the back of the range, cover closely and let stand ten minutes. This causes the white to be of creamy consistency, and the yolk not hard and dry. For hard boiled eggs boil eight minutes—some like them fifteen minutes.

Poached Eggs.

Butter the bottom of dish that you poach them in, so they will not stick and break when you take them up; put in two inches boiling hot water. The dish or spider must be flat-bottomed; lay in muffin rings, break one egg at a time in a saucer, put one in each ring (no salt, as it hardens the white); do not have the water boil, but only simmer; with a spoon dip the water over each egg; be careful not to break the yolks; as soon as the whites look like a thick veil over the yolk they are done; they will cook in from three to four minutes. Take a half slice of toast, sprinkle salted hot water on it with a spoon and butter it as for eating, lay one egg on each piece of toast, salt and pepper and lay a bit of butter on the center of each egg. This can all be done while the family are getting seated at table, as their relish depends much upon their freshness. There are pans made out of heavy tin now on purpose for poaching eggs, which hold from two to six or more eggs, but the bottom cooks harder than it does in spider.

Scrambled Eggs.

For four persons take five eggs, break them in a deep earthen pie-plate, half beat them, then add half a cup of cream if you have it, if not, milk and salt, stir a little, taste to see if salt enough; before this place spider on stove with a piece of butter the size of a large hickory nut, to get just sissing hot, pour in the eggs and scrape one way with large spoon constantly (do not stir round and round) cooking gently and evenly; when it is as delicate as a boiled custard, take it off quickly and pour into a hot dish. If you do not beat the eggs too much, it will be in stripes of mingled white and yellow, but we like them best well beaten. Turn them out before you think them quite done, they will cook more; a good sprinkling of white pepper on top. They will cook in three minutes or less.

Omelet.

Three eggs beaten slightly together, two even teaspoons of flour, two-thirds cup of cream, or milk and salt, stir till well mixed, place in hot buttered spider, when browned turn one-half on the other half with two knives.

Omelet.

If you prefer a dry fluffy omelet to a moist flaky one, beat the white and yolk of the eggs separate. If not, together slightly, add a tablespoon of cream for each egg and salt. Have a flat spider hot and well buttered, pour in the omelet, brown slightly on the bottom having the top soft, roll one-half over the other half deftly and serve in hot covered dish. Some set it in oven on top of grate to brown instead of doubling, but it is not so moist.

Eggs, Point Shirley Style.

Separate the yolks and whites of three eggs. Beat the yolks two minutes; add three tablespoons of cream, one-half even teaspoon salt, beat a little more. Melt half a tablespoon of butter in a hot spider, pour in the yolks, when they thicken slightly pour the whites in without beating. Let them be until they look nearly like the white of a boiled egg, then gently mix them with a silver fork. Serve in hot dish or if you like on buttered toast. Chicken or ham omelet is made by placing either of them hashed and seasoned over the omelet before turning it over.

BOB THE SEA COOK'S OMELET.

A real French omelet is a natural dish. It don't want all the fixing most cooking folks put on her. One would think by reading the books that it was as big a thing to do as a suffler. Most books tell you to beat up your whites till they stand, but it ain't right. A Frenchman don't take no time in making an omelet. While the butter is in the pan heating, he gets his eggs ready. There ain't no use to separate whites and yellows. Break the eggs in a bowl, stir them so whites and yellows is mixed thoroughly and that's all. Two minutes does that. Now don't you add water, nor milk, nor nothing. You can put cream in, but then that don't make the old original Johnny omelet, but something else that may be good enough but new fangled. If you have any parsley, chop that up before you begin, that is, if you want a parsley omelet; the parsley, about a teaspoon to six eggs, ought to be as fine as possible; add a little salt and very little white pepper to your eggs and when your butter is a sizzing, tilt over the frying pan a very little and pour in your eggs. It don't take half a minute to cook. If your butter is hot enough a minute will do it all. Don't go to turn your omelet with a fork but sling her. She ought to take a whole turn in the air and fall on her other side. But anyhow, if you ain't up to that trick, you might help her over with a spoon. An overcooked omelet is just a disgrace. It ought to be mellow and a little underdone in the middle. Don't you never go to give people as knows what an omelet is, something in a flat sheet as tough as a canvas and call it an omelet.

Eggs à la Lavallette.

Pour into a flat tin dish cream to the depth of a quarter of an inch; bring to a boil, then drop in the eggs and cook until the whites are set. Season to taste with salt, pepper and butter. Serve in the same dish or take carefully out and pour the seasoned cream over the eggs.

Eggs à la Créam.

Boil six eggs eight minutes, drop in cold water a minute; remove the shells, cut in halves; slice a bit off each end so they will stand on end. Mix a tablespoon of butter with a teaspoon of flour; stir it into a pint of boiling milk, stirring constantly; season and pour over the eggs.

Egg Gems.

Two cups of sweet milk, two eggs, one tablespoon of butter, one-half teaspoon salt, three and one-half cups sifted flour, one heaping teaspoon of baking powder. Bake in gem pans.

To Fry Egg Plant.

Always choose fat, plump ones, they are much better than the long slim ones. Cut in slices not quite a half inch and peel them. Rub a little salt on each side and pack them in two piles, putting the largest at the bottom, in a dish. Place a plate on top, upon which put a laundry iron weight. Fill dish with water; let stand an hour and then throw off this water; rinse and repeat the same process for another hour. This is to take out that unhealthy bitter taste. Rinse, wipe dry, dip in beaten egg and then in rolled cracker or in batter, and fry in spider; brown on both sides in half butter and half suet. If you have a fresh plant, not wilted by being picked too long or by drought, they are very fine.

VEGETABLES.

All vegetables in summer should be freshly gathered the day they are to be cooked. Peas, beans, and asparagus, if laid over for one day lose their own peculiar sweetness and relish. Soft water is better for all vegetables except potatoes, turnips and cabbage, these three should be put in just as the water comes to a boil. Some one says that a teaspoon of common salt put in a gallon of soft water hardens it at once, and a half teaspoon of bi-carbonate of soda to a gallon of hard water renders it soft. Rainwater, if fresh and pure; gives a relish to sweet corn and peas that hard water does not, and I put the salt in when it is first put over. When any vegetables are wilted they should soak for an hour or two, in very cold water. Peas, beans and lentils are the most nutritious of all vegetables (lentils are raised more in the old country), and are said to contain as much carbon (that is heat-giving) as wheat and nearly twice the quantity of nitrogen (for muscle).

PLAIN BOILED POTATOES.

Never boil potatoes with their skins on. They contain three-fourths water and nearly one-fourth starch, with a small proportion of other elements, thus supplying what is lacking in lean meat and other nitrogenous food. When the sprouts begin to appear in the spring they must be rubbed off at once, as they exhaust the most nourishing part of the potatoes. Rub them off three times and they will cease to grow. Keep them in cool place. I presume there are more potatoes consumed than all other vegetables put together (excepting grains). Select potatoes of medium size, without blemishes and of a yellowish white color. Those that grow on a rich heavy soil are most nutritious. To boil potatoes wash them clean, then pare them thin, and lay them in cold water till ready to boil, then put in boiling hot water just enough to cover them, boil fifteen minutes, then add salt. Boil slowly until nearly done, then put in half a cup of cold water, to render the potatoes more mealy. As soon as tender enough to admit a fork easily, pour off the water; take the cover off and shake the potatoes in a current of cold air, at either the door or window, place the kettle on back part of the stove, and cover with a clean, coarse towel until serving time. The sooner the potatoes are served the better. This is for whole potatoes. Or cut them in quarters after shaking them and put on a half cup of cream, a little butter, salt, and let come to a scald, then dish and sprinkle with pepper. You only need half as much cream for mashed potatoes; mash and stir with a fork a few times. Season as the others, and do not pack them in the dish too solid.

CREAMED POTATOES.

Take cold boiled potatoes, slice one-fourth of an inch thick; put in your spider with salt and half cup of cream, and boil it fifteen minutes, chopping it a little with spoon and stirring; boil slowly or it will burn. If one has no cream, take twice as much milk and boil it slowly with the potatoes; till it creams. It will need a little more butter. Dish and sprinkle with pepper, serve hot.

BAKED POTATOES.

Select medium sized potatoes wash and rinse and clean and place in very hot oven for forty or more minutes; when done crack each one in your hand, with a towel over it. If baked crisp they will snap and be mealy as this process lets off the steam.

PLAIN FRIED POTATOES.

Slice cold boiled potatoes one-fourth of an inch thick, put in spider a bit of butter and lard; salt them, lay them in the hot spider brown lightly and slowly on both sides. Pepper.

MASHED POTATOES.

Prepare the potatoes the same as for boiled potatoes, as soon as a fork will go through them easily, drain off the water, dry them by setting kettle on top of stove, put in salt and butter, according to quantity, mash with a wire masher, then stir in a little cream or milk as you like with a fork. Dish and smooth over the top. Some brown the top in oven. There is no vegetable so much used as the potato, yet how few know how to cook them properly. Most people think they certainly know how to boil a potato. Some will throw them in cold water just when it happens to be convenient, whether it lacks one hour or two before meal time, when they should be put in just as the water begins to boil and taken off as soon as a fork can easily pierce them. A common sized potato will boil in thirty minutes. We should not allow our daughters to lose sight of the fact, that to be able to boil an Irish potato well, is an accomplishment of more importance to the human race, than to know the science of banging the hair, and will go farther to beautify the human face.

CURLED POTATOES.

Take freshly mashed potatoes and press through a colander into your table dish. Brown the top in oven. Season just right first.

SCALLOPED POTATOES.

Wash and rinse your potatoes, peel them, boil nearly done, and slice thin; butter the pudding dish or a good basin, put in a layer of potatoes, then a seasoning of salt, pepper, and bits of butter, fill with potatoes, remembering to season every layer; cover the top with cracker crumbs, then heat boiling hot, one cup of cream and one cup of milk and sprinkle it over till it is half full or over. Cover with a good plate that fits, and bake in the oven one hour and a quarter for two quarts. Some like chopped parsley in, and a thin layer of rolled cracker between each layer of potatoes. Take off the plate fifteen minutes before they are done, to brown the top. Others sprinkle a little flour between each layer; or make a nice drawn butter of your cream and milk, with one tablespoon of flour no thicker than cream and put it between each layer of potatoes. For one quart or less bake thirty minutes, having the oven just at boiling point. Take off the plate and brown the top when nearly done. These are very nice for supper, and if there are some left over, they can be used for breakfast, by adding a little cream to moisten them and heat hot in the oven. If raw potatoes bake one hour or more.

French Fried Potatoes.

Select long potatoes. When peeled and rinsed put in cold water for one hour, wipe dry, cut lengthwise into six or eight pieces, place on a dry clean cloth and clap them dry; have ready a kettle of hot lard, or half suet and lard, fill a skimmer with the potatoes and drop into the hot fat. The fat must be hot or they will not be good, but care must be taken not to have your lard spatter over, as you put them in and so set fire to the spider; when ready to put the potatoes in, set the spider on the back part of the stove for a minute or two to avoid this. They generally cook in ten minutes; try with a fork, skim out. and lay on drab paper and sprinkle salt on both sides, and serve hot.

Parisienne Potatoes.

Peel large potatoes and throw into cold water for half an hour, dry with a cloth, and with a vegetable scoop cut out tiny balls, dry with a cloth again and cook in hot suet cooked through and of a light brown; the fat must be very hot, then they will be dry and mealy. Skim out on clean drab paper and sprinkle with salt.

Potatoes a la Royal.

Allow one pint of hot boiled potatoes, half cup of cream, two tablespoons of butter, the whites of four eggs and yolk of one and salt; mash the potatoes fine, then beat light with a fork. Gradually add the butter and cream, and beaten egg to a froth, mix well, turn into a dish that can be set on the table, well buttered, smooth the top or pile it in a rocky form and brush over with the yolk. Set in hot oven till brown.

Potato Puffs.

2 cups mashed potatoes 2 eggs beaten separate
2 tablespoons butter ½ cup cream
Salt and pepper

Make in puffs large enough for each person; bake in oven till brown.

Brown Potatoes with Roast Beef.

Peel and put in cold salt water for an hour, then put into boiling water (salt it) and cook fifteen minutes; take out and drain, then put in dripping-pan with the roast beef on the frame. When you baste the meat every ten minutes throw the gravy on the potatoes also.

Lyonnaise Potatoes.

Put one tablespoonful of butter in your spider, slice one good-sized onion, stir and cook in butter till done; add one tablespoon of parsley chopped fine for one pint of cold boiled potatoes cut into dice; salt and pepper to taste. Fry and stir gently till the potatoes are a nice light brown. Put in a hot covered dish.

Another Lyonnaise Potato.

To a pint of thin sliced cold boiled potatoes put a chopped onion cooked in one tablespoon of butter, one half pint of milk, with pepper and salt; cover and stew fifteen minutes. Wet a half teaspoon of corn starch in cold milk and stir in a spoon of minced parsley. Can add more milk and butter if liked.

New Potatoes à la Cream

Wash new potatoes and scrape off the skin; put them in boiling water, a little salt; as soon as tender take up and cut into four pieces. While these are boiling put some new milk or cream, say half pint for a pint of potatoes, a piece of butter the size of a small egg and salt. Mix an even tablespoon of flour with cold milk, stir into cream, boil enough to cook the flour and pour over the potatoes.

Small Potatoes Creamed or Hashed.

Chop cold boiled potatoes, put a spoon of butter in spider, put in the potatoes, salt, enough sweet milk and cream to nearly cover them; wet a spoon of flour with cold milk and stir in. Anything warmed over needs enough cooking to give it a flavor, that merely being warmed can not give it.

Saratoga Potatoes.

Wash and peel the potatoes and cut them in very thin slices, either with a knife or a slaw cutter; lay them in cold water for a time, then drain them in a dish, and put them on a dry cloth, patting the top with another dry cloth. Have in your spider hot fat as for fried cakes. When ready to put some in the fat, have it boiling hot and remove it to back of stove till they are in, so as to avoid its running over. Put in only a few at a time or they will stick together. Have ready a piece of cheese-cloth thrown over a colander, when light brown skim them into the cloth and drain; sprinkle salt on both sides, and set in the heater till all are done; going through the same process till all are cooked. Serve hot. What is left can be heated over the next day

POTATO CROQUETTES.

To one quart of hot mashed potatoes, add one-half cup of hot milk, two generous tablespoons of butter, one teaspoon of salt, well beaten in. Beat the whites of two eggs stiff and stir in. Form into croquettes (if you wish to fry them in spider flatten them, if in hot fat, do not) roll them in the yolks of the eggs and then in cracker crumbs, lay in a croquette basket and immerse in boiling hot fat till brown.

POTATO SALAD.

One pint of cold boiled potatoes cut into dice, two hard boiled eggs cut fine, one teaspoon of finely minced cold onion and one tablespoon of chopped parsley; mix well together. For dressing, stir into three tablespoons of butter gradually three tablespoons of vinegar; one saltspoon salt, and half spoon pepper. Mix well. Keep dressing in cold place.

BAKED SWEET POTATOES.

Lay nicely cleaned medium sized potates on the upper grate, in a hot oven, in their skins; when nearly baked, take a towel in your hand and crack them; leave them in five minutes longer to let the moisture evaporate. Serve hot after the family sits down.

STEAMED SWEET POTATOES.

Steam them in a steamer with skins on; do not let them get over done. Peel them quickly with a white metal or silver knife or fork. Never use a steel one for sweet potatoes as it turns the potato black whereever it touches it. Sweet potatoes are too watery to boil in water.

Fried Sweet Potatoes.

Cold steamed potatoes are nice for breakfast cut either long or round, salt them, and fry in spider in half butter and half lard or drippings. A little brown on both sides.

Cooked Over Sweet Potatoes.

Cut cold steamed sweet potatoes in dice like pieces or bits; to one pint of potato put two tablespoons of butter, salt and pepper to taste, fry till a nice brown, or not as you like, then to a half pint of beef stock, one even tablespoon of flour and one well beaten egg, let boil two minutes.

Sweet Corn Boiled.

Husk and silk the corn, put the ears of corn in a kettle, in cold soft water, let come slowly to a boil, boil for five minutes. Put it in hot covered dish. Set the kettle on back of stove and keep it in the water till ready to eat it. It will be sweet and juicy. I prefer no salt in it, but put salt and butter on as I eat it. A common mistake of otherwise good cooks is to boil corn half an hour. This could not fail to make it hard and indigestible. Overcooking brings it into disrepute as a vegetable, while if freshly picked and cooked properly it is delicate and healthful. For eating at the table, some score each row of corn with a sharp knife, then butter and salt it and eating the center of the grain, leave the hull on the cob, it is for some more healthy.

Succotash.

Shell one pint of fresh green beans, after washing the pods clean. (Never wash the beans after shelling.) Boil the beans till tender in soft water. When half done add the salt. Score and press from the cob twice as much corn by measure as there are beans. When the beans are well cooked with hardly enough water to cover the beans then set the kettle off the fire. Add to the corn three-fourths of a pint of cream or milk, two tablespoons of butter, salt and pepper to taste; pour this slowly on the beans; when hot stir in one even tablespoon of flour to make the consistency of thin cream. Boil it five minutes. This can be made in winter from canned corn and beans. Canned corn can be cooked for table in same way.

To Dry Corn.

Husk and silk it, then place it in boiler in cold rain water (water must be pure); let come slowly to a boil; boil five minutes, take out as fast as you can in a large dish; cut it while hot, but not too close to get the hulls, picking off all the silk you see (much of it comes off in the water); then run your fingers through it and dip your fingers in a bowl of water, and pick it all over carefully to get the silk all out, for it is too much like a hair to be pleasant in the mouth. Then spread on the drier if you have one. I dry one and a half bushels at a time on mine in one-half of a day and evening. It takes three of us one-half a day to get such a quantity ready to put on the drier. It needs scraping up together and respreading as fast as it dries, and almost constant attention. It will dry in six or seven hours. If you have no drier put it on plates and platters around the stove, changing and turning often. This will dry in eighteen hours. Put it in tight bags and hang in a dry cool place.

To Cook Dried Corn.

One cup full of the corn will be sufficient for six or more persons. Put cold water on it, and the hulls that rise on top pour off, then put on cold soft or rain water about one pint and a half, all it will soak up, set it where it will keep quite warm, in an earthen dish or a good tin basin. It will soak in five or six hours. Then put in sweet cream and milk, butter, salt, pepper and a little flour. Just boil long enough to cook the flour. This is delicious when rightly proportioned, according to quantity of corn. The sweet corn must be of the best.

Mrs. Rorer's way of drying sweet corn: "Score the corn down the center of each row of grains, then with the back of the knife press out all the pulp, leaving the hull on the cob." Spread this pulp raw on plates and dry around stove. It will brown easily, so watch it closely.

Roast Green Corn.

Mrs. Herrick says that " corn is excellent roasted in this way. Select tender ears, turn the husks and remove the silk, then re-cover the corn with the husks. Lay on the bottom of the oven with grate under, turning often." I should think in a hot oven it would roast in from twenty to thirty minutes.

Mock Oysters.

Grate six good sized ears of sweet corn; rub it through a hair-sieve to rid it of the hulls; add two well beaten eggs, two tablespoons of thick cream, one tablespoon of butter, two of fine rolled cracker, one teaspoon salt, one-fourth of pepper. Beat this all well together; have a lump of good butter about the size of half an egg; when hot on griddle drop the corn mixture in tablespoonfuls, allowing space that they do not run together; when they are a nice brown turn them over and brown the other side; it requires about five minutes to cook them. This will make about two dozen oysters; serve them hot. They can be cooked while the table is being waited on.

Corn Fritters.

Prepare one dozen ears of corn the same as for mock oysters and put it in fritter batter made of two eggs beaten separately, one cup of flour, one teaspoon of baking powder, one-half pint of milk, salt and pepper. Fry in hot fat, drop in by spoonfuls in the fat. So soon as brown on both sides they are done. Take out with a wire skimmer, drain on good plain brown paper.

Beets.

Wash the beets but do not break the skin. It takes from one to four hours to boil, according to age. An old or wilted beet will never be eatable. When tender put them in a pan of cold water and quickly rub off the skins with the hand, keeping them as hot as possible, slice them round and put butter, salt, pepper and hot vinegar on them and set in the heater. Be sure you have the rich, long, blood beet.

Baked Beets.

It is not, perhaps, generally known that common beets baked in the same manner as potatoes are much sweeter and drier than when boiled; peel them and dish them up the same as boiled beets.

Curing Beets for Winter Use.

Take up the beets before freezing time, boil tender, skin and slice round, put them in glass fruit jars, pack in as tight as you can, then fill jars with cold cider vinegar (this is done to know how much vinegar is needed), pour off and bring vinegar to a boil. For each jar add one tablespoon of sugar, a small amount of cayenne pepper, a little salt, pour it over the beets hot; then screw tight as you would fruit. Take medium sized beets and good blood red. This is a good way to have sweet and tender pickled beets for winter use.

Boiled Turnips.

Wash and pare the turnips, cut into quarters, put into boiling water, boil till tender, say thirty minutes, pour off the water and set on stove to dry, then press out all the water, add butter and salt, mash fine, dish and sprinkle with pepper. They are drier to be steamed; or you can slice and fry them to eat with roast duck. Good turnips or beets are seldom found now-a-days.

Stewed Tomatoes.

Scald them by pouring boiling water on them, let stand for five minutes, pour it off, peel them, cut out the hard stem end and hard cores, as you slice them. Cook them in a granite or a porcelain lined saucepan, put to about a quart of tomatoes a tablespoon of butter, salt and pepper (they do not bear much salt) stew thirty minutes or more and pour on to one heaping tablespoon of rolled crackers in dish.

To Can Tomatoes.

Prepare in the same way leaving out the butter, pepper and rolled cracker.

Raw Tomatoes.

Scald and pour off the water, peel, slice them into dish, pour off the juice, salt and pepper them, let persons put on sugar and vinegar to suit themselves, or prepare a mayonnaise dressing.

Carrots Stewed and Fried.

Pare and boil whole, salt the water, boil till tender, from thirty to sixty minutes, then slice round, put butter, salt and pepper or a cream sauce, or slice and brown them in spider. All vegetables must be *taken up* the minute they are *done*.

Boiled Parsnips.

Scrape and put in boiling water, add salt, boil till tender, say from thirty to fifty minutes; drain and dry them, then slice, put on butter, salt and pepper, or a cream sauce; or, take the boiled parsnips sliced and brown them, after seasoning, or mash them and stir into fritter batter.

Green Peas.

Peas are better if picked and shelled just before cooking. Wash the pods clean before shelling, as washing the peas takes off the juices which we always find in young peas, and gives them their delicious flavor, but you can not find it in an old pea. Boil in cold rain water for about thirty minutes, add salt. When tender add cream, butter, salt and pepper, a very little flour, according to quantity. Everything depends upon the seasoning of peas, beans, or oysters or anything else in the cooking department.

Lima Beans.

Green beans of all kinds should be cooked the same as green peas, also string beans after they are strung and cut in half-inch pieces, being careful to remove all that is stringy. All dried beans are dished in the same way, after being cooked tender in rainwater, add the salt.

Boston Baked Beans.

Put three quarts of warm soft water on one quart of the small white bean, after washing, let soak over night (this to soak out the rank oil contained in the thick skin) turn off this water and rinse them thoroughly. Add cold water and boil ten minutes, pour this off and put on boiling water and boil till half done, then put in about one pound of well salted pork until half cooked to season the beans, if they are not sufficiently salt add more. Have a teakettle of hot soft water on stove to replenish with. (If you have to use hard water soften it with a little soda.) Take out the pork and boil the beans until they can be easily mashed between the thumb and finger; then put the beans into a deep earthen bean pot, and the salt pork buried in the beans all but the rind, which should be gashed one-half inch apart. Some like one tablespoon of molasses in the beans. If you prefer you can leave out the pork and the molasses, and stir in instead two tablespoons of good butter. Put on cover and bake from six to eight hours, taking the cover off the last hour to brown and crisp the top and rind of pork.

Add boiling water from time to time, as it may need to prevent burning. This is Boston baked beans. But if you do not wish to bake them so long you can bake them from one to two hours in a tin dish.

PICKLED BEANS.

Wash and string tender green beans, put into a kettle of boiling water, add salt and boil till tender, say twenty-five minutes. When done, drain in a colander and let stand until cold; then put into a glass jar, sprinkle over a little cayenne pepper, add a tablespoon chopped horseradish and cover with good vinegar. A nice relish.

ASPARAGUS ON TOAST.

Wash it well, tie it in bundles of ten or fifteen stalks, with a well-washed cord, and cut them of equal lengths, from three to four inches long, boil in hot water, a little salt; when it first comes it will cook in fifteen minutes, and at the last it may take thirty. Great care should be taken not to over-cook it, as some do. As soon as tender, pour off nearly all the water, and add sufficient cream and milk, butter, pepper, and salt, according to quantity, to season and make sufficient gravy to put on toast or plain bread (one-half slice each) enough for the number of persons. Butter the toast or bread as for eating; thicken it only as thick as thin cream. This is nice for dinner or supper. Do not cut off the cord till you lay it on the toast, then cut it and let one bunch be for each half-slice and fall open, then pour on the gravy or sauce and a sprinkle of pepper; serve soon. Some cut the asparagus in inch long pieces.

Salsify and Parsnips.

Grate a bunch or two of salsify, as you would horse-radish, add a raw egg beaten, rolled cracker or flour, and fry as you would oysters. Parsnips prepared in this way are extremely nice.

Fried Salsify or Mock Oysters.

Scrape the roots, lay in cold water fifteen minutes, put them in boiling water, cook till tender, then drain and mash fine, picking out all the fiber. Moisten with one teacup of cream, a little milk; add a tablespoon of butter and three eggs for every two cups of salsify. Beat the eggs light. Make into round cakes, dredge with flour and fry brown.

Boiled Cauliflower.

Select close heads, trim and open the flower in water to remove any insects. Soak in salt and water for an hour before cooking, then put them in boiling water with a little salt, cook till tender, slowly. Can tie up in piece of cheese-cloth to prevent them breaking, or if not lift out with a skimmer. Serve with drawn butter, adding a well beaten egg or mayonnaise sauce.

Boiled Onions.

Pour boiling water over the onions, drain off, this will prevent the smarting of the eyes, then peel, put them over to boil in cold water and boil slowly for fifteen minutes, then pour off this water to take out the strong taste, and put in more boiling water and cook till tender; put salt in when cooking; pour off this water, and put on cream and butter or milk, season, and thicken a little and boil it five minutes, put it in covered dish. Do not boil vegetables on the gallop as it makes them fall to pieces.

CELERY AND RADISHES.

Clean with a brush (a new stiff tooth-brush is the best), put in a celery glass with water and eat with salt.

CELERY—COOKED.

Clean and cut in pieces one-half inch long, cover with soup stock and boil till tender, remember the salt. Rub one tablespoon of butter and one of flour together and stir in and dish.

DANDELIONS.

These are used for greens in the early spring. Do not use them after they blossom, as then they are bitter. Cook only the leaves; wash them in two waters, leaf by leaf. It is safer for the lady of the house to see to this herself, as then she can feel sure there are no bugs or stray weeds. Simply boil in water with a little salt, until tender, from twenty to thirty minutes; drain well and eat with vinegar or mayonnaise sauce.

COOKING CABBAGE.

Almost every one likes cauliflower if it is properly cooked, while few admit a fondness for cabbage. Yet it belongs to the same family and is improved by cooking well. It should first be parboiled one-half hour in a porcelain kettle; a little salt, then drained, and put on fresh boiling water and cooked until tender two hours. Serve with this dressing:

Cabbage Dressing.

Three tablespoons of vinegar, one teaspoon of salt, a piece of butter the size of an egg; mix altogether and let them just come to a boil. Let them cool off a little and then thicken with a beaten egg; boil up again, then thicken with milk or cream, as you have.

Sauerkraut.

Squeeze the cabbage out of the brine, wash it in one or two cold waters, drain; put it in porcelain kettle, cover with cold water, boil two hours; pour into colander, press out the water, replace in vessel. Prepare a dressing of one tablespoon of butter and one of flour, stir in pan on the fire until a light brown color. Mix this well with one quart of kraut.

Wiesbaden.

Baked Macaroni.

Use about half a pound of macaroni, break it up in pieces, put it in boiling water; salt and boil rapidly for twenty-five minutes to prevent it from sticking together. Drain well, then throw into cold water to blanch for ten minutes; drain again. Have a buttered pudding dish, place a layer in the bottom, then cover with grated cheese and a few lumps of butter, then another layer of macaroni and more butter and cheese until all is used up; pour on one-half cup of cream. Bake covered for half an hour; then remove the cover and bake the top to a golden brown on grate. Serve in dish.

Mollie.

Macaroni à l' Italienne.

¼ pound macaroni   ½ pint cream or milk
¼ pound grated cheese   Butter size of a walnut

Cook the macaroni the same as for baking. Put the milk into a farina-boiler add the butter then the macaroni and cheese; stir until thoroughly heated, add salt and pepper, and serve.   *Mrs. Rorer.*

Oyster Macaroni.

Boil macaroni the same as above, put a layer in a dish with butter, salt and pepper, then a layer of oysters and alternate until the dish is full. Mix some grated bread or rolled cracker with a beaten egg. Spread over top and bake.

Cream Macaroni.

Select macaroni that is of a brownish color, rather than of a pure white. Spaghetti is the most delicate form of macaroni that comes to this country.

For a dish holding three pints one-half pound of spaghetti will be required. Have ready a kettle full of boiling water, salted. Take the spaghetti all up together, in the long sticks without breaking. Hold the ends in the boiling water; in an instant it will all go down into the water. Whirl it round and round with a fork to thoroughly separate it, then allow it to boil hard for twenty minutes. When done, put it in a colander and pour cold water through it (this is called blanching). After it is drained, put it into the dish in which it is to be baked.

For the Cream Gravy.

Put one and one-half pints of milk on in double boiler. Stir smoothly together three tablespoons of flour and three scant tablespoons of butter. When smooth, stir carefully into the boiling milk, stirring till flour is cooked. Then add three tablespoons of grated cheese. Parmesan is best, but any strong cheese will answer. Pour it over the macaroni in the dish, sprinkle a little more cheese over the top and put in the oven to brown. Do not put the cream and macaroni together till ready to go into the oven, as the cream will curdle if allowed to stand on the macaroni.

Mrs. Rorer.

TOASTED CHEESE.

One-half pound of rich cheese is enough for four slices of toast. Cut the cheese thin in slices a little smaller than the toast, and put it in buttered tin in oven to toast. While this is toasting, toast the bread, salt and butter it. Put cheese on toast. Serve hot.

Mrs. Rorer.

CHEESE STRAWS.

2 ounces flour	A little cayenne and salt
3 ounces grated Parmesan cheese	Yolk of one egg

Mix flour, cayenne, salt and cheese together, and moisten with the egg; work all into a smooth paste. Roll out on a board, one-eighth of an inch thick, five inches wide, and five inches long. Cut some of the paste in small rings and some in strips of one-eighth of an inch wide. Place both on greased sheets and bake ten minutes in an oven (240 Fahr.) till a light brown. Then put the straws through the rings like a bundle of sticks.

Mrs. Rorer.

Stock for Sauces and Gravies.

In every family of five or six persons or more, there will be many bones and fragments of meat left from roasts and steaks either cooked or uncooked or both which can be utilized for making stock or puree for gravies and sauces for various kinds of meats, fish or croquettes. Put into a granite or porcelain kettle, the bones and pieces of meats from yesterday's and to-day's cooking (do not use any older bits for they loose their virtue by standing); with as little water as will cook well, and boil slowly for three hours, covered tight; salt it just right for eating; have the quantity of broth according to the nourishment contained in the meat. This will not often be rich enough for soups; strain it through a soup strainer, when cold take off the fat. In winter it will keep a week. In large families it can be prepared twice a week. To make nice gravies is only difficult to the inexperienced. You will soon learn to use good judgment and be a good taster.

Maitre d' Hotel Sauce.

2 tablespoons butter
1 tablespoon lemon juice
1 tablespoon chopped parsley
Salt, a little

Mix all the ingredients well together. Served with salt fish. *Mrs. Rorer.*

Anchovy Sauce.

Add to the above recipe two tablespoons of anchovy paste. Try it for fried fish.

Apple Sauce.

Nice tart apple sauce can be served with all dishes of fresh pork.

Bearnais Sauce.

Yolks of three eggs
3 tablespoons butter
3 tablespoons stock or water
¼ teaspoon salt, red pepper
1 tablespoon gooseberry catsup
1 tablespoon vinegar

Beat the yolks, add the stock and butter, standing the new basin in boiling water stirring until the eggs thicken, then add the other ingredients. Nice for meat croquettes. Add one cup of cream to this and a little flour and it is good for steamed fish. And you have also Bechamel sauce.

Brown Sauce.

2 tablespoons butter
2 even tablespoons flour
1 tablespoon parsley
1 pint stock or water
1 teaspoon onion juice
2 tablespoons gooseberry catsup.
Salt and pepper
2 tablespoons Worcestershire sauce.

Melt and brown the butter in spider, stir in flour, add the hot stock; stir continually; simmer gently for ten minutes then add the other ingredients. This is nice for warmed over roasts.

Caper Sauce.

Is made by adding two tablespoons of capers to the drawn butter sauce. See the recipe.

CURRANT JELLY SAUCE.

Add five tablespoons of the jelly to the drawn butter and let it boil up once. Serve with any wild game.

CRANBERRY SAUCE.

This should always be served with roast turkey, either in the form of jam or jelly.

LOBSTER SAUCE.

Add one cup of lobster to drawn butter, chopped fine, and rubbed to a paste with a spoon of butter. Nice with fish. Oyster sauce for roast turkey is made the same way, using the oyster broth and chopping the oysters.

CELERY SAUCE.

5 roots celery
1 even tablespoon flour
1 tablespoon butter
1 pint cold water
½ pint milk
Salt and pepper

Clean the celery, cut it into small pieces, put it in a saucepan (granite); stew slowly about thirty minutes; press it through a colander. Mix the butter and flour to a cream; put all together; stir continually, letting it boil two minutes. Good with boiled fowl.

CREAM DRESSING NO. 2.

When oil is disliked in salads the following dressing will be found excellent: Rub the yolks of two hard-boiled eggs very smooth with a silver spoon. Stir gradually in a teaspoon of mixed mustard, a tablespoon of softened butter, half a cup of thick cream, a a saltspoon of salt, cayenne pepper the size of a small pea, a few drops of anchovy or Worcestershire sauce or gooseberry catsup as you like. Slowly add sufficient vinegar to make it a creamy consistency. Good for any salad or lettuce.

A PLAIN SAUCE

Salt and a sprinkle cayenne pepper
½ pint softened butter
2 teaspoons lemon juice
5 yolks of eggs

Add the butter gradually to the well-beaten yolks, add the seasoning; put in a double boiler; stir continually until it thickens, but do not let it boil, as it will curdle. Take it off and add the lemon juice. For salads.

PASTRY AND PIES.

Practice and good judgment are as necessary as good recipes to become a good pie-maker. Pies are not as economical as puddings, neither are they as healthy. Dyspeptics should seldom if ever eat them. A good pie is very relishable where there is a good appetite. One needs to save some of their appetite for pie, so do not eat a full supply beforehand, nor too large a piece. Pie crust should be light, crisp and flaky. Use fine flour and the best of butter. The rolling board should be heavy, smooth and level, the rolling-pin should be of hard wood, smooth and even; the water very cold, even ice cold. Never knead or work the dough as it makes it tough, but stir it only with your fingers in as slight a way as possible; take it out to roll in all its roughness. Flour the board (some like a marble board) and rolling-pin, and always roll from you. It is better to mix the crust and let it stand in a cold place or in ice-box till cold before rolling out. The secret of success with puff paste is to put it in a cold place for fifteen minutes after rolling it three times. Then roll it twice more to secure the greatest number of layers of butter and dough alternately as the result of folding (not rolling over and over as one would for a roly-poly) and rolling out without breaking it. It must be just stiff enough to handle easily and not stick much to the floured board, or pin, neither roll hard. Three-fourths of a pound of butter to one pound of flour is the least that can be used for good puff paste. For common use one-half as much butter as flour by weight, if not worked any, only stirred, makes good crust. I always use butter for shortening for pie crust, biscuit, fried cakes, muffins, etc. Pastry requires a quick oven and of even heat, and must bake the fastest on the bottom. Take out the grate; can put it on the upper grate to brown the top. Pies should be baked on earthen plates. Three medium-sized coffee cups of flour is one pound. One coffee cup and nearly one-third is one pound of butter. This is the proportion of a pound of flour to to a pound of butter by measure. The cup full is just one-half pint.

Puff Paste.

1 pound sifted flour
1 teaspoon salt
1 pound washed butter
1 pint nearly very cold water

Scald a large earthen dish and rinse it so the butter will not stick to it, then fill it with ice-cold water and put in butter; with a cool hand work it in the water for eight minutes. Drain it well and let it stand on ice to harden. Then divide the butter into five parts; work one-fifth of it with the salt into the flour with a knife, cutting it quickly in small pieces, at the same time mixing it with the flour; add the ice water, gradually, stirring it with your fingers. Not all the water, perhaps, as some flours swell more than others. Then put it on board in the roughest form (never knead or work it); dredge it with flour and roll quickly into a long, thin sheet. Cut one-fourth of the butter you have left in little bits and put on crust; sift on a sprinkle of flour; double it over, roll out the same way; repeat this three times, using all the butter. Then put it in cold place to stiffen and it is ready for tarts, pies or patties.

FOR TARTS OR PATTIES.

Cut out with a cooky cutter three layers. Take a pepper-box cover and cut out the center of two layers and lay on top of the whole one, which makes one tart. The crust should be rolled very thin; bake, then fill with jelly a short time before using. Another very pretty way is to take an open-top thimble or something as small and cut three or five holes in the two top layers; after baking lift them off, put a slice of jelly on the lower layer; put the two upper layers on, squeezing up the jelly through the holes; this has a pretty effect. For patties use a little larger cutter; a sharp cutter is the best. The oven should have a strong under heat, so they will rise before browning. If oven is too hot open the draughts, or put a basin of cold water in oven.

TART CRUST.

The white of one egg	1 tablespoon white sugar
1 cup butter	1 even teaspoon salt
3 cups sifted flour	5 tablespoons cold water

Beat the egg stiff, and prepare the same way as for puff paste.

PIE CRUST.

1¼ pounds flour   1 pound butter

Wash the butter, have every thing as cold as possible, use less than a half pint of very cold water. Rub the butter and teaspoon salt in the flour with the hands, then stir the water in with the fingers, put it in the rough on the molding board, roll out, cut it in wide strips, put one upon another, then cut in squares to make the size for each plate and roll out for the pie plates. It will be better to set the dough on ice before rolling out. Never press on the crust after it is on the plate. Wet the rim of under crust with water to make the crusts unite, so as to retain the juices.

PLAIN PIE CRUST.

Plain but good family pie crust is made with one pound of flour and one-half bound of butter, or three cups of sifted flour and one cup of butter, rub them well together, so that when you squeeze it in your hand it will remain in form; add cold water enough to make a stiff dough; do not make it too wet, as it makes it tough to work it over. Roll out just enough for the one plate. This last quantity is enough for two pies.

PIE CRUST WITH LARD.

4 cups sifted flour   1½ cups lard or butter
1 heaping teaspoon salt   ½ cup ice cold water

Rub the lard and salt lightly into the flour and stir in the water with fingers of one hand, flour the board and roller, and roll it in the rough, do not work it at all, as it makes it tough. I have eaten very flaky and tender crust made of lard, also of half lard and half butter.

A Good Plain Pie Crust.

Sift one quart of flour (which is one pound) into your bowl and a teaspoon of salt, heaping. Lard requires more salt than butter. Rub in one teacup of fresh lard, stir in one cup of very cold water to make it stiff enough to roll; handle it deftly and as little as possible; flour the board and pin, roll out very thin; remember to roll from you. Have ready one teacup of good butter that has been washed in two cold waters, spread one-third of the butter on the dough, sprinkle with flour; fold it over, then roll it out thin again; spread with bits of butter again and roll out, making four times, to use all the butter. Then roll out, after setting the pan in ice water to get cold, just enough for one crust at a time. This will make crust enough for two or three pies according to size.

Apple Pie.

Wash and peel tender sour apples, slice them very thin. Put the under crust on the pie plate and fill it sufficiently full to be right when cooked. Flavor with either nutmeg or cinnamon as you like or allspice, put bits of butter all around, cover with sugar one-half cup of water, dip the fingers in water and always wet the rim of crust all round, then roll out the upper crust neither too thick nor too thin, double it together and cut three gashes in center, lay it on the pie, cut the edges smooth, prick it with a fork five times to let the air out. If the apples are not tender partly cook them, but you must have tart apples to make a good pie. Some expert cooks put nothing in but water, till the pie is baked, then lift the upper crust off whole while hot and stir in the sugar, butter and flavoring.

PIE PLANT OR RHUBARB PIE.

Wash the stalks of rhubarb and peel off the thin stringy skin by stripping it down, then cut it in one-half inch pieces. Line a deep pie plate with crust, fill it nearly full of pieplant, grate nutmeg on it, sift a little flour, put bits of butter on, one cup of sugar, one-third cup of molasses, no water, as it is juicy of itself. Roll the crust out the same as for apple pie, only squeeze the edges together to retain the juices. The oven must be only just to a slow boiling heat or the syrup will all boil out.

PUMPKIN PIE.

This requires only the under crust with a rim; this is best made by rolling the crust about an inch larger than the plate, then you have a continuous circle to lay on the edge of plate, about three-fourths of an inch wide, wet the edge of under crust where you lay it on; put the rim all around, do not press on it, and it is ready to fill. Be sure you have a good pumpkin, cut in two, dig out the seeds and inside, bake on grate in a hot oven until soft, or steam it, it is richer baked. (In cold weather you can bake enough for twice, keeping in a cool place; they should be eaten the day they are baked, though you can scald them over.) Scrape out the pulp, press it through a colander. The most delicate pie is made by using one-third pumpkin, one-third milk, one-third eggs and cream or milk as you have it, nutmeg, a little salt, one teaspoon ginger, one-half teaspoon cinnamon. Some like it half pumpkin, it is more solid. This is for one pie. Two eggs are good, but three are better. Two large spoons sugar; some pumpkins are sweeter than others. Heat the mixture hot when ready to fill the pie and bake; have a hot oven. Beat well into the pumpkin all the spices and sugar, then the milk, and last the well beaten eggs.

HUBBARD SQUASH PIE.

1 large coffee cup new milk	1 large coffee cup squash
	1 teaspoon salt
1 large coffee cup of 2 or 3 beaten eggs filled up with cream	¼ nutmeg
	½ cup sugar
	1 teaspoon Jamaica ginger

The squash is prepared the same way as the pumpkin. In baking it cover it with thick brown paper, stand it on grate or a brick, bake double the quantity you need, as it will keep in a cold place two or three days. The crust and filling prepared the same as the pumpkin. This is the measure for one pie. You will see the proportion is one-third squash to the other ingredients.

HUBBARD SQUASH OR PUMPKIN PIE.

4 eggs beaten separately	4 tablespoons sugar
2 cups squash or pumpkin	2 cups milk or 1 of cream
1 teaspoon cinnamon	¼ grated nutmeg

Last thing stir in the whites. 1 teaspoon ginger

CHERRY PIE.

Wash the cherries, take out the pits; line a deep plate with crust, fill with the fruit having two thick layers (first drain off the juice) sift a good tablespoon of flour, bits of butter on it, one full cup of brown sugar, three-fourths cup of molasses (no water or juice) then cover, not forgetting to wet the edge of under crust and pressing the edges together. Bake in hot oven. Whenever your oven is too hot always put in a basin of cold water or open the dampers. If the heat is just at a boiling point, the syrup will not run out and the pie is delicious. A handful of cherry pits scattered in the pie, adds to the flavor; but do not do it if there are any children in the family.

PEACH PIE.

Line your plate with good crust, peel and slice the peaches with a silver knife, fill the plate, sift one tablespoon of flour, sprinkle one-half cup or more of sugar on, add one-third of a cup of water. Be careful to wet the edge of lower crust before covering the pie, so the edges will adhere together and retain the juice in the pie and add much to its richness. Crack five or six of the pits and put the meats in the pie, for flavoring if you like.

CREAM PIE.

Line a deep pie plate with a rich paste and fill with a custard made of the yolks of three eggs, three tablespoons of sugar, one tablespoon of flour, one teaspoon or more of vanilla, one pint of milk or part cream. When the pie is baked, carefully spread a layer of orange jelly or any jelly or jam you like over the top (warm it if too stiff to spread easily), then a meringue made of the whites of the eggs, two tablespoons of powdered sugar and vanilla. Spread the meringue evenly but not smoothly and brown slightly in a moderately heated oven. Serve cold.

CREAM PIE NO. 2.

Beat two eggs well, add four even tablespoons of sugar, one pint of sweet cream, flavor with nutmeg or vanilla. Great care should be taken not to bake any custard too long, as it will soon turn to whey, after it is at boiling point.

CUSTARD PIE.

To one pint of milk add two beaten eggs with three tablespoons of sugar, a dust of salt, flavor with nutmeg. Line the pie plate with crust and a rim and bake as in the above recipe.

COCOANUT PIE.

1 cup grated cocoanut	3 eggs
4 tablespoons sugar	1 teaspoon butter, salt
1 lemon	1 pint milk

Grate a cocoanut after removing the outer shell and the inner skin, strain the milk it contains through a cloth if you like to use it, if not, use a pint of boiled milk, stir in the cocoanut, then the butter and beaten yolks, sugar, the grated rind and strained juice of half a lemon, lastly the stiffly beaten whites or make a meringue made by sweetening the well-beaten eggs with two large spoonfuls of sugar and spread it on top with a good sprinkle of cocoanut after it is baked, and return on the grate until delicately browned. Line the pie plate with best pie crust and fill. All pies with only one crust must have a rim laid on it.

LEMON PIE NO. 3.

1 large or 2 small lemons	1½ cups hot water
Yolks of 3 eggs	3 soda crackers
1 cup sugar	Whites of three eggs

Grate the rind, strain the juice of the lemon, roll the crackers, stir and pour on the hot water, beat the yolks, mix all together; pour it in the crust, which should be of the best, and bake while hot; make a meringue of the whites beaten stiff, then sift in three heaping tablespoons of powdered sugar, spread on top, and brown.

LEMON PIE NO. 2.

1 lemon
1 cup sugar
Butter the size of an egg
1 tablespoon corn starch
2 eggs, salt a little
2 cups hot water

Stir up the corn starch in a little cold water and pour it in the hot water and let boil enough to cook the starch (say one minute), let cool, then add the butter, sugar and beaten eggs, and lemon, grated rind and strained juice. Make a meringue of the whites of two eggs and three spoons of sugar. Some bake the shell or crust first, lightly, then fill and bake the filling, for all lemon or custard pies.

LEMON PIE NO. 1. (Very Fine.)

2 lemons
8 tablespoons sugar
3 eggs
1 cup water
2 even tablespoons flour

Grate the rind and strain the juice of the lemons, stir the flour up with the water, then add the sugar and beaten yolk, then the juice and grated rind. Bake with an under crust; have ready when it comes from the oven, the whites beaten to a stiff froth, with four tablespoons of pulverized sugar; spread over the pie, set in oven, and brown as quickly as possible, to avoid being leathery. *Home Messenger.*

ORANGE PIE.

Slice three or four oranges into a plate lined with paste, sprinkle well with sugar, two tablespoons of water, cover with paste. This is nice, but orange shortcake is better.

Sponge Cake Cream Pie.

One teacup of sugar, one teacup of flour with one teaspoon baking powder, three eggs beaten separately. Bake it in two layer cakes. Whip a pint of very cold sweet cream until very smooth and stiff; first sweeten and flavor to taste, then spread it on one of the layers, placing the other on top. If one likes one can spread the top with cream and cocoanut. Should be eaten the same day.

Lemon Tarts.

1 cup sugar	3 teaspoons flour
2 eggs	1 pint boiling water
	1 large lemon

Make the tart shells of puff paste and fill with this mixture. Grate the rind, strain the juice of lemon, wet the flour with cold water, beat the eggs separately, reserve one white for the top, stir sugar and all in the hot water and boil enough to cook the flour. Stir it constantly till clear and smooth.

Huckleberry Pie.

This has two crusts, top and bottom. Wash the berries and drain well; fill the crust pretty full; sprinkle two tablespoons of flour on top, bits of butter, a little salt; cover the berries with a cup of brown sugar and a sprinkle of water. Pinch the edges together and keep it just at the boiling point, or you will lose the syrup.

Washington Pie.

1 cup sugar	½ cup butter
2 eggs	1 teaspoon baking powder
½ cup milk	2 cups flour

Bake in two layer cakes and put between them the filling. Filling: Make a custard with one-half pint of milk, two tablespoons of sugar, one spoon of flour, one egg, a pinch of salt; flavor with essence of lemon; beat well together and boil a minute to cook the flour. Flavor them both with the same flavoring. When cold spread on one cake and lay the other on top. Or if you like it better, instead, spread any kind of fruit jam or apple marmalade or cocoanut on top.

Mince Pies.

4 pounds solid beef	6 pounds tart raw apples
3 coffee cups chopped suet	1 quart boiled cider
2 pounds raisins	1 quart molasses
4 pints brown sugar	4 pints water
4 teaspoons cinnamon	4 teaspoons cloves

2 nutmegs

If you wish the whole quantity, purchase five pounds of solid lean meat (the best of the round is good), as there is some waste; in boiling the meat allow one pound for loss, in boiling such a quantity. Salt it right for eating when you put it over, in boiling hot water; boil until just tender; set away to get cool over night, then cut in small pieces and chop it fine, so it will be neither coarse grained nor pasty, then weigh it. Peel the apples, quarter, core and chop them; wash and wipe them before peeling, and then weigh the quarters before chopping. Wash and seed the raisins, but do not chop them; chop the suet fine, mix all together in a large earthen dish. Do not use all the water, let the mince meat stand for two days (as it will swell some), in a cool place; you can add more water, cider, or sugar, as you think it needs, after baking one pie to try it. They do not taste so sweet after baking. Bake well done, three-fourths of an hour. These are nice to make in winter, as you can bake up as many as you like, according to the size of the family, from ten to twenty at a time. Keep them in a cold room, but do not freeze them. Put the mince meat that is left in a crock and cover the top with writing paper. It will keep in a cold place three months, only it must not freeze. For a small family of four I only make one-half the quantity. I grate the nutmeg in each pie as I make it, with bits of butter before putting the crust on. It requires practice to learn to make good pastry for mince pies (I do not mean puff paste), and also not to fill them too full. I have used this recipe ever since 1843, and have never wished for any better for any occasion. It it is palatable and healthy.

The two following recipes I take from the Messenger, but I think them too rich for health; neither do I think it a good plan to boil the mince meat:

MINCE PIES.

- 3 pounds fresh beef
- 4 or 6 pounds suet
- ¾ pound citron
- 8 pounds chopped apples
- 1 pint molasses
- 1 teacup mace compound
- 1¼ ounces salt
- ½ ounce pepper
- 1 fresh beef tongue
- 3½ pounds raisins
- 3 pounds currants
- 4½ pounds sugar
- 3 ounces cinnamon
- 2 ounces cloves
- 1 nutmeg
- 1½ gallons sweet cider

When mixed put into a kettle and scald, stirring it all the time. Put it hot into Hero or Mason jars—two quart or gallon jars—and the longer you keep it the nicer it will be. When making up your pies you can add a teacup of finely chopped apples for each pie.

Home Messenger.

MINCE PIE.

7 pounds meat
14 pounds chopped apples
1½ gallons boiled cider
Nutmeg and cinnamon to taste.
1 teacup mace compound
6 pounds suet
4 pounds sugar
7 pounds currants
7 pounds seeded raisins

Boil together cider, apples and sugar, and when hot pour over the other ingredients. If citron is liked, put in slices just before baking. The vinegar from pickled peaches is a nice addition; to this quantity use one pint. *Home Messenger.*

PUDDINGS.

Fifty-six years ago there were but few recipes for puddings or pies, both being considered as an extra dish for company. A recipe book of 1838, which was the one I tried to follow, when I first went to housekeeping in 1842, gave recipes for only twelve puddings and seven different kinds of pies. How uncertain I found them. I shall never forget my first baked Indian pudding. I mixed it ready to bake, and left it for the girl to bake (as I was invited out to dine), according to directions in the book, three to four hours. It was more like a rock than a delightful suet pudding. I soon left the book to lie on the shelf for future ages to explore. Some puddings are good either cold or hot. A baked pudding is not as acceptable immediately from the oven as one covered and cooled for ten minutes. A blistering hot pudding is anything but acceptable, no matter how delicate the article may be.

A Delicate Baked Rice Pudding.

5 tablespoons rice
6 tablespoons sugar
½ cup raisins
3½ pints milk
1 teaspoon salt
Flavor with nutmeg

Stir the ingredients well together, and cover the pudding the first hour of its moderate baking, stirring every fifteen minutes, so it will form the cream which makes it so delicious. Then uncover and cook slowly stirring it every ten minutes twice, then let it slowly brown on the top for ten minutes more, taking one and a-half hours to bake. The rice kernels should be perfectly soft, amidst the delicate cream that has formed of the starch of the rice and the milk. This simple pudding when perfectly made and baked, eaten cold in summer is as delicious as ice cream. Much depends upon the careful baking. It is a delight to the housekeeper when she has made a good dish, to have it baked well, for baking either makes or prevents success.

Rice Pudding.

3 tablespoons rice
3 tablespoons sugar
½ cup raisins
1 quart milk
1 even teaspoon salt
Grated nutmeg

Bake one and a-half hours, same way as the former. Serve cold or hot with cold sweet cream.

Baked Batter Pudding.

1 quart sweet milk
9 tablespoons sifted flour
8 eggs beaten separately
1 teaspoon salt

Measure the flour and gradually beat in the milk; beat it ten minutes with salt, then beat the yolks well and beat them in, beat the whites stiff and beat them in well. Butter the pudding dish and pour in and bake immediately from thirty to forty minutes. Serve with lemon or cream sauce. Plan so as to eat on taking out of the oven, as it is liable to fall when exposed to the air. Take one half the quantity for four persons. Serve with cream sauce.

BOILED BATTER PUDDING.

1 quart sweet milk
8 eggs beaten separately
1 pint sifted flour
1 teaspoon salt

Mix this the same way as the baked pudding preceeding this. Boil steadily for two hours. Do not let the water slacken its boiling for an instant as it will fall. Keep a teakettle of boiling water to replenish with as it boils out. Get a tin pudding bag or make a bag of drilling (unbleached), wash it; you need one half a yard long, not quite one half wide, hem both ends and run a string in long enough to tie it tight so both ends of the pudding will be shaped alike. Sew it up with double seam, scald and flour the inside, pour in the pudding, leaving one third of the room in bag for swelling; have the water boiling when you plunge it in. Keep covered tight. Serve with cream or lemon sauce.

STEAMED OR BOILED PUDDING.

1 cup molasses
1 cup sweet milk
½ cup softened butter
½ teaspoon soda
2⅓ cups flour
1 teaspoon salt
1 teaspoon cloves
1 teaspoon cinnamon.
1 cup seeded raisins.

Stir soda in the molasses; mix all together. Can steam it in a tin basin or a tin pudding dish, or boil in a bag; follow the directions for boiled batter pudding.

Steam two hours. Use any sauce you like. Cream sauce is the most healthy. Lemon sauce is the most relishable.

Genuine English Plum Pudding.

1 10-cent loaf bread	1 quart rich milk
1 pound raisins	1 pound currants
1 pound brown sugar	3 tablespoons flour
¾ pound beef suet	2 grated nutmegs
3 teaspoons cinnamon	2 lemons or oranges
½ pound cut up citron	10 eggs beaten separately

Wash and seed your raisins, wash and dry the currants, chop the suet and get everything ready the day before making; also slice the baker's bread in thick slices and dry it in oven and grate it, stir your milk in it; then add the other ingredients beating it well, adding the whites last. Stir the flour on the fruit. Grate the orange peel, just the yellow rind (the white is always bitter), squeeze the juice and strain, making one-half cup of juice. Mix well and pour into a scalded and floured pudding bag if you wish to boil it, and place in a kettle of boiling water, and keep hot water to replenish with. Boil steadily five hours. Or put it in a tin mold or basin and steam it; if your mold has a tube in the center it will steam in three hours, if not, steam it five hours. This will keep three weeks. Leave it in bag and boil or steam it over one hour the day you use it. Some add to this two teaspoons of extract of nectarine, and three dozen of bitter and sweet almonds blanched and powdered. (I use no fruits in this pudding, but the raisins and oranges or lemons and the spices. I do not think it well to put everything into the stomach at once.) Use foaming or lemon sauce.

English Plum Pudding.

1 pound raisins
3/4 pound grated bread
1/4 pound flour
1 pound suet chopped fine
5 eggs, salt
1 grated lemon rind
1/2 nutmeg
1/4 pint brandy
1/4 pound brown sugar
1 pound dried currants
1/2 pound mixed candied orange peel

This is the plum pudding winning the two-guinea prize (ten dollars, our money) offered by Queen Victoria.

Clean, wash and dry the currants, stone the raisins, mix all the dry ingredients together. Beat the eggs and pour them over the dry ingredients and thoroughly mix. Put it into your buttered mold, or your scalded and floured bag (this will make about six pounds), and boil eight hours at the time of making, and two hours when wanted for use. This, of course, can be made several weeks before Christmas, as the longer it stands the better it is. Serve with lemon sauce. Do not eat much.

A Plain Steamed Pudding.

1 cup sweet milk
1 teaspoon salt
2 teaspoons baking powder
1 teaspoon cloves
2 eggs
5 cups flour
1 cup raisins
1 teaspoon cinnamon

Steam three hours. Seed and chop the raisins, sift the flour, baking powder and salt, twice together, then mix, beat the eggs separately and mix last, and put over to steam at once over boiling water.

STEAMED GRAHAM PUDDING.

2 cups Graham flour
1 cup sweet milk
1 cup raisins
1 teaspoon salt
½ teaspoon cinnamon
1 cup molasses
1 teaspoon soda
1 egg
½ teaspoon cloves
A little nutmeg

Put the flour in the dish, then add all the other ingredients, beating the soda well into the molasses. Mix thoroughly. Flour the raisins, put the mixture in a buttered pan, steam three hours. A very excellent pudding. *Home Messenger.*

A MORE SIMPLE GRAHAM PUDDING.

3 cups Graham flour
1 quart milk
1 teaspoon soda
3 cups corn meal
1 cup molasses

Steam three hours in mold. *Home Messenger.*

SWEET CORN PUDDING.

12 ears corn
2 tablespoons sugar
1 quart rich milk
2 tablespoons flour
1 tablespoon butter
3 eggs, salt

Gash each row of corn with a knife straight down; then grate it, mix it in the milk, rubbing it well to get the hulls free from the corn; then rub it through a fine seive to relieve it of the hulls. Work the flour and butter to a cream, then beat in the sugar and well-beaten yolks, then the beaten whites, then add all to the corn and milk, with salt. Bake. Eat with cream; sugar if liked.

Boiled Indian Pudding.

1 quart milk
1 cup molasses
2 or 3 eggs
1½ pints corn meal
1 teaspoon soda
Salt

Put in bag; boil four hours.

Bread Pudding.

1 qt. bread crumbs nearly
1 quart sweet milk
1 tablespoon butter
¾ cup sugar
6 eggs, beat separately
1 lemon, salt

Slice and dry the bread in oven and grate it or break it up and soak it in milk and put through sieve. Grate the rind of lemon, squeeze the juice and strain. Put all together. Save two of the whites for a meringue after it is baked. Bake thirty minutes or more. Spread on a layer of jam, jelly or cocoanut and the beaten stiff whites of egg, with four tablespoons of powdered sugar in it and brown the top quickly.

The Sauce.

1 cup sugar
1 tablespoon corn starch
2 eggs, a little salt
½ cup butter
1 cup hot water
2 teaspoons vanilla

Stir butter and sugar to a cream; wet the starch with cold water; beat the eggs light; put all together. Boil three minutes to cook the starch.

Lemon Pudding.

½ cup sugar
2 eggs
1 tablespoon butter
1 lemon

Grate the lemon, squeeze the juice and strain. Work the butter and sugar to a cream, add the well beaten yolks, beat well, then add the stiff whites, last of all the lemon juice a few drops at a time beating it till it becomes like thick cream. Then stir in slowly one pint hot milk. Bake as a pudding or as a pie with under crust. Serve with cream.

LEMON PUDDING.

3 tablespoons corn starch 3 coffeecups hot water
2 teacups sugar 2 eggs
2 large lemons 1 teaspoon salt

Wet the starch thin with cold water, then pour on the three cups boiling water, and boil to cook the starch, stirring all the time, then add the sugar and slowly, the grated rind and juice of the lemons. Bake twenty minutes. To be eaten cold with cream. This makes two pies. *Home Messenger.*

BAKED INDIAN PUDDING.

6 tablespoons corn meal 1 cup molasses
1 quart milk 1 even teaspoon soda
½ pint cold water 1 tablespoon ginger
½ cup suet chopped ½ teaspoon cinnamon
2 even teaspoons salt ⅓ of a nutmeg
3 tablespoons brown sugar 4 eggs

Put the milk over to boil, wet the corn meal with the cold water, and as soon as it boils stir in the corn meal, salt and suet, boil fifteen minutes, stirring all the time. Chop the suet very fine, taking all the skin off. Take it off of the fire, put in one-half cup of cold milk, the sugar, molasses—stir the soda into the molasses—add the spices, beat the yolks well and beat in lastly the stiff beaten whites. Butter a two-quart pan and bake immediately over one hour. When done there will be whey in the center. Let it cool a little. Serve with cream.

Ground Rice Pudding.

¼ pound rice flour   3 tablespoons butter
2 quarts milk   ⅔ cup sugar
8 eggs, salt   1 lemon, or essence lemon

Wet the rice flour with one pint of the cold milk, add salt, and pour into the three pints of boiling milk, boil it five minutes to cook the rice, stirring well. Stir the butter and sugar to cream, then add the beaten yolks of the eggs and stir it in the rice, add the grated rind and juice of the lemon or essence, as you choose; the whites, last, beaten to a stiff froth. Bake thirty minutes. When baked, can add a spread of jell and a meringue if you like. Cream sauce.

Batter Pudding.

1 pint flour   ⅔ cup sugar
1 pint milk   6 eggs, beaten separately
        1 even teaspoon salt

Add a pint of cream just before baking. Bake about one hour. Flavor the cream sauce.

Cup Cake Pudding.

2 cups sugar   5 eggs
1 cup butter   1 cup milk
3½ cups flour   3 teaspoons baking-powder
½ pound raisins   1 teaspoon cinnamon
        1 teaspoon cloves

Stir butter and sugar to a cream, then add the well beaten eggs, beat in; pour on the milk but do not stir it in till you sift in half or more of the flour mixed with baking-powder; then add the spices and rest of flour, the seeded and chopped raisins with an extra half cup of flour stirred on them. It is nice without raisins. Serve with this

VINEGAR SAUCE.

6 tablespoons sugar
10 of hot water, salt
4 tablespoons butter
1 tablespoon corn starch

Heat the water and sugar very hot, stir in the butter till melted, but do not let it boil. Add the starch or flour as you like, and two tablespoons or more of vinegar or other flavoring.

TAPIOCA PUDDING.

6 tablespoons tapioca
1 pint cold water
1 small cup sugar
1½ pints milk
3 eggs
1 teaspoon salt

Wash in two or three waters the tapioca and soak it five hours or over night in the pint of cold water, put it in heater (salt it) to keep quite warm till perfectly soft, then put it in double boiler with milk, sugar, two teaspoons vanilla, add gradually the well beaten yolks and stir until boiling a minute, till it thickens and gradually stir in the well beaten whites. Let partly cool, then pour it in glass dish. Serve cold with clear cream. A nice dessert to prepare on Saturday for a Sunday dinner.

A BAKED TAPIOCA.

Prepare it the same way, only using a quart of milk and 4 eggs, do not stir the eggs in till you take it off the fire; bake 30 minutes. Use two of the whites for a meringue, putting on a layer of jell first; set back in oven and brown.

Apple Tapioca or Sago.

This is prepared the same way, only take out the cores and fill with sugar six tart apples and bake well done; then put them in the pudding dish, and when your pudding is ready for baking pour it over the apples and bake 30 or 40 minutes. Serve with cream. Sago pudding is made in the same way, using sago instead of tapioca.

Apple and Tapioca Pudding.

Prepare the boiled tapioca or first pudding and stir in it one pint of tart apple marmalade. Prepare and stew tart tender apples with sufficient sugar for eating, rub through a sieve and stir it in pudding. It is very relishable. Serve with cream.

Baked Corn Meal Pudding.

1 quart milk	3 tablespoons molasses, a
4 tablespoons corn meal	little soda
3 teaspoons ginger	3 tablespoons brown sugar
3 tablespoons suet	Nutmeg and salt
3 eggs	

Wet the meal with cold water so it will pour. Put the milk in spider, when it boils, stir in the corn meal, suet and salt. Boil and stir fifteen minutes, take it off, add all the other ingredients and one cup of cold milk and lastly eggs beaten separately.

Mrs. B.

Snow Pudding.

Dissolve in one pint of cold water one-half box of gelatine, next add one pint boiling water, one teacup of sugar, bring to a boil; add the juice of two lemons or essence. Take from the fire; add the beaten whites of six eggs, beat well, just before it sets, and put into cups or molds. Set it on ice or in a cold place. Serve with whipped cream, sweetened cream, or a soft custard.   Mrs. B.

ORANGE OR LEMON SNOW PUDDING.

Dissolve one-fourth of a box of gelatine in three tablespoons of cold water, then pour on a pint of boiling water, one cup of sugar, juice of four large oranges or two lemons, strain and put it on ice or set in very cold water till it begins to stiffen, then add the whites of three eggs beaten stiff; beat well together fifteen minutes; put it into molds over night. Serve cold with a custard made of the yolks, or with cream, or lemon sauce. I like it better served on table from a glass dish. This, if good, all depends upon the flavoring and sweetening.

DELICIOUS STEAM PUDDING.

1 half cup butter	1 half cup sugar
1 cup butter milk	1 egg
1 teaspoon soda	

Add flour until stiff as cake, then a cup of stoned raisins chopped a little. Pour it into a tin pudding bag or a tin basin and steam an hour and a half. Serve with boiled sauce.

APPLE SNOW BALLS.

Take one or two cups of freshly boiled rice; peel as many tart apples as there are persons; core, but do not go through the stem end, fill with sugar and grate on nutmeg. The rice must be cool and stiff enough to handle. Take enough rice in your hand and make a hollow in it, place an apple in it, having the rice a good half-inch thick all around the apple; set each ball in a cloth large enough to cover and tie up. Set them in a steamer over boiling water. Steam three-fourths of an hour and eat as soon as cooked. These are nice to eat with roast duck or goose, or with the following sauce as dessert: Braid together two-thirds of a cup of butter, one cup sugar and one tablespoon flour; pour over it, slowly stirring, one-half pint boiling water, and grate in nutmeg, boil a minute to cook the flour. Can double this quantity.

PEACH BALLS.

For a dozen peach balls pick over a cup of rice, wash it in cold water till you have poured off all the specks, then in double boiler add a quart of water or milk, a heaping teaspoon salt, cook till soft, then stir in four tablespoons white sugar, and the yolks of two or three raw eggs, and nutmeg; stir together over a moderate fire until the yolks begin to thicken; if the heat is too intense, the yolks will curdle. As soon as the yolks thicken remove the rice from the fire and let it cool sufficiently to handle, then heat in the spider half lard and half suet, as you would for fried cakes. Let this fat get boiling hot, but not burning hot. Have ready a plate of rolled cracker and two well beaten eggs; wet the hands in cold water, put a heaping tablespoon of the well boiled rice in the palm of the left hand, and hollow it until it is about half an inch thick, into this hollow lay two halfs of a fresh peach or canned peaches or other fruit as you like. Inclose the rice around it, adding more if necessary, being careful to have the rice half an inch thick all around the fruit. The rice must be the right softness and stiffness to cling together. Roll each of the balls in the eggs, then in the cracker crumbs, put them in the smoking hot fat and fry them a golden brown, as fast as they brown turn them and drain them in a skimmer, and lay them for a moment on brown paper to drip, serve them in covered hot dish; sprinkle with powdered sugar or with sweetened cream, flavored as you like.

Chocolate Pudding.

Grate one and one-half squares of Baker's chocolate, not sweet, wet it with a little warm milk, then stir it into one quart of boiling hot milk, in double boiler; when cooled a little, beat the yolks of six eggs and add with one cup of sugar and a pinch of salt, set it on stove again (but do not boil it as it will turn to whey) till like custard, put it in a pudding dish. Can flavor with vanilla. Beat the whites to a stiff froth and sift in six tablespoons of powdered sugar and pile it lightly on top. Put it in oven just to brown the top.

Easter Pudding.

1 quart milk	2 tablespoons corn starch
4 eggs	1 even teaspoon salt

Place the milk in double boiler, when it boils stir in two tablespoons of corn starch, wet in a little cold milk, the well beaten yolks of four eggs and stir constantly for five minutes. Remove from the fire, add a little salt, and the well beaten whites, stir briskly for two minutes and pour it in a buttered pudding dish (fit for the table). Spread a layer of jam or jelly on top and then a meringue made of the whites of two eggs and three tablespoons of powdered sugar and bake lightly in a moderate oven. Serve with sweetened cream and nutmeg.

Plain Boiled Rice.

For a family of four, one small teacup of rice, well washed, boiled in one pint and a half of milk, with one teaspoon of salt; boil one hour and thirty minutes. Serve with a sauce or sweetened cream and nutmeg. There will be enough left to make a rice pudding for the next day.

Rice Pudding.

Take two cups of cold boiled rice and put it in nearly one quart of hot milk, take your clean washed right hand and mash it fine; add an even teaspoon of salt, three tablespoons of sugar, two beaten eggs, and nutmeg. Bake thirty minutes.

Frozen Pudding.

The scraps of stale cake, enough milk to moisten them; beat four eggs with a quart of milk, and stir them over the fire in double boiler until they begin to thicken; then remove, and beat the stale cake into the custard, about two cups to each quart. If you like add a cup of fresh fruit or canned to each quart. Add enough cream or milk to make it semi-liquid. Make it over-sweet, as it looses by freezing; then freeze like ice cream and serve it in the same way.

Pudding Sauce No. 4.

1 cup sugar ½ cup butter
1 egg, beaten 1 teaspoon lemon extract

Stir butter and sugar to a cream, then add all together, beat well and set it in hot water and moderately heat it through, stirring all the time.

Cocoanut Corn Starch Pudding.

Put one quart of milk in double boiler. Wet four tablespoons of corn starch with a little cold milk; as soon as the milk boils stir in the corn starch and boil five minutes, a little salt, add the well beaten whites of four eggs, six tablespoons of sugar and a cup of grated cocoanut. Turn into a mold. Serve with a boiled custard made of the yolks, and a pint and a half of milk.

Cocoanut Rice.

1 quart milk	1 teacup rice
½ grated cocoanut	1 teaspoon salt
1 cup sugar in cocoanut	2 eggs, the whites only

Put into a double boiler the milk, well washed rice and salt, boil it one hour and a half, sweeten it with three tablespoons of sugar if you like; put it in a dish for the table, (or in cups set in water) grate the cocoanut, stir in the cup of sugar, the whites of eggs, beat well and spread it upon the rice, set in oven to brown, eat with cream, or stir all the top in the rice; try both.

Poor Man's Pudding.

1 cup molasses	1 cup beef suet chopped
1 even teaspoon soda	½ cup sweet milk
1½ cups flour	1 teaspoon salt

Chop the suet fine, have all things measured, then dissolve the soda in a little boiling water and beat it well into the molasses, and mix while foaming having one teaspoon of baking powder in the flour. Put in pan or pudding bag, steam or boil two hours.

Puff Gems for Tea.

6 eggs, a little salt
1 quart milk
6 heaping tablespoons flour
1 teaspoon, heaping, butter

Stir the beaten yolks into the milk, stir it gradually into the flour and softened butter, beating it five minutes, then quickly add the stiff beaten whites. Bake in little cups or gem pans, well buttered, in a quick oven for twenty minutes or thirty.

German Puffs.

3 eggs, well beaten
1 pint flour
1 pint milk
1 even teaspoon salt

Beat the milk and flour for eight minutes; bake in gem pans in a quick oven. Serve hot with the following sauce: Beat to a cream one cup of sugar and half a cup of butter; add gradually four tablespoons of cream and flavoring. Set it in hot water and beat smooth for a minute or two, but do not melt it.

Lemon Puff.

4 eggs, ½ teaspoon salt
3 tablespoons milk
4 tablespoons sugar
4 tablespoons flour

Beat the eggs separately, stir until very smooth, then add the grated rind and strained juice of a lemon and the whites of the eggs. Put in a buttered dish or gems and bake fifteen minutes. Serve hot.

Lemon Meringues.

2½ tablesp'ns corn starch
Yolks of 3 eggs
3 lemons, the juice
1½ pints boiling water
1 coffee cup sugar
1 even teaspoon salt

Put the water in double boiler; when boiling hot

wet the corn starch with a little cold water and stir in for five minutes with the salt. When it is cold add the rest of the ingredients. Bake in pudding-dish, cups or gem pans. If you wish it to look extra nice cover with a meringue made of the whites beaten stiff and sweetened.

CREAM PUFFS.

1 cup hot water   ½ cup butter
1 cup sifted flour   3 unbeaten eggs

Stir the butter in the boiling water; while boiling stir in the flour beaten to a smooth paste; after this cools stir three unbeaten eggs one at a time. Stir five minutes. Drop in tablespoons on a buttered tin two inches apart. When light they should not touch each other, and do not open the oven door more than is necessary. Bake in a quick oven twenty-five minutes. For the filling:

1 cup milk   ½ cup sugar
1 tablespoon corn starch   2 eggs, little salt

Put the milk in a double boiler, wet the corn starch in a little cold milk; when the milk is hot, after beating all the ingredients well together, cook until like a custard; flavor with vanilla. When both this and the puffs are cool, open one side of the puffs and fill with cream. This makes one dozen.

CUSTARD SOUFFLE.

Rub two scant tablespoons of butter and one and a half of flour to a cream, with two tablespoons of sugar and pour on gradually one cup of hot milk. Cook five minutes in double boiler, stirring all the time. Separate the whites and yolks of three eggs, beat them separately; add the whites last, and bake about thirty minutes, in a buttered pudding dish, in a moderate oven, and serve at once with this creamy sauce:

Creamy Sauce.

Cream together two tablespoons of butter and five of powdered sugar until a perfect cream. Stir constantly as you slowly add what flavoring you wish, either lemon extract or orange peel, or nutmeg, with two-thirds of a teacup of cream. When ready to serve set the dish in hot water and beat smooth, but do not melt the butter.

PUDDING SAUCES

* Foaming Sauce.

1 cup sugar   ½ cup butter
⅓ cup cold water   1 tablespoon vanilla

And two tablespoons orange flower water or lemon juice, or one of mace compound. Beat the butter and sugar to a cream, add the flavoring and water, a few drops at a time, stirring all the time. It will become very light. Place it in a double boiler on the back of the stove; let it simmer for one hour, but it must not boil. Do not stir it until you are ready to serve, then give a good stir and serve. This is the most delicious sauce for all kinds of boiled and steamed puddings.

Bath Lemon Sauce.

One cup sugar, one-half cup butter, stirred to a light cream; beat well the yolks of two eggs and mix well, then beat in gradually one pint of boiling water, and the juice of one lemon strained, then the well beaten whites of two eggs. Very nice for batter pudding when you have no cream. *Home Messenger.*

Fairy or Nun's Butter.

One cup of sugar, one-half cup of butter stirred to a cream. Grate in nutmeg and on top; or add a well beaten egg, the juice of a lemon (a wine glass of brandy improves the flavor).

Strawberry Sauce.

One half cup of butter, one cup of sugar stirred to a cream, then add a cup of crushed strawberries. This can only be made in strawberry time.

Cream Sauce.

One cup of powdered sugar, one-half cup of butter stirred to a cream. Take one pint of rich sweet cream (very cold) whipped to a froth, beat all well together. Flavor with extract of nectarine or vanilla.

A Pudding Sauce.

One-half cup of powdered sugar, one-half as much butter stirred to a cream, with one even tablespoon of flour, then pour on gradually one teacup of boiling water and flavoring, then set it in a pan of boiling water, stirring it constantly to cook the flour.

A Creamy Pudding Sauce Without Cream.

1 cup sugar
2 tablespoons water
1 orange
½ cup butter
1 teaspoonful extract nectarine

Beat the butter to a cream, add powdered sugar gradually, then slowly the juice of one orange, then place your dish in boiling water and stir for two minutes; it should be light and creamy.

Puff Pudding.

Take six eggs and drop them into six tablespoons of milk, add six tablespoons of sifted flour, beat well into a batter (say fifteen minutes). Put them in buttered cups; bake in a fairly hot oven, turn them out and eat with sweet sauce.

A Steam Batter Pudding.

1 cup sour milk
1 teaspoon soda
½ cup sugar
2 eggs, well beaten

Stir up quickly, add one teaspoon salt and flour enough to make it as stiff as cake, then stir in fruit or berries, put it in a buttered two quart basin; steam two hours. Do not uncover nor let the cold air blow on it, keeping a supply of boiling water to replenish. It must not cease to boil.

Lemon Sauce.

Boil one cup of granulated sugar in two cups of hot water; wet a tablespoon of corn starch in cold water and boil ten minutes. Add juice and grated rind of one lemon and a tablespoon of butter. In all these recipes you can double or treble them, or use one-half the quantity as desired.

CREAMS.

Italian Cream.

1 quart milk
1 pint rich cream
⅔ cup sugar
½ box gelatine

A little salt
Flavor with lemon or vanilla.

Soak the gelatine in some of the milk, then bring the milk to a boil in double boiler and add all the ingredients except the cream, set it in the coldest place till it shows signs of beginning to stiffen; then sweeten and whip the cream, stir in quickly and put in a mold on ice. Very nice.

Strawberry Cream.

1 quart strawberries
½ box gelatine

1 coffee cup sugar
1 pint sweet cream

Pick over the berries and wash and drain, then mash in earthen dish with silver spoon, add the sugar and set away for half an hour; then soak the gelatine with a little water till dissolved; strain the berries through a sieve or colander, add the gelatine to the berries, set the dish in a basin of very cold water or a pan of pounded ice, stir until it thickens, then beat in the whipped cream; pour into mold and set on ice over night is best. Serve with cream.

Lemon Snow.

Take one-half box of Cox's gelatine, just cover with cold water, set it in warm place till dissolved, then pour on it one quart of boiling water (in hot weather one pint and a half of water); when dissolved add two cups of sugar and the juice of two or three lemons; according to size; strain, set away in cold water or on ice till it begins to thicken, then add the stiffly beaten whites of four eggs, with the dish on ice continue to beat for fifteen minutes or until white as snow; turn into a mold or on ice. All gelatines are firmer to be made over night. Very nice.

WHIPPED CREAM.

Allow one quart of thick sweet cream for one dozen persons, set in a pan of broken ice until very cold, sweeten to taste, and flavor, then beat with a cream whisk, take off the top as it stiffens into froth and beat again and so on till it is all beaten; one-half pound sugar, whites of four eggs. Serve in sherbet glasses. It will whisk better if you add a half cup of milk to the thick cream. It is very nice served on top of grated cocoanut.

COFFEE CREAM.

This is an inexpensive dessert. Soak half a box of Cox's gelatine in a cup of cold water, till dissolved. Wet half of a large coffee cup of Java coffee with cold water, then pour on a pint of boiling milk and let stand on hot stove for fifteen minutes, add one cup of sugar, let dissolve, the yolks of five eggs, well beaten, Strain through a cloth. Set over the fire and stir until it begins to be creamy. Take from the fire, add the gelatine, stir well, set in a cool place, when it begins to get stiff, stir into it one pint of whipped cream, beat well, pour into a mold. Serve cold.

Spanish Cream.

½ box gelatine   2½ pints milk
6 eggs   8 tablespoons sugar

Dissolve the gelatine in a little of the milk, bring the milk to a boil, add the sugar and gelatine and the well beaten yolks, let it simmer until it begins to thicken a little but not boil; take from the stove, then beat in the stiffly beaten whites. Flavor with lemon or vanilla.

Chocolate Cream.

¼ box gelatine   ½ cup sugar
1½ pint milk   2 oz. grated chocolate
1 pint whipped cream   A little salt

Dissolve the gelatine, bring the milk to a boil, add all but the cream, then the yolks of six eggs well beaten, heat till it thickens a little, then cool and set it on ice then beat in the whipped cream. Put it in mold and let stand over night, on ice in hot weather. Serve with cream.

CUSTARDS.

Fluff.

1 pint milk   1 tablespoon corn starch
½ cup white sugar   3 eggs, the whites
1 lemon or essence   ½ even teaspoon salt

Put one pint of milk in double boiler. Wet the corn starch in quarter cup of cold milk, add salt and stir it into the hot milk, let it slowly boil for six minutes stirring often, adding sugar; take it from stove and stir in the well beaten whites of three eggs and flavoring. Turn into a mold, wet with cold water; let stand some hours in a cold place, over night is better. Serve it with cream or a thin custard made of the yolks.

FLOATING ISLAND.

Bring to a boil one quart of new milk, beat stiff the whites of four eggs sweetened, take up a large spoonful at a time, and lay on the hot milk for one minute as fast as you can till all is scalded, or put it all on as one island, take up with a skimmer, drain and set in the cold. Make a custard of the milk, yolks and four tablespoons of sugar well beaten, a little salt, as it begins to thicken take off and strain through coarse sieve if it is not smooth. Put it in a cold place, when ready to use, place the custard, flavored, in the dish, the float on top, dot it with bits of jell. This can be made in the forenoon for supper. It needs an open pan or spider to cook it in. If you drop it in spoonfuls you can put it in custard or lemonade glasses, placing a little jell at the bottom and another on top.

BAKED CUSTARD.

1 quart milk	½ cup sugar
4 eggs	Flavor to taste, salt

Heat a quart of milk hot in a double boiler that it may not whey when boiled, let it stand till cold. Beat the eggs and sugar, stir in with salt and flavoring, put it in basin, set in baking pan of water, in oven, cover till nearly done then take off and brown. When the center is thickened like jelly and shakes it is done. Watch it closely, as one minute too long will turn to whey, and the least bit of that destroys the beauty of the custard.

BOILED CUSTARD.

Prepare the same as above, using five eggs instead of four, and cook in double boiler, taking it off as soon as it clings to the spoon, stirring it often; if you wish, can put it in custard cups, with a meringue on top and jell.

ORANGE CUSTARD.

Soak two cups of baker's stale or dried bread, dried in oven and grated, in a pint of cold milk. When it is soft, beat it smooth, add the grated rind and juice of three oranges, and sugar according to the acid of the oranges; the beaten yolks of three eggs; then the well beaten whites, set the cups in pan of hot water, cover till hot and bake till it thickens in middle, be careful and take it out before it turns to whey.

COCOANUT CUSTARD.

To one pound of freshly grated cocoanut allow one quart of scalded milk in double boiler and one heaping teacup of sugar. Beat well the yolks of six eggs and stir in alternately in the milk with the cocoanut and sugar. If you like it light colored, use the whites instead of yolks, or beat stiff, sweeten and drop on top of cups. As soon as it begins to thicken set off of stove.

CHOCOLATE CUSTARD.

Make one quart of boiled custard, adding four tablespoons of grated Baker's chocolate, take off the minute it thickens, just to boiling point.

LEMON CUSTARD. (May keep three days.)

Two lemons, the rinds and juice, strained and sweetened to taste, beat the yolks of eight eggs till very light, stir this all into one pint and a half of water that has been boiled, stir it on the fire (adding one teaspoon cornstarch), take it off as soon as it begins to thicken. Can add almond or nectarine flavoring; put in cups, eat cold.

PEACH MERINGUE.

Put on in a double boiler one quart of new milk; take out enough of it to wet two tablespoons of corn starch; when the milk boils stir in the starch till cooked; remove from the fire and stir in one tablespoon sweet butter; let it cool a little and add the well beaten yolks of three eggs; beat till light and creamy; add one-half cup of sugar. Cover the bottom of a buttered pudding-dish with two layers of cut up ripe peaches; sprinkle sugar enough to sweeten and pour the custard on top. Bake in a quick oven twenty minutes. When done cover with the well-beaten whites sweetened; brown lightly in oven. Eat warm with sauce or cold with cream. I think it nice cold without baking if it is brought to a boil after the yolks are in.

AMERICAN CREAM FOR DESSERT.

½ box Cox's gelatine   1 quart milk
6 tablespoons sugar   4 eggs

Soak the gelatine in some of the milk, add it to the rest in a double boiler with the well-beaten yolks with four tablespoons of the sugar. Put on the stove and heat again (but not boil); take off the stove, add the stiffly beaten whites and the two tablespoons of sugar Flavor with vanilla or lemon and pour in molds.

Fresh-Made Jelly and Whipped Cream.

2 quarts berries	½ box gelatine
2 cups sugar	½ pint cream

Take strawberries or raspberries; put in granite kettle with just water enough to not quite cover; cook till soft, strain through a jelly bag; add the sugar and enough boiling water to make the quantity one quart. Let it boil up, add the gelatine soaked in half a pint of water. Strain and pour in cups. Put the whipped cream on top before serving.

Chocolate Blanc Mange.

1 quart milk, salt	1½ squares chocolate
4 tablespoons sugar	4 tablespoons corn starch

Use Baker's chocolate. Place the milk in double boiler; when it boils add all the ingredients, stirring well as it boils for eight minutes. Flavor with vanilla. Wet the molds with cold water before filling. Serve with cream or whipped cream.

Blanc Mange.

1 quart cream	½ box gelatine
4 oz. sweet almonds	½ ounce bitter almonds
	¾ cup sugar

Crack the almonds take out the meats, pour boiling water on them and skin them, pound them in a wedgewood mortar, moistening them gradually with orange-flower water; mix this with the cream in double boiler. Dissolve the gelatine in half cup of cold water. When the cream comes to a scald stir in slowly all the ingredients; just let it come to a boil stirring constantly. Put it in molds. Stand on ice over night. Serve with cream. A plainer but nice blanc mange can be made with milk and almond extract or vanilla. Put it upon the ice and when about to thicken, stir it until it is very smooth; then stir in lightly a pint of cream, whipped, and put into a mold. I prefer putting it in a glass dish ready for the table, as the cream is on top; it is more relishable and looks better.

THE ORANGE.

How true it is with fruits, as well as metals, that the laws which govern supply and demand are quickly adjusted. No sooner was it realized that fresh fruits and vegetables were as necessary for health as animal food, then our most enterprising growers set themselves not only to increase the quantity, but to improve the varieties and preserve them for the longest time possible in their natural state. In the month of January, before home grown fruits have become scarce and high priced, Florida oranges are at our door, cheap enough that all may indulge in some of these well tested recipes on the delicious fruit.

ORANGE SHORTCAKE.

1 pint flour
2 teaspoons baking-powder
1 cup milk
2 tablespoons butter
½ teaspoon salt
1 egg beaten

Sift the flour, salt and baking-powder twice, rub the butter in flour, mix soft as you can handle, roll out in two cakes long for a long square tin; just butter the under one and lay one on top of the other; mark the top one with a fork. Stand in a cold place or in ice-box fifteen minutes, then bake in hot oven about thirty minutes, then take out of oven, let stand three minutes, then separate the two layers, butter the two insides, as for eating. Before making the cake, peel five or six sweet oranges and cut in small pieces around the core, taking out the seeds, let stand till cake is in the oven, then drain off the juice and sprinkle a cup or more of sugar on them; spread between the layers and set in oven three to four minutes. Do all this quickly and serve immediately.

LEMON OR ORANGE SAUCE.

If one wishes a sauce for it (I do not), cream a cup of sugar and half a cup of butter, or that proportion, add the grated rind of one lemon or orange, one beaten egg; beat it well; set the bowl over hot tea kettle, where it will become hot, but not boil, beating constantly. Before serving add the juice that came from the oranges, or the juice of a lemon.

STRAWBERRY SHORTCAKE.

This is made the same way as the orange shortcake. Wash the strawberries, pick them over (all berries need washing quickly); put the sugar on them just as the cake is done, and half chop them a little with the spoon. Some like a layer of strawberries on top of cake also. We prefer a dish of berries and sugar for each one. *Mrs. B.*

ORANGE JELLY.

Put one pint of cold water on one-half box of Cox's gelatine; soak until dissolved; add two cups of sugar, the juice of one lemon and one orange, strained, one pint of boiling water; let come to a boil, set away to cool; when it begins to thicken pour it over eight oranges sliced by cutting around the core and taking out the seeds, and sprinkle well with sugar in dish for table; put it in ice-box to harden. *Mrs. B.*

ORANGE JELLY No. 2.

To half a cup of cold water put half a box of gelatine, set in a warm place till dissolved, then pour over it a cup of boiling water. Put half a cup of granulated sugar on the board and roll a large lemon in it until the oil is extracted from the rind. To a pint of the juice of sour oranges add the juice of the lemon, one cup of sugar and the half cup flavored with the oil of the lemon. Add all to the gelatine; stir well; strain into wet molds or a flat dish, and cut it out in small blocks when solid. Other ways of serving are to cut the oranges in half, take out the fruit carefully, and drop the skins in cold water. When the jelly is made dry these inside, notch the edges prettily, fill with the jelly and set on ice or in a cold place; or the oranges may be cut so as to leave half, and a half-inch strip over the top for the handle, notching the edges. Place the baskets in a pan of chopped ice, fill with the jelly, and put a teaspoon of whipped cream on top of the jelly.

MERINGUES.

4 eggs, the whites   9 heaping tablespoons sugar

Beat the eggs very stiff, add gradually the powdered sugar till stiff enough to lie in oblong shape on paper. Butter white foolscap paper, lay it on bottom of dripping pan and drop the mixture on the paper, by tablespoonfuls, allowing two inches between each, they must not run together. Flavor with lemon. Bake or dry in a slow steady oven to a delicate tinge of brown. Place the flat sides together, when dry, with sweetened and flavored whipped cream.

GOLDEN MERINGUES.

Made the same way as the previous recipe, only using the yolks and the white of one egg. The yolks will not beat stiff but they will beat very light. They must be stiff enough to drop.

ALMOND MACCAROONS.

Shell half a pound of soft-shelled almonds, pour boiling water over them until the skins are loose, peel and throw into cold water, take out, drain in dry towel, pound to a paste in marble or some hard mortar, put in a dish and gradually add one pound of pulverized sugar, and the whites of three stiffly beaten eggs, and two teaspoons of extract of lemon. Mix well with a mixed metal spoon (not iron spoon). Wet the hands in cold water and make the mixture quickly and deftly into balls the size of a small hickory nut, put sheets of buttered paper in sheet iron pans, lay the balls on the paper two inches apart, wet the hands and smooth over the top so they are glossy, set in a moderate oven for half to three-fourths of an hour till dry.

LEMON SAUCE.

½ cup sugar
1 tablespoon corn starch
1 lemon, rind and juice
1 tablespoon butter
1 pint boiling water
1 egg, salt

Beat the egg separately, stir the butter and sugar to a cream, boil the water in double boiler, wet the starch in cold water, put it in the boiler and boil ten minutes, beating all the time till smooth, now add all together, take off the stove, add the rind and strained juice of lemon.

Orange Sauce.

This is made the same way as the above recipe, using the juice, strained, of two oranges, and the grated rind of one.

Hickory Nut Maccaroons.

These are made the same way as the almond maccaroons, taking off what skins you can, chopping the meats fine and mashing in mortar.

CANDY.

Molasses Candy.

1 cup N. O. molasses   1 cup brown sugar
1 tablespoon butter   1 tablespoon vinegar

When warm, stir the ingredients together, let boil till brittle, but do not stir it. Be careful not to burn; it must slowly boil. Test it by dropping a little in water. When brittle, pour out on a greased platter, turn up the edges as it cools, butter your hands and work by pulling long lengths until a bright and golden color. Butter the fingers when it sticks to them, draw it into stick size. When cold, cut it in lengths you like, flavor with what you like, or put different kinds of nuts in different dishes, chopped fine; stir them in.

Candy of Any Flavor.

3½ pounds best sugar   1½ pints water
1 teaspoon cream tartar

Boil for fifteen minutes, test it by dropping a little in cold water; if the threads are brittle as you pull it, it is done; then flavor differently, or put nuts, chocolate, cocoanut, or whatever kind of candy you wish to make, by stirring them in, in different dishes. Add the cream tartar just before you take it up.

Ice Cream Candy.

3 pounds best coffee sugar   ¼ pound butter
1 teaspoon cream tartar   2 teaspoons extract lemon

Add just water enough to melt the sugar. Boil without stirring, till it is brittle when dropped in cold water; then it is done; add the lemon and cream tartar, then pour it into as many buttered plates as there are pullers. Pull when partly cold till very white and creamy.

SHERBETS.

Peach Sherbet.

1 quart peaches chopped fine   1 quart, heaping, of sugar.
4 tablespoons gelatine
2 quarts water boiled

Soak the gelatine, then pour the boiling water onto the sugar and gelatine, add the peaches and set to cool, then pack to freeze, when partly frozen add one quart of whipped cream sweetened. Pineapple can be frozen in the same way. Freeze the same as ice cream.   *Mrs. B.*

Orange Sherbet.

Soak one tablespoon of gelatine in cold water. Boil one quart of water and one pound of sugar for five minutes, then add the gelatine and stir till dissolved. Remove from the fire; as soon as cool set it on ice to get ready to freeze, after adding the juice of ten oranges and two lemons, when it is all very cold, freeze, adding the beaten white of one egg sweetened. Freeze the same way as ice cream.

Pineapple Sherbet.

To one quart of grated pineapple add one and one-half pounds of sugar, the juice of two lemons and one quart of water boiled, dissolve the sugar in hot water, stir in the lemon and pineapple, let stand one hour, then strain through a sieve. When very cold pour into the freezer to freeze, stirring it until stiff. Beat the whites of two eggs to a stiff froth, add two tablespoons of sugar. Stir these in when partly frozen, then finish. It will need two large pineapples or three small ones. For freezing see freezing ice cream.

Cocoanut Sherbet.

Two good sized cocoanuts, save the milk that is in them, break in pieces and grate all the meat into a deep dish, pour over it two quarts of water and let it stand two hours, strain through a jelly bag or sieve; to this liquid add the cocoanut milk and three-fourths of a pound of sugar; mix well. If not sweet enough add more sugar, as freezing always requires more.

LEMON SHERBET.

5 lemons, the juice
1 quart water
1 pint sugar
1 tablespoon gelatine

Soak the gelatine in a little of the water; boil the quart of water and pour onto the gelatine and sugar, add the lemon juice, strain, turn into freezer and freeze. This is light and creamy.

ICE CREAMS.

How to Freeze Creams and all kinds of Ices.

The first requisite is to have perfectly sweet cream and use only the best materials, for it will be tainted with the least defect. Next get a good freezer, one working with a crank. There are new ones nearly every year, or some improvements. Begin to make preparations four hours before you wish to serve it. A four-quart freezer will require twelve pounds of ice, two quarts and a half of coarse salt, rock salt is the best. Put the cut-up ice in a coarse coffee sack, pound with a hatchet back till as fine as hickory nuts, see that the freezer is properly set in its own tub, put the cover on and tie a double cloth over it, to prevent the possibility of any salt getting inside. Place at the bottom a layer of ice three inches thick then a layer of salt, then ice again, then salt, and so on till packed full, with a layer of ice last. Pack very solid with a stick. Then remove the cloth and cover carefully (see that there is no salt inside), and pour in the cream having just added the well whipped whites, leaving two inches for expansion. Replace the cover, adjust the crank, and soon begin to turn the freezer, after fifteen minutes pack the ice down again, drain off most of the water by taking out the plug from the bottom, put it in again, add more ice and turn again, repeating the draining and packing. Turn the crank steadily till it turns pretty hard. If all is right it will freeze in about thirty minutes. Water ices take longer time than creams. When frozen wipe the lid of the can, open, take out the crank, remove the dasher, scrape it off, take a flat mush stick and scrape down from the sides of can, and beat and work thoroughly for ten minutes; this makes the cream smooth. Put the lid on, cork up the crank hole, drain and pack with salt and ice, keeping a cloth on cover to protect from salt; covering the top with pure ice; then throw a piece of double carpet over it and stand in a cold place to ripen. In tasting when the cream is first frozen, you taste each ingredient separately, but after standing one or two hours, they seem to blend and form a pleasant whole. When ready to serve dip the can quickly in cold water and wipe it and turn out on platter and serve. If you have no freezer you can use a tin pail for the can, setting it in a bucket or some crock the right size for pail, packing into the space between them, very firmly, a mixture of one-third salt, to two-thirds pounded ice, or snow in winter. Shake the pail back and forth, scrape down often. Ice creams can be served in fanciful shapes by the use of molds. These you have to buy, and unless you have much use for them, it is cheaper to buy the cream, as it can be obtained in almost every city. It must be placed in the molds after it is frozen and well beaten with the spatula, upon this *beating* depends the fineness of the cream. I will give a few general directions here, which I will not repeat in the recipes for creams. To freeze custards, puddings, sherbets, or water ices, follow the same directions.

If you use eggs or any thickening always strain. Do not handle the ice with your hands but use a skimmer or dish to dip it with, nor think you must freeze it in a cold place like a cellar and endanger your health and life. It can be frozen in any comfortable place. The more rapid the melting of the ice the quicker the cream freezes. Bring your cream to a boil and melt the sugar in it while hot, reserve one pint of cream for whipping to stir in after it begins to freeze; remember to sweeten and flavor it before whipping. When raw cream is frozen it has a strong taste and will never be perfectly smooth or velvety. For ices also boil the water and dissolve the sugar, boil and skim and set to get very cold, then prepare and freeze. Berry flavors are prepared by allowing the whole berries to stand awhile with a good allowance of sugar. Mash them, strain the juice, add it to the cream. It must be too sweet before freezing.

To one quart of cream, allow one quart of fruit, and one pint of sugar. Before it is quite frozen add one pint whipped cream sweetened and flavored. If a cream is too rich it will not freeze at all. If too poor it will be rough and scaly. A pint of berries or peaches cut fine (without the juice) and sweetened added to a quart of ice cream, while in process of freezing makes a delicious fruit ice cream. Water-ices are made from the juices of fruits mixed with water, sweetened and frozen the same way as cream, only it takes longer time for freezing. They must both, cream and water, be very cold before stirring.

Ice Cream. Very Nice. No. 1.

2 quarts cream
4 eggs, the whites
2 cups sugar, heaping
4 teaspoons vanilla

Scald the cream in double boiler, (saving out one pint for whipping) dissolve the sugar in hot cream, set where it will get very cold before stirring in the stiffly beaten whites and whipped cream. Freeze.

Ice Cream No. 2.

3 pints cream
1 quart milk
1 pint sugar
2 eggs, the whites

This is a different proportion and good. Flavor with lemon extract or vanilla. Follow the directions on the previous page for freezing.

Ice Cream No. 3.

2 quarts new milk
3 quarts fresh cream
2 even tablespoons corn starch
3 pounds sugar

Bring to a boil in double boiler the milk and two quarts of the cream; dissolve two pints and a half of the sugar in it hot; set it where it will get very cold or on ice. Then flavor it and flavor and sweeten the other quart of cream with the other half pint of sugar. Whip and skim off, having it very cold, with a cream whisk, taking it off as fast as it rises, wet the corn starch with cold milk very smooth and boil five minutes, stirring all the time. Then strain it. After all this is done it is ready for freezing when cold. This makes two gallons. For this quantity it will take nearly one peck of salt and two pecks of fine ice. Please remember that you can divide or double any of these recipes, as your needs may be. Freeze; following directions for freezing.

Ice Cream, Not So Rich.

2 quarts new milk	4 eggs beaten separately
3 teaspoons lemon extract	2 cups sugar
1 pint whipped cream	1 pint strawberry juice

Scald the milk in double boiler, beat the yolks and add and scald five minutes, dissolving the sugar in it. Let it get very cold, and add the beaten whites and cream sweetened and flavored. Prepare the strawberry juice as directed, it gives the cream a pretty pink color. Always remember to strain all creams that have been boiled. You can leave out the whipped cream and strawberry juice, if you wish.

Frozen Custard.

2 quarts milk	2 tablespoons vanilla or lemon
1½ pounds sugar	
4 eggs	

Boil the milk, taking one cup out to beat in with the well beaten yolks. Put in the sugar; boil two minutes, put away to get cold, then add flavoring and the well beaten whites. From one pint to a quart of whipped cream is a great addition. These must be very cold before beating, as they beat stiffer.

Strawberry Ice Cream.

It is simply adding one pint of well sweetened juice to one quart of ice cream, putting it in cold when ready to freeze.

Peach Ice Cream.

Peel and mash six large ripe peaches, put through a sieve, for every quart of cream well sweetened.

Pineapple Ice Cream.

To one quart of cream, peel, grate or mash one pineapple, with one-half pint of sugar, strain through a sieve; add it to a regular ice cream.

Chocolate Ice Cream.

To two quarts of regular ice cream add four heaping tablespoons of Baker's sweet chocolate, stirred smooth in a few spoons of hot water and the yolks of two eggs, then pour it into your hot milk or cream and scald three minutes, set away to cool, and proceed as for ice cream.

Orange Ice Cream.

To one quart of cream, allow one pint of sugar, " a pint is a pound the world around " is the old adage; the grated rind of one lemon and one orange, (only the outside, remembering the white is bitter) and the juice of six large oranges, after it is cold. After scalding the cream put in one-half of the sugar very slowly to prevent its curdling. The other half dissolve in orange juice.

Lemon Ice Cream.

Grate the rind and strain the juice of two large juicy lemons, or three small ones, to one quart of cream. Put half a pint of the sugar in hot cream.

Dissolve the other half in a little water and lemon juice, adding it when slightly frozen. Add the juice slowly beating carefully. It will not require so much sugar if you use lemon extract. The flavor is different. All creams are lighter if you add the stiffly beaten whites of one or two eggs just before freezing. All fruits should be sweetened before mixing with the cold creams just before freezing. All creams should be frozen two hours before they are needed.

Cocoanut Ice Cream.

The same as ice cream No. 1, adding nearly one pint of finely grated cocoanut to one quart of cream.

Coffee Ice Cream.

To one quart prepared cream, put one pint of strong coffee (the best Java or Mocha) well settled. It must be perfectly clear. One pint of sugar. In using fruits or coffee, use no other flavoring. Cook one teaspoon of corn starch in boiling coffee.

Biscuit Glace.

4 yolks of eggs ½ pint sugar
2 quarts whipped cream

Beat well the yolks of eggs, add the sugar slowly, and vanilla to taste; scald three pints of cream in double boiler, stir in eggs and sugar, when cold add the pint of whipped cream and freeze. When nearly frozen, stir well with the spatula, color part of it red (if you wish) with confectioners' sugar and put in bottom of paper capsules, or individual molds, or paper cases, then fill up with the uncolored cream. Pack these in ice and salt putting ice only on and near the top. It must be frozen smooth before putting it in these biscuit molds. Let freeze two hours.

French Cook.

WATER ICES.

It takes a little longer time to freeze water ices than creams. Stir the crank for five minutes then let it rest five minutes, for four or five times, then freeze the same as for creams. Whatever the desired quantity make a syrup of the proportion of one pint of water to one pint of sugar, and boil for fifteen minutes, skimming it as soon as the skum rises, then set away to get cold. Add the lemon juice or whatever fruit is desired, adding the whites of three eggs, stiffly beaten, to every two quarts of the mixture, stirring them in when partly frozen.

LEMON ICE.

3 quarts water 3 quarts sugar
18 lemons 6 eggs, the whites

Strain through a fine sieve. Follow directions for freezing as above and for ice cream. Or make a very strong lemonade and very sweet, the juice of five lemons, strained, to one quart of water. When it begins to freeze stir in the six beaten whites of eggs.

Mrs. B.

PINEAPPLE ICE.

1 pint water 1 pint sugar
2 ripe pineapples 5 eggs, the whites.

Prepare the syrup as directed; beat the whites of two of the eggs stiff, stir it in to clarify the syrup, skimming as fast as it rises; boil fifteen minutes; let it get very cold. Peel and grate the pineapple, strain through a sieve. To one quart of the syrup add the juice of one lemon and stir in the pineapple; when very cold freeze as directed. When about half frozen beat in the whites of three stiffly beaten eggs, adding four tablespoons of powdered sugar in eggs. Freeze.

Cherry Water Ice.

Prepare the same as the above recipe, allowing one pint of mashed pitted cherries to one quart of syrup, adding one cup of sugar to cherries and rub through a sieve. Freeze the same as other ices.

Coffee Ice.

One pint of strong coffee (perfectly clear), one pint of water, one pint of sugar. Prepared as other ices and frozen the same way.

Orange Ice.

Peel and cut up eight large oranges; put on one cup sugar; let stand an hour, squeeze them well and strain through a sieve, add the juice of two lemons; add all to one quart of the prepared syrup, as heretofore stated, and the whites of three stiffly beaten eggs when partly frozen, then freeze.

Currant and Grape Ice.

These are made the same as other fruits; allowing one pint of the juice to one quart of the syrup. With all these fruits be sure they are sweet enough, as the acids vary.

Tutti Frutti.

When a rich vanilla cream is partly frozen, candied cherries, chopped raisins, citron or any other candied fruit chopped fine are added; add about half the quantity of fruit that there is of ice cream. Freeze in molds or not.

CAKE.

Cake Mixing.

There is a best way of doing everything, even to boil an egg, to cook it so as to be palatable and nourishing. So there must be a best way to go to work to make a cake. How very difficult it seems to a beginner, while to one of experience it is very simple and a delight. Knowledge gives us power in all things. A clean calico dress and apron is the first necessary thing when one is going to work with flour. The next is to get every thing ready to work with, on the clean kitchen table. Line the baking pans with best wrapping paper. Turn the cake pan bottom side up and cut two papers the size of the bottom, butter the top one by warming the pan, then put the dry one under the other; for the sides shape the paper inside to the pan and then crease it and cut it the depth of pan and butter them. Cake baking pans should have a tube in the center, it bakes more even, but do not forget to butter it. Now get all the ingredients together, and be very exact in all your measurements. For a cupful of flour, sugar or butter, run a knife straight across the top of cup; this is even full for a cup or tablespoon. Roll the sugar (using the powdered for nice cake, the granulated is too coarse a grain), and measure the butter you need; in cold weather let the butter stand long enough to soften so as to cut easily, but if it melts at all, it will make the cake heavy or soggy. Sift and measure the flour, then sift the second time, after you have stirred the baking-powder in it. In hot weather lay the eggs for one-half hour in very cold water as they will beat lighter. This should be the first thing to do. I always take for all kinds of cake just half as much butter as sugar, except fried cakes. This gives the best grain to the cake. For fruit cake, seed the raisins, clean, wash and dry the currants the day before. Sprinkle two tablespoons of flour on every pound of raisins after slightly chopping them, using the dryest and best brown sugar. Add the raisins after the flour and milk is stirred in. Stir the cake in an earthen dish (never in tin) with a wooden spoon. In cold weather warm the dish by letting warm water stand in the dish till warmed through, not hot enough to melt the butter. First put the rolled sugar in the dish, then in the center put the cut up butter and stir to a perfectly light cream. This is best for all cakes, even cookies or or fried cakes are more delicate. Always beat the yolks and whites separately on a flat plate or platter with a steel knife, using it deftly by slightly lifting it and not stirring, to give it a light foam. I have purchased several egg beaters and tried two of our own invention, but have discarded them all and gone back to the steel kitchen knife; the eggs are much lighter. Stir the well-beaten yolks in next till very light color, then the whites, then the flour and milk, about one-fourth at a time gradually, till all is in, adding the flavoring. Do not leave the cake after you once begin to mix it; always stir the same way and put right in a moderate oven that you can hold your hand in to count thirty. It must be heated through to the center ere it bakes, so as to rise even; the heat must not decrease, or it will fall, but be kept a steady heat. It must rise fully before a crust is formed. If the cake browns too fast cover it with brown paper, and open one of the oven dampers for a short time. As much depends on the heat of the oven and your intelligent management of it as in mixing. Count the number of minutes it takes to bake bread, for cake a little less. When the cake rises and cracks open you may be sure there is too much flour. Some flours swell more than others. Open the oven door as little as possible and close it quickly, do not turn it round till it is set in center. There are three simple tests to tell when cake is done. It will cleave from the pan around the edges; will not stick to a broom corn run into the center of cake; and put your ear to the cake and if you hear it tick or sing loudly it is not done; return it to the oven; if very faintly it may be done. Do not take out of pan till half cooled, then put it on the flat bottom of a larger cake pan and frost if you wish to Remember to use only good, fresh eggs and perfectly sweet butter. It is well to weigh and measure one pound each of flour, sugar and butter and get cups that twice even full of sugar will be one pound and four times even full of flour will be one pound, and once full and one-third or more one pound of butter. Do not allow these cups to be used for any other purpose, and they are always ready. It is more convenient than weighing. I shall give my recipes by measure as far as possible. I do not wish to enlarge the book by repeating how to mix every recipe. I will give it in more condensed form. Beat the butter and sugar to a cream, then beat the yolks well and stir in; beat the whites to a stiff froth and stir in; next the flour with baking powder and milk, a part of each gradually, and flavoring. All cakes are mixed this way, except when otherwise mentioned. If the inexperienced will read all these directions they will be thoroughly equipped to make a cake.

FRUIT CAKE.

2 cups sugar
1 cup butter
1 pound raisins
¼ pound citron
1 cup brandy

4 cups flour
10 eggs
2 pounds currants
2 even teaspoons cloves
2 even teaspoons cinnamon

Prepare the raisins, currants, and slice the citron very thin the day beforehand, and follow the directions for mixing cake. Remember the former directions, to rub the dried or Zante currants first in a crash towel to break off the little stems, and they are sometimes very dirty; wash in two or three waters, press the water out between two dry towels and dry them over night by the stove. You can leave the currants and citron out of any cake you wish, and some like it better without either. I am certain the cake is more healthy without and more relishable. A slow oven for all cakes with fruit or molasses in them.

LOAF CAKE. VERY NICE.

3 cups sponge
3 eggs
½ cup flour
1 teaspoon cinnamon

1 cup butter
2 cups sugar
1 teaspoon cloves
¾ pound raisins

1 teaspoon soda

Wash and seed the raisins the day before you make it. In the morning take three large cups of the bread sponge before working the dough. Cream the (brown) sugar and butter and beat eggs the same as for other cake. Dissolve the soda in a little hot milk. Mix all well together and lastly add the partly chopped raisins, putting two tablespoons of flour on them   Put it in a warm place to rise forty minutes. Bake one hour.

Confectionery Cake.

2 cups sugar
1 cup milk
3 cups flour
½ cup butter
3 eggs, the yolks
2 teaspoons vanilla

Mix all together for a three layer cake. For the middle layer take one cup of the above mixture, add one cup of molasses, one cup chopped raisins, one teaspoon each of cinnamon and cloves, one tablespoon of brandy, one-half cup of flour. Bake in one layer and put between the other two white layers. Frost each layer.

Plain Fruit Cake.

2 cups brown sugar
1 cup butter
2 teaspoons baking-powder
4 cups flour, nearly
½ cup milk
6 eggs, or 8 eggs
1 pound raisins,
1 teaspoon cloves
1 teaspoon cinnamon

Can make half the quantity, or double it.

Rich Fruit Cake.

4 cups sugar
2 cups butter
2 pounds raisins
20 eggs
4 teaspoon baking-powder
8 cups flour
2 pounds currants
1 pound citron
½ cup milk
½ pint brandy

Mix as before directed.

Fruit Cake. Good.

1 cup brown sugar
½ cup butter
1 cup molasses
½ teaspoon soda in molasses
½ cup milk
3 cups flour
4 eggs
1 even teaspoon cloves, cinnamon and mace.
1 pound raisins

Sift two spoons of flour on the slightly chopped raisins.

Mrs. H. M. D.'s Reliable Fruit Cake. Good.

2 cups dry brown sugar
1 teaspoon almond extract
4 cups flour
1 teaspoon mace
1 tablespoon rosewater
1 cup butter
2 teaspoons baking-powder
2 pounds raisins
½ teaspoon nutmeg
8 eggs

When all is mixed put one-fourth of the quantity in a baking pan, then a layer of thin sliced citron dredged with flour, then another layer of batter, then of citron, and so on until all is in, this being an excellent way of putting in the citron; finish with a layer of the cake batter, and bake forty-five minutes or more.

Imperial Cake

2 cups sugar
10 eggs
1 lemon, grated rind and juice
½ pound raisins
1 tablespoon orange flower water
1 cup butter, heaping
4 cups flour
1 pound almonds
½ pound citron
1 tablespoon nectarine extract in 1 teaspoon water
1 tablespoon rosewater

Pound the almonds after skinning and splitting them. Put two extra tablespoons of flour on the fruit.

This is a delicious cake, and when cut is very distinguished looking. Will keep a long time.

These two last recipes will make two medium-sized cakes, that is, two three-quart pans, or one five-quart. For fruit cake it bakes more even with a tube in the center of the pan.

WHITE FRUIT CAKE.

1 cup white sugar
½ cup butter
1 pound raisins
2 teaspoons baking-powder
7 eggs, the whites
2 cups flour
⅓ cup milk
2 teaspoons flavoring

Mix as directed before and flavor with any light colored extract. Boil the raisins in a little water a few minutes to bleach them; then wipe dry and stone them, then chop them a little. Can add two layers of citron if you like. Sprinkle the raisins with flour.

Mrs. B.

DRIED APPLE CAKE.

2 cups dried apples
1 cup sugar
⅔ cup butter
2 teaspoons baking-powder
1 cup raisins
1 cup molasses
1 cup milk
1 teaspoon, even, soda
2 eggs
3 cups or more of flour   Nutmeg and cinnamon

Make it as stiff as fruit cake. Pick over and wash the apples and soak in just enough water to soak soft, say, two hours. Then chop them as raisins, and boil them fifteen minutes in the molasses, then dissolve the soda in a little hot water, and put it in the molasses when cold.

Delicate Cake.

2 cups sugar
1 cup butter
4 cups flour
10 eggs, the whites
¾ cup milk
2 teaspoons baking-powder
2 teaspoons almond extract

Stir the butter and sugar to a cream, beat the whites stiff and stir into the cream; add the baking-powder to the flour and sift it twice, then add it with the milk gradually and the extract.

Delicate Cake.

1¼ cups sugar
¾ cup butter—scant
2 teaspoons baking-powder
6 eggs, the whites
2 cups flour
2 teaspoons lemon extract

Mix baking-powder well with flour, pass it through the sieve three times. This is mixed contrary to the usual rules. Beat the butter alone, to a light cream, and add the flour to it, stirring it in gradually with the ends of the fingers, until it is a smooth paste. Beat the whites to a stiff froth, and mix in them the sifted sugar; now stir the egg and sugar gradually into the flour and butter, adding the flavoring, and mix it smoothly together with the egg whisp. For frosting, see frosting.

Hickory Nut Cake.

2 cups sugar
1 cup butter
5 eggs
1 cup milk
4 cups flour
2 teaspoons baking-powder

One pint hickory nut meats cut fine, sprinkled with flour and rolled. Rich and excellent.

Fig Layer Cake.

For the cake:
1 cup sugar
½ cup butter
2 cups flour
2 teaspoons vanilla
1 egg, and yolks of 2
⅔ cup milk
2 teaspoons baking-powder

For Fig Paste.

¼ cup water
8 figs
1 cup sugar
1 egg, the white

Bake the cake in three layers. Boil the water and sugar till a little brittle when you string it in cold air; then take the sugar from the stove, cool a little, beat the white to a stiff froth and add to it, chop the figs very fine, and add gradually. Spread the paste on top of each cake and sides, if you wish. It (the cake) may need more flour.

Plain Loaf Cake. Very nice.

1¾ pounds brown sugar
⅓ pint of yeast
2 pounds raisins
3 eggs
1¼ pounds butter
1 pint milk
1 teaspoon each cinamon and cloves
3 pounds flour

This measures three quarts sifted, well heaped of flour, one pint rounded of butter, one quart of sugar. Stir butter and sugar to a cream, warm the milk and stir with the yeast in flour, let rise over night, saving out one cup of flour to add next morning with the other ingredients, beaten eggs and floured raisins. Put in pans and let rise forty minutes. This recipe makes three loaves. Bake in moderate oven.

Pound Cake.

2 cups sugar
1 ⅓ cups butter
4 cups flour
10 eggs
Flavor as you like

This is very rich and fine, and needs to be made and baked in a skilfull manner. One teaspoon baking-powder is surer of being light and a tube in center of baking pen. Can bake it in one large loaf, or two smaller ones. Can flavor with one tablespoon nectarine of orange flower water.

Cup Cake.

1 cup butter
2 cups sugar
2 teaspoons baking-powder
3 cups flour
4 eggs
Flavoring.

Mix as for other cakes. Can add, if you wish, a half cup of milk, and then more flour.

Sponge Cake.

2 cups sugar
2 cups flour
10 eggs, salt
1 lemon, juice and rind
Baking-powder, if you like

Beat the yolks light, beat in the sugar until very light, then add half the flour. Beat the whites to a very stiff froth, add half of them to cake, then the remaining half of flour, then the remaining half of the whites, the grated rind and strained juice of lemon; stir lightly and put in buttered paper pan. Bake in a quick oven, but not too hot, about forty-five minutes; to one hour. Great care should be taken not to butter the paper too heavily; lay the paper in hot pan and grease with small cloth.

White Sponge Cake.

6 eggs, the whites   1 cup sugar
½ teaspoon cream tartar   ¾ cup flour
1 teaspoon almond extract

Beat the whites to a stiff froth, then gradually beat in the sugar, mixing lightly, add the cream tartar to the flour, sift it twice, then sift it into the cake, mix the cake quickly, but carefully, add one teaspoon of flavoring. The recipe says turn into an ungreased pan and bake in a moderate oven thirty minutes.

A Small Sponge Cake.

1 cup sugar   1½ cups flour
6 eggs   Flavoring

Beat eggs separately and mix as above.

Sponge Cake.

1 tumbler sugar   1 tumbler flour
5 eggs   1 teaspoon vinegar

Another Sponge Cake.

1 cup sugar   1 cup flour
4 eggs   1 teaspoon baking-powder
Flavoring

A Smaller Sponge Cake.

1 teacup sugar   1 teacup flour
3 eggs, lemon extract   1½ teasp'ns baking-powder
2 tablespoons water.

Ice-Cream Cake.

2 cups sugar ¾ cup butter
1 cup milk 7 eggs, the whites
1 cup corn starch 2 cups flour
2 teaspoons baking-powder 2 teaspoons lemon extract

Bake in three layers with boiled frosting between. Two cups sugar, one-half a cup of water boiling hot; boil until it candies; do not stir it. Cool a little and try it between the thumb and finger; if it threads it is done. Beat the whites of three eggs to a stiff froth; pour over them slowly (beating) the candied sugar and beat until cold. *Mrs. Sarah B. Smith.*

The above recipe is a nice delicate cake baked in one loaf.

Delicate Cake.

2 cups sugar 3 cups flour
6 ounces butter 14 eggs, the whites
1 lemon juice and rind.

Almond Cake.

2 cups sugar ¾ cup butter
8 eggs, the whites 1 cup milk
1 or 2 teaspoons orange flower water ¼ pound almonds mashed
  4 cups flour
2 teaspoons baking-powder

This must be carefully put together and it is very nice.

To Blanch Almonds.

Shell them, throw them into boiling water, place on back of stove about six minutes; then put them into cold water and remove the skins by rubbing with the hands. Mash in an earthen mortar.

White Mountain Cake.

2 cups sugar
¾ cup butter
2 cups flour
7 eggs
1 cup corn starch
2 teaspoons baking-powder

Bake in layers, three or four, with this filling: Pour one-half a pint of boiling water over four cups of sugar (powdered) and boil till a spoonful on a cold saucer will stir to a cream. Pour the boiled sugar gradually (beating all the time) into the whites of four well-beaten eggs. Stir until the whole is cold and creamy. Spread between and on top of layers.

Cocoanut Cake.

1 cup sugar
½ cup butter
2 cups flour
⅔ cup milk
2 eggs
1 teaspoon baking-powder

This is a good foundation for any layer cake. I have made it in one loaf, stirring one-half of a grated cocoanut in the cake, frosting the top and sprinkling thick with cocoanut. For the icing, take two whites, beat to a stiff froth and beat in (sifting through a piece of lace) one cup of powdered sugar or more, till it is stiff enough not to run, spread it thin on each layer and sprinkle with cocoanut, then lay on the other and frost the same till all three layers are together, frosting and sprinkling the top one the heaviest. Set in the heater to dry.

Chocolate Cake.

1 cup butter
4 cups flour
4 eggs, flavoring
2 cups sugar
1 cup milk
2 teaspoons baking-powder

Three or four layers.

Frosting.

Two ounces of grated Baker's chocolate; and one cup and a half of powdered sugar sifted through lace into the stiffly beaten whites of three eggs; beat fifteen minutes, spread on each layer and put them evenly together.

Washington Cake.

2 cups sugar	8 eggs
⅔ cup butter	2 cups flour
Lemon extract	2 teaspoon baking-powder

Bake in three layers. This is good for any layer cake and is just the thing for a picnic.

Filling or Frosting.

1 quart milk	2 eggs
1 small cup sugar	2 tablespoons corn starch

When both are cold, spread it between; but does not keep good over night.

Lemon or Orange Jelly Cake.

2 cups sugar	1 cup milk
⅔ cup butter	2 cups flour
3 eggs	2 teaspoons baking-powder

This makes three layers, flavor with lemon—The jelly: One cup of water, one tablespoon corn starch, one cup sugar, one lemon, two oranges, grate the rinds, add the juice, let boil to cook the corn starch, beating, making it very smooth.

Or this filling:

1 cup sugar	1 lemon or 2 oranges, grate
1 tablespoon butter	the rind, squeeze juice
1 egg	

Beat well together and let boil. This is much richer.

Marble Cake.

Light Layers:
1 cup sugar
½ cup butter
1 ¾ flour
2 eggs, the whites
½ cup milk
1 teaspoon baking-powder
¼ nutmeg

Dark or Dash:
½ cup brown sugar
½ cup butter
2 cups flour
1 teaspoon baking-powder
½ cup molasses
½ cup milk
1 teaspoon cloves and cinnamon
2 eggs, the yolks

Can bake as layer cake, or as one cake by putting in first a layer of light, then the dark, making four layers, or in two cakes. If one prefers can use two tablespoons of grated chocolate instead of the spices.

Queen's Cake.

2 cups sugar
½ cup butter
2 teaspoons baking-powder
16 eggs, the whites
4 cups flour
½ cup sweet cream

Flavor with almond or lemon.

Plain Cup Cake.

1 cup sugar
½ cup butter
2 ½ flour
1 cup milk
3 eggs
1 teaspoon baking-powder

Flavor with nutmeg.

Can leave out the cup of sweet milk and use sour cream our sour milk and soda if you like it better.

Silver Cake.

2 cups sugar
¾ cup butter
8 eggs, the whites
2½ cups flour
¾ sweet milk
2 teaspoons baking-powder

Gold Cake.

1 cup sugar
½ cup butter
2 cups flour
¾ sweet milk
8 eggs, the yolks
2 teaspoons baking-powder

Mix and bake the same as other cakes. Flavor as you like.

Cream Sponge Cake Pie.

3 eggs
1 teacup sugar
2 tablespoons cold water
1½ cups flour
1 teaspoon baking-powder

Beat all well together and bake in layers. Use this filling: Boil one pint of milk, stir in smoothly one tablespoon corn starch dissolved in cold milk, two eggs, one-half cup sugar, a large teaspoon of butter; flavor as you wish. Vanilla or grated cocoanut in the cream. Or bake the above cake in one loaf; when cold split it open and put in the above filling, or this, whip a pint of sweetened cream stiff, the whites of two eggs beaten stiff, flavor with vanilla, beat all together, having it on ice or snow, and spread it upon the split sides of the cake. Do not let the cream appear on the outside and it looks like an ordinary cake. This is a delicate and delicious dessert.

Real Angel's Food.

11 eggs, the whites
1 tumbler flour
1 tumbler sugar
A pinch of salt

Sift the flour five times with the baking-powder (one

teaspoon) and salt; sift the sugar three times. Beat the eggs to a stiff froth. In mixing beat as little as possible; bake twenty minutes in a moderate steady heat.

ANGEL'S FOOD.

½ pint flour
4 tablespoons hot water
1½ cups powdered sugar
11 eggs
1 even teaspoon corn starch
3 even teaspoons cream of tartar
1 teaspoon flavoring

Sift the flour, corn starch, and cream of tartar together five times; put the water and sugar in a granite basin on the stove; stir well together, let it simmer slowly while you beat the eggs to a stiff froth after you sprinkle on them one-half teaspoon of salt. Boil the syrup until it will thread, and pour it slowly over the beaten eggs; beat all briskly until the mixture is light and cool; then sift the flour over it a little at a time, and stir it gently until all the flour is in and no lumps, stir in the flavoring, and pour the batter into a three-quart pan with a tube in the center; bake in a moderate oven about forty minutes. Stick a straw into the cake, if it comes out clean, the cake is done. Turn the pan upside down and let it rest on the table until the cake is nearly cold, then remove it from the pan, and place it bottom up, on a larger cake pan. Cover with boiled icing.

N. B.—In making the angel's food, the beating and mixing must all be done with a wire spoon egg beater (not a Dover). The eggs must be very cold. Grease the pan very slightly—do not use a piece of butter larger than a pea; do not cut this cake until it is ten or twelve hours old. Better when two days old. Saw the cake with the knife when cutting it.

Home Messenger.

Sunshine Cake.

10 eggs, the whites   7 yolks
1 tumbler flour   1½ tumblers sugar
1 teaspoon cream of tartar 1 lemon, juice and rind
½ teaspoon carbonate ammonia, or extract lemon

Beat the yolks very light with half the sugar; beat the whites to a stiff froth, beating in lightly the rest of the sugar; then add the beaten yolks, sugar and flavoring; stir in the flour gradually, sifting the ammonia last. Bake in a tin the same as angel's food, without greasing it; sift the sugar once and the flour four times; turn the tin upside down to cool as in angel's food.

N. B.—Carbonate of ammonia can be powered fine and dissolved in lemon juice or sprinkled over and stirred into the batter the last thing.

Home Messenger.

One Egg Cake.

1½ cups sugar   1 cup milk or cream
½ cup butter   1 egg,
3 cups flour   2 teaspoons baking-powder
Grated nutmeg to taste

Molasses Cake.

1 cup molasses   1 teacup butter
⅓ cup hot water   1 teaspoon soda
1 even tablespoon ginger

Heat the molasses hot, dissolve the soda in the hot water, stir it with the softened butter, ginger and one teaspoon baking-powder in the two and a half cups of flour, sifting it twice. Not quite so stiff as other cakes.

ICINGS.

Icing for Cakes.

The whites of three large eggs beaten so stiff they will not slide or drop from knife, sift in through a piece of lace or fine sieve two cups of powdered sugar, sifting and beating in gradually, till you can spread it on cake and not run. This will frost two cakes top and sides. Flavor with one teaspoon of lemon extract or a half teaspoon cream of tartar.

Rule for Frosting.

For the white of one egg, one cup of sifted sugar. Beat the egg stiff and gradually add the sugar, beating till light and not thin enough to run when you spread it. Flavor or not as you like. This is the proportion. For boiled icing, I refer you to the icing under the head of mountain cake and ice cream cake.

Boiled Icing.

Boil until it will thread one and one-half cups of sugar, one tablespoon of vinegar, and one tablespoon of water; pour the boiled sugar into the whites of two stiffly beaten eggs, beat well; when cool spread. After a little experience in nice cake making and frosting, one needs to be guided by their own judgment as regards the stiffness of cake or icings; as eggs vary in size and flour in thickening qualities. Be particular to use the same sized cup for all measures of the same cake.

Soft Ginger Bread.

1 cup brown sugar
1 cup butter
2 eggs
1 tablespoon ginger
1 teaspoon cloves

1 cup N. O. molasses
1 cup milk
1 teaspoon soda
1 teaspoon salt
1 teaspoon cinnamon

About 4 cups flour

Heat the molasses boiling hot; dissolve soda in a little hot water and beat it well into the molasses, beat this into the creamed butter and sugar, add a part of the flour, then the well beaten eggs, milk, spices and the rest of flour. Be careful not to burn it or bake too fast. It must rise up, before the top browns. If oven is too hot cover the top with paper. There should be a paper or two in bottom of pan.

Plain Soft Ginger Bread.

1 cup sour cream
1 cup N. O. molasses
1 even tablespoon ginger

1 teaspoon soda
1 pint flour or two cups
1 teaspoon salt

Hard Ginger Bread.

2 pounds butter
2 teaspoons powdered alum
2 tablespoons ginger

2 quarts molasses
4 teaspoons saleratus
¼ teaspoon sal. ammonia

About 10 pounds flour

Put the flour, sifted twice, in the bread pan; make a hollow in the center; cut up the butter and put in; heat the molasses; dissolve the alum in one pint of boiling water; also the saleratus in another pint of hot water. Let both settle and pour off carefully (leaving the sediment at the bottom) into the molasses and pour all quite warm on to the butter. Sift on the ginger, ammonia and a teaspoon of salt; work and mix it with the hands. Mix it soft, as you can roll it easily and nicely three-fourths of an inch thick, and bake on long square tins. Make it up without delay and put it in oven immediately, as anything with soda or saleratus loses its rising qualities. Bake in moderate oven, as molasses burns easily. This is the old-fashioned gingerbread, such as our grandmothers used to make on training days after the revolutionary war and was called Trainers' Gingerbread.

GINGERBREAD.

2/3 cup molasses
1/2 cup brown sugar
1 cup sour cream
2 teaspoons ginger

2 eggs, well beaten
1/3 cup butter
1 1/2 teaspoons soda
1 even teaspoon cinnamon

About three cups flour.

Mix as other cakes. Dissolve the soda; put half in the hot molasses and half in the sour cream. Bake in a moderate oven. It requires more care and longer baking than a cake made from all sugar. Always put one or two papers in bottom of pan for cake that has molasses in it.

GINGERBREAD.

1/2 cup sugar
1/3 cup molasses
1 teaspoon soda
2 cups flour, about

1/3 cup butter
1 cup sour cream
1 teaspoon ginger
1/2 teaspoon cinnamon

Put half of soda in cream and half in molasses; mix and bake as others.

GINGER SNAPS.

1 cup brown sugar
1 cup butter, heaping
1 good teaspoon soda
1 cup N. O. molasses
⅔ cup hot water
1 tablespoon ginger

Cream the butter and sugar, bring the molasses to a boil, let partly cool, stir in one-half the soda, putting the other half in the hot water. Stir all together, then take the hand, stir in flour just right to roll. Roll out very thin and bake quick and dry in a moderate oven. This makes a pan full. Remember, you can make one-half, or double any of these recipes. Keep dry in tin box. If they gather dampness, dry them in heater.

GINGER COOKIES.

2 cups molasses
2 teaspoons soda
2 teaspoons ginger
1 cup butter
1 cup sour milk
2 teaspoons cinnamon

Boil the butter and molasses five minutes. Dissolve the soda just half in molasses, and half in sour milk. Mix stiff enough to roll.

GINGER COOKIES.

1 cup brown sugar
1¾ cups butter
1 tablespoon cinnamon
1 quart N. O. molasses
4 even tablespoons ginger
1 teaspoon cloves

Cream the sugar and butter, boil the molasses five minutes, then add a large teaspoon of soda, put all in the center of flour and mix with hand; do not knead it, but roll out and cut for cookies. Bake in a moderately quick oven.

Chocolate and Cocoanut Jumbles.

1 cup butter
2 cups sugar
4 eggs, ½ teaspoon salt
2 teaspoons baking-powder

Cream the butter and sugar, beat the eggs light. Mix all together, then take one-half of mixture and add three-fourths of a cup of grated chocolate, mix it in flour to roll, to the other half add one cup of grated cocoanut, mix and roll, and you have two kinds of cookies with one mixing. Cut with scallop cutter, or in fancy shapes. The oven should be hot enough to bake in ten minutes.

Sugared Cookies.

2 cups sugar
1 cup butter
1 cup sour cream
2 eggs, nutmeg
1 even teaspoon soda

Mix as the others, soft, with little mixing, roll out and sprinkle with granulated sugar through a sieve, and cut with round or scallop cutter. These are very nice and white.

New England Cookies.

1½ cups sugar
½ cup butter
1 cup sour cream
1 teaspoon soda
2 tablespoons caraway seeds

Sufficient flour to roll out easily; if too stiff, will not be good; roll them half an inch thick. Bake cookies in dripping or sheet iron pans. Keep dry in tin box.

Crullers.

2 cups sugar
½ cup butter
1 cup sour milk
1 even teaspoon saleratus
4 eggs

Cream the butter and sugar, beat the eggs, put all

in the flour, mix soft, roll out long, one-fourth of an inch thick, cut strips one and a half inches wide and three inches long, with a jagging iron, running it three times through the center leaving the ends whole, double the ends together diagonally and fry a light color in hot fat as fried cakes.

BAKERS' COOKIES.

1 cup sugar, brown
½ cup butter
½ cup milk or sour cream
1 egg
1 teaspoon baking-powder

CANNING FRUITS.

The four months from the time of strawberries in June, till October, is the harvest time for fruits for every housekeeper, as well as for the industrious farmer, to go earnestly into the work of securing the winter and spring supplies of relishes, preserves, canned fruits, pickles and condiments of various kinds. To an ambitious housekeeper it is a genuine pleasure and satisfaction, that she may be fully equipped to supply the needs of those who are depending upon her for much that goes to make life a pleasure. We should not be content until we have become familiar with caring for fruits as well as cake-making; though not as essential as a good bread-maker and cook of meats and vegetables. She will be constantly gathering new ideas and making improvements. Let us try and not make too hard work of this extra annual labor; but make our plans for it before hand, thinking of all the materials we will need to purchase for the fruit that is to be cared for in the coming weeks, such as sugar, spices, cans, covers and rubbers. More vinegar, etc. We do not need to can as many fruits as formerly, as we can obtain fine oranges in the early spring, which are a very pleasant change.

The lack of having things in readiness only goes to annoy and tire the one who is hoping to make a success of it.

Select your fruit carefully yourself; reject all that is imperfect. Wash and wipe it dry with a crash towel. Strawberries, raspberries and blackberries, wash in very cold water quickly and drain through a colander or sieve. Some years raspberries have a small white worm inside, the water brings them out, but take them to a bright light when washing. For canning only cook enough for three or four quarts at a time, as it breaks the fruit. The best way to test the covers of cans is to fill the cans with water the day before you wish to use them and screw tight with good new rubbers the same as for canned fruit, and lay them on the side over night. When you put the rubber on the Mason jar run the thumb all around the inner edge to make sure it is pressed down and neither too large or too tight. If they do not leak water you may be sure they are good. Put a breakfast plate in the bottom of a kettle, fill it half full of water, fill three or four cans two-thirds full of water and set in on the plate, to keep from breaking them. Let these get boiling hot while you are heating the fruit. Another way is to wrap a cold wet cloth twice around and under the bottom of can while filling can, excluding the air from the outside it will not break; put in funnel and fill gradually with boiling hot fruit, run the handle of a silver spoon next to the inside of can to let out any air bubbles, fill full, let stand ten minutes as it will settle some; screw tight as possible; when cold tighten the cover again, let lie over night on their side, if they do not leak they are probably all right, and ready to put in a dark, cool place. You can try them and see if they are tight. In one week examine them closely. If any are fermented take off the top of them, and scald and recan and use up soon. Some set the can on a cold wet cloth and put a silver tablespoon inside, letting the handle run up into the funnel, and fill with hot fruit as others. The fruit should be perfectly fresh and nearly ripe enough to eat by hand. All berries should be canned the day they are picked, and so should peaches. Pears should be picked as soon as seeds are more than half turned dark, put in boxes in cellar and covered with matting or old carpet, till they are nearly fit for eating. This is the only way they have a rich flavor; they never get it on the tree. Look them over every day after the first three days. Quinces should not be picked till in October and turning somewhat yellow. They can stand a few days. The rubber rings should have an even edge all around, when the cover is screwed on, for if it slips up (drawn in) or swells out, air is admitted. Be sure the glass cans, covers and rubbers are perfectly clean when put up. Keep your rubbers on a ribbon roller, to keep in shape. If not kept in shape, they will not probably be air-tight again. Wash all the syrup off of jars, before putting them away after filling.

New glass cans often contain fine bits of glass; they should be washed well with hot soap suds and use a swab.

CANNED APPLES.

Take tart late fall apples, wash and wipe clean. Peel and quarter, or if large cut in six or eight pieces. Allow one cup of sugar for each pound of apples after they are cored; wash them again that the syrup may be clear. After weighing the apples keep them covered from the air (as it turns them dark) till you have made a syrup of the sugar and one quart of water or more according to quantity of fruit. Boil and skim. If the sugar is specky strain it, and then put in apples enough for four quarts at a time, let get hot slowly, as soon as tender, can them as directed in canning. Do not can them till cold weather as they will keep better. A nice way is to mix a few quinces with the apples, by partly cooking the quinces first. To two quarts of apples put one quart quinces, they require more sugar than apples. Never cook nor eat what seems to be the sound part of decayed fruit of any kind; its very breath is tainted. The Duchess and Maiden Blush are superior for cooking. Always use a porcelain-lined or granite kettle for cooking all kinds of fruits and pickles. Apple preserves are made the same way, only, three-fourths pound of sugar to one of apples.

Canned Peaches.

Select fruit just ripe, but not soft, the late Crawford is the best, though there is a very rich white peach if you can obtain it. Peel and cut in halves, take out the pit, cover them with a paper, as they turn dark in the atmosphere; (have a wet cloth in your dish, to wipe knife and fingers on often for paring all fruits). Rinse quickly in water and drain. One cup of sugar to two quarts of peaches, or as you like it. Prepare the syrup as for apples. Do not boil as they will boil to pieces, but keep them boiling hot and press down dipping the syrup on top. Do not stir fruit that you wish to keep whole. When clear or boiling hot can them.

If you wish them rich as preserves put one cup and a half of sugar to one pound of peaches.

PEARS.

Pears should be pared and halved and cored, not only taking out the seeds, but all the core to the stem; keep them covered, rinse in cold water, drain, make the syrup, skim and strain if necessary, they require much less sugar than peaches, and require to be cooked twice as long or more, till they can be pierced easily, with fork. Some like sliced lemon in them. A little green ginger root added to the syrup gives a very pleasant flavor, as pears are quite tasteless.

PLUMS.

To can plums allow one-half pound of sugar (or a coffee cup) to one pound of fruit; wash and pick off the stems; prick each end of the plums quite through with a darning needle, put in a stone jar; make the syrup, putting as little water as possible to melt the sugar, for the plums are very juicy. Put one cup of water in the kettle with what sugar it will melt slowly and then keep adding till all is melted, boiled and skimmed, then pour it boiling hot over the plums. Put a nice clean plate on them, to keep the plums under the syrup, and let stand until the next day; pour the syrup from the plums and let boil again, pouring it on the plums, repeat this process three days; then put the syrup over the fire, and when it comes to a boil add the plums, and cook slowly fifteen minutes, then fill your cans and seal. The object of scalding them so many times is to prevent them from breaking to pieces. This is good for all kinds of plums. Plum preserves are made the same way, using pound for pound, or some will only require three-fourths of a pound of sugar to a pound of fruit.

Plum Marmalade.

Pour boiling water over the plums to take the skins off easily; take off the skins, take out the pits, then weigh; if sour use pound for pound, if not, three-fourths of a pound of sugar to a pound of fruit. To make the syrup add as little water as possible to melt it, then put in the fruit and cook till smooth, say thirty minutes, if not smooth put it through a sieve; put it in cups or small jars.

Quinces.

Quinces should be thoroughly ripe and one meets with the best success when they are of a bright golden yellow. There are two or three kinds of quinces, some cook to pieces in the syrup, not bearing much boiling; other kinds require cooking soft in water first.

I use what is called the lemon quince and I find it cooks tender in the syrup. If it turns red you have cooked it too long. Can them as soon as tender. Wash the fruit and rub with a dry cloth, pare and cut in eight pieces, and cut out all the white core, as it will turn dark. Keep covered while paring and wash, to take off all specks. In making the syrup allow one-half pound of sugar to one of fruit and hardly water enough to cover, when cold put in the fruit, cook slowly till tender (not red) and can. A tea saucer is the best to dip all fruit into the funnel. For preserves use three-fourths of a pound of sugar, to a pound of fruit and can air tight.

STRAWBERRIES.

Take fresh picked berries, wash quickly in very cold water, hull and pick over carefully; one coffee cup of sugar to one quart of berries or richer if you like. There are two ways of canning them, one is, put one-half a cup of water into a porcelain kettle, put in the sugar then the berries on top and stand on back of stove. Let stand till the juice moistens the sugar; put it over a slow fire till all the sugar is melted, then gradually increase the heat till the berries are heated through, say to the boiling point, and can. Do not be too long about it, or let them be on the fire too long, as they will loose their beautiful color and turn white. Another way which I have never tried, but is recommended by good authority is, to fill the can with the fruit, fill up with the syrup, put on cover without rubber, set the cans in an old boiler with rack under them, have the cold water not reach the top of can by two inches, then let come to a boil, fifteen minutes boiling is usually enough; the berries must be boiling hot through, then fill full, put on rubbers and screw on covers. This is the most difficult fruit to keep, as it is very acid and comes in the hottest weather.

STRAWBERRY PRESERVES.

Prepare them in the same way, taking a pound of sugar for a pound of fruit, only as soon as the fruit is boiling hot through skim it out into can (the proportion), and boil the syrup with cover off twenty or thirty minutes; then make the cans air tight.

RASPBERRIES:

These are canned and preserved the same way as strawberries.

PINEAPPLES.

The sugarloaf is one of the sweetest and best pineapples for preserving. The season for this is at its height about the last of June or 4th of July, when these delicious fruits may, when plenty, often be purchased for $1 a dozen. The best come from Havana. In June the choice Ripley and the Queen Anne are choice varieties and come from Jamaica. They are exceedingly rich in flavor and sweet. These fancy pines are quite small, selling on an average at 30 cents apiece. These are considered superior to any other variety for table use because of their rich flavor. The most delicious way of preserving a pineapple is in its own juice without using one drop of water. Peel the pineapples carefully after, cutting them in slices one-half an inch thick cut out all the eyes and allow three-fourths of a pound of sugar to every pound of pineapple. Put a small layer of sugar in the bottom of a stone crock, then a layer of pineapple and a layer of sugar and one of fruit, and so on till all is used; cover them tight after putting a pressure on them and let stand twenty-four hours. A clear juice will nearly cover them then. Now take each slice and tear the pulp in pieces off the core, using a silver fork. Drain off all the juice from the pulp and also the juice and sugar out of the dish; put this juice and sugar in granite kettle. Let it come slowly to boiling point; skim and boil for five minutes, then strain through a fine sieve or sheer cloth over the pulp. Let the pulp boil up in the syrup once, then can it immediately, as longer boiling darkens the fruit. If you wish use the whites of two eggs beaten up to clarify the syrup.

Serving Pineapple.

A nice dessert for dinner or a tea dish, is to slice it the same as the above, cover with sugar in layers, let stand for two hours. Then tear the fruit from the core with a silver fork. Preserved pineapple is especially fine served with whipped cream. A pineapple Bavarian cream is one of the best desserts we have, and there is no better water ice or sherbet. But do not buy the coarse-grained, flavorless early fruit.

Canning Tomatoes.

Scald, peel and slice the tomatoes as for cooking for table, rejecting the cores and every one that is imperfect. One teaspoon salt to every peck; put over to cook one-half hour or more stirring very often, till it is fine, then can hot and seal tight.

Preserved Citron Melon.

Pare, core and cut the melons into slices; cut up the slices an inch and a half long. Weigh them, and to every six pounds of fruit put six pounds of granulated sugar, the juice and yellow rind—pared off thin—of four lemons; also half a pound of race ginger; put the slices into a granite kettle, cover with water and a layer on all of peach leaves; boil about half an hour, or until clear, and a broom-corn will easily pierce them; drain them, spread them in a pan of cold water, and let them stand all night; next morning tie the ginger in a thin muslin cloth and boil it in three pints of water until the water is highly flavored; take out the ginger; dissolve the sugar in the ginger-water, put in the lemon peel and boil and skim it till

no more scum rises; take out the lemon peel, put in the citron slices and juice of lemon, and boil in the syrup till the slices are transparent and a straw will go through them; put the slices, while warm, in jars, and pour the syrup on slowly; seal in air tight cans.
Home Messenger.

CRANBERRY SAUCE, JAM AND JELLY.

Pick out all the soft berries and stems, wash and put over to stew with water enough to come to the top. To every quart of berries put one pint of sugar, stew till tender and thoroughly cooked, either to a jell or with a syrup, as you like. The jell is made the same as currant jell, and the jam or marmalade the same as plum marmalade.

PRUNES (Stewed).

Wash thoroughly in two waters, put in stew kettle with water enough to cover, to one quart of prunes put two tablespoons of sugar, be very careful not to get them too sweet, as the flavor of good ones depends upon the proportion of sugar and fruit. Let steep on back of stove till tender, perhaps two hours or more. Do not buy cheap ones, they are insipid.

APPLE SAUCE.

This is a favorite dish to be eaten with fresh pork, roast pig, goose and duck. Use Rhode Island greenings or any sour, juicy apple; wash and wipe clean. Pare, quarter and core, put in granite kettle, with water to cover well, cook till nearly tender then add sugar according to the acidity of apple. If you wish marmalade add a little more sugar and rub through a sieve. Some like a teaspoon of butter stirred in.

JELLIES.

Jelly making requires skill and care; only the best quality of fruit and best coffee sugar should be used. It must not be cooked too long as it makes it ropy, strong and dark-colored. The same rules must be observed for all jellies. I will give a perfect one for currant jelly and all others are made the same way, such as strawberries and grapes. Try to obtain the fruits when they are just ripe—not too ripe, for then they are liable to be watery and the jelly qualities destroyed to a greater or less extent.

Currant Jelly.

Have the currants picked as clean as possible from leaves, pick them over but not off the stems, pick out all that are dried or green; wash and drain well, then squeeze a few at a time with the hands, in a large bowl, and put them in a porcelain-lined kettle, when all are in, put it on a slow fire stirring often, let come to a boil for twenty minutes; then strain through a coarse three-cornered cloth strainer. Wash out the kettle. Let the strainer hang and drip for an hour, (let them cool before you fill the strainer), then squeeze lightly only. Measure the number of pints of juice; allow one pound of best coffee sugar to each pint of juice; set the sugar on platters in moderate oven to get quite hot, while the juice is boiling twenty-five minutes; skim the scum off as soon as it rises, then have a strong fire, and slowly stir in the hot sugar, which will take five minutes. Jelly will form one side of spoon and kettle while the stirring is going on, let it just come to a boil, wrap a cold wet cloth around the glasses and fill with a cup, if it is right the cold cup will be loaded with jelly. Such juicy fruits as currants, grapes and strawberries require no water to make jelly. Pulpy fruits, such as peaches, apples and quinces, should be cut up small, after being pared and cored, and just water enough to come to the top of fruit in the stew kettle. Boil slowly, keep covered, stir often, till tender and no more, then strain, (without much squeezing) measure and allow one pound of sugar for every pint of juice, and proceed the same as with currant jelly. A friend, who is always successful in her jellies, says the juice for jellies must never be squeezed through the jelly-bag; and also that she always cooks the strained juice twenty minutes without the sugar, after it is measured, but has the sugar on platters in the oven, carefully stirring it occasionally, and watching that it does not get too hot so as to brown. Then she stirs the hot sugar into the juice, and lets it boil up just once; then takes it from the fire immediately. Her jelly always " sets."

LEMON JELLY.

1 oz. gelatine 3 cups sugar
3 lemons 2 oranges, the juice

Wet the gelatine with a little cold water, when partly dissolved pour on one quart of boiling water; add the juice of lemons and oranges and sugar, then strain and pour in molds, set on ice. Make it the day before using it.

WINE JELLY.

To a package of Cox's gelatine put one pint of cold water, put in a warm place for a while to dissolve, then add one quart of boiling water, the juice of three lemons, three cups of sugar, one pint of wine. Bring to a boil, strain and put in molds. If it is cold weather, or stands over night, one pint more of water can be added and it will come to a jelly easily. This makes nearly three quarts.

Charlotte Russe.

To one ounce of Cox's gelatine, put one cup of warm milk, keep warm till dissolved, then add one cup sugar; strain, add·a little salt, flavor with lemon, extract or vanilla. Flavor and sweeten one quart of cream. Whip it, and add it to cold gelatine. One can put it in dish and serve when cold as it is with cake, or line the dish with sponge cake and pour it in when it begins to stiffen. This must be eaten the day it is made.

Charlotte Russe.

The day before wanted make a stiff plain jelly of calves' feet, or you may use Cox's gelatine, but the feet are best; put four calves' feet in a gallon of water and boil slowly until the meat drops from the bones and the water is reduced to less than two quarts; strain, and let stand over night in a cool place; in the morning scrape off all the fat, then turn it out, scrape off all the sediment from the bottom; have just three pints. Boil one pint of milk, flavor it highly with vanilla, let get cold. Take three pints of rich cream, put it in a shallow pan, set on ice and whip it with whisk, skimming it off as fast as it rises; then add the vanilla milk to the cream, and beat both together; melt the jelly by setting it over the fire. Beat very light the yolks of six eggs, beating in one cup of sugar; add by degrees the melted jelly to the sugar and eggs, stirring very hard; keep the vessel setting on ice and continus stirring till the mixture is firm enough to retain the mark of the spoon; then stir in the whipped cream as quickly as possible; have ready your dish for table, lined with sponge cake and pour in the charlotte. Put ice around it in refrigerator. It will be ready to serve in two hours. Some prefer it without the sponge cake and eat it with cream and cake. For cleaning feet, see souse.

Calves' Foot Jelly.

Clean well, and cut off the toes of a calf's feet, put the feet into a gallon of water, boil till reduced one-half, then strain, let stand over night. In the morning take off all the fat, remove the sediment, and put the clear part over the fire, the strained juice of three lemons, two cups sugar, a blade of mace, a stick of cinnamon, the beaten whites of three eggs. Boil fifteen minutes, strain, and if not clear strain again through a jelly bag. The bag should always be wrung out of hot water before using, and the jelly should always run through of itself, never squeeze it, as it makes the jelly muddy. This jelly is amber color. Half of it may be colored red and a little at a time put into glasses, as it begins to set, then the amber, then the red, and so on till the glass is full. This makes a very showy, as well as palatable dessert; can cover the top with frosting of whites of sweetened beaten eggs. This is the old English way.

Neapolitan Blanc Mange.

Measure three pints of milk, put one pint in the double rice boiler, mix two and a half even table-spoons of corn starch with cold milk, make it smooth. When the milk is hot, before it scalds, stir in the starch, with two large spoons of sugar and a pinch of salt, stir all the time until smooth and as thick as custard, remove from the fire and add one-fourth teaspoon of rose extract and enough cochineal extract (which you can find at the druggist's) to color it pink. Put it in a mold or dish that will hold three or more pints. Wash the boiler and put in another pint of milk and proceed as before. When the pink is cold, pour this (flavored with lemon extract) over it and set away to cool; when the kettle is washed and you cook the last pint of milk the same way. Grate two teaspoons of chocolate in a cup and set in a dish of hot water to melt. When the blanc mange is smooth, add chocolate and half a teaspoon of vanilla, cool a little, and when the other is solid pour this over it, and set in cool place till next day. Serve with sweetened whipped cream for dessert.

Pure Grape Wine for the Sick.

I give this recipe as a safe preparation of wine to be used when necessary, in cases of great prostration. It may prove of value where a pure wine is needed. Pick the grapes when ripe and sweet, remove all that are green, imperfect or broken, pick from the stem, wash thoroughly by hand, drain them, then mash by squeezing a few at a time in a large earthen bowl; then put them in a sweet earthen vessel (say four-gallon jars) and let stand two or three days, or until the skins rise and form a scum and the first fermentation begins to stop. Then strain through a wet and somewhat sheer cloth strainer; do not squeeze too close, as there will be too much sediment; add to the juice as much of best brown sugar as required to make it (when dissolved), bear an egg above the surface, the size of a two shilling piece. Pour off carefully into a good clean cask or beer keg, that you can fill full and have two gallons over to fill up with every day as it runs over. Leave the bung out, and keep the cask so full that the scum may run over until the fermentation begins to stop, which will be in eight or ten days. Then stop it up very tight and keep in a good cool cellar for three months, when it will be fit for use, but will improve with age, whether bottled or kept on the lees. Three bushels of grapes will make five gallons of wine.

"A minister in New York," says the Chicago Inter Ocean, "visited a number of the best liquor stores in his neighborhood and bought pint samples of their gin, whisky, port wine, etc. In the analysis of the 'Pure Holland Gin' were found neutral spirits, rotten corn, juniper berries, turpentine and vitrol. The fine old hand-made Kentucky whisky contained neutral spirits, glycerine, sulphate of zinc, chromic acid, creosote, unslacked lime and fusil oil, and the rare old port had licorice, zinc, mercury, antimony, muriatic acid and alum. The result of this analysis is sufficient apology for my recipe of 'Pure Grape Wine for the sick.'"

Baked Quinces.

Wash and wipe clean, take out the cores from the blossom end with a tin apple corer, fill with sugar, bake in pan with a little water in hot oven, one and a half hours. Serve hot with sugar and cream. A nice dessert.

Sugar Vinegar.

Dissolve twenty-five pounds of good brown sugar in hot rain water, or soft water, then strain it into a clean vinegar barrel with iron hoops, then fill up with soft water strained; get a piece of what is called "the mother" from some other vinegar barrel and put in the barrel. It ought to stand in the sun for six weeks with a glass bottle in the bung. Then put it in a warm cellar till it is good, perhaps six months, but you will be provided with good vinegar for years to come, and always have the pure article at hand. We know not what injurious acids are in the vinegar we buy for cider vinegar. The sugar vinegar is the healthiest vinegar that is made and makes the best flavored pickles.

CUCUMBER PICKLES.

Pick the cucumbers early in the morning, the smallest are the best, about three inches long; put a layer of salt in bottom of crock or cask and a layer of cucumbers, and then salt, and so on till it is full. Put a little water in at first, after that it makes its own brine. In the fall pour off this brine and wash them nicely. Scald a brine strong enough to bear up an egg; let it get very cold then pour it on. Cover the top with a double cloth and cover this with salt; the brine must cover it all. Take off the cloth and rinse it every two weeks to prevent any scum from rising, as it eats in and turns them soft. There must always be a double cloth on pickles whether in brine or vinegar, and rinsed off every two weeks, or they will soon mold. When you wish to put them in vinegar, take out what you wish and soak them three or four days in soft water; change it every day till they are freshened enough; then put them in cold vinegar; add a few peppers, ginger root and horseradish if you wish. They will be ready to eat in a week. It is better to put them in glass jars. Nasturtiums are a pleasant addition. Pick them with the steams on; they are ornamental. Add them to any pickle you wish. Always use a granite or porcelain-lined kettle for all pickles or fruits; indeed, I think they are the nicest for soups and all cooking. As pickles of all kinds are indigestible eat sparingly, as a relish only.

Spiced Sweet Pickles.

Sweet pickles should be rich and not cooked soft; can put in one-half ounce of ginger root if one likes it.

Always prepare pickles in a porcelain-lined or granite kettle; use wooden spoon. If you wish your cucumbers green, put them into cold vinegar in a granite kettle, stand them over a moderate fire, and heat slowly until they become green.

Pears, quinces and plums are pickled in the same manner as peaches.

Mangoes.

Use young or small musk or nutmeg melons or cantaloupe (which is a delicate variety of musk melon), wash and rub the melons well, cut out one section, scrape out the inside and wipe it out with a cloth, tie each section on to its own melon. Lay the mangoes in a good brine for three days, then drain off the brine, rinse it all off, and freshen in pure warm water for twenty-four hours (green them as cucumbers if you wish). Then fill each one with four string beans, two small cucumbers, a gherkin, a small tomato, just to fill them; then put in one tablespoon of the following mixture to each one.

4 tablespoons English mustard seed
4 tablespoons grated horseradish
1 teaspoon mustard
2 teaspoons mace
2 teaspoons ginger
1 dozen pepper-corns
1 teaspoon celery-seed
1 cup brown sugar
6 nasturtiums

Put the section on, sew it in with coarse thread, and pack in a deep stone jar; pour scalding vinegar (the sugar vinegar is the richest) over them, repeat this process three times more at intervals of two days, then put a double cloth over them a plate and a weight to keep them under the vinegar. These are fine and will keep for months. Watch them closely.

Sweet Pickle of Watermelon Rind.

Take firm thick rind, scrape the inside, pare off the green, cut in small pieces one inch wide and two long; boil in water until clear and a straw will pierce them; drain well, dry with a napkin, place in a jar; pour over the following, boiling hot, three days in succession: for ten pounds of melon rind take four pounds of brown sugar, one quart best vinegar, one ounce of whole mace, one ounce whole cinnamon, half ounce of whole cloves; put the spices in a thin bag and boil in the vinegar, but not left in with the pickle, as it discolors the melon; put in a jar, having them fully covered with syrup; add more vinegar if needed.

Spiced Cantaloupe.

Select small nutmeg melons, a little green, not hard, neither quite ripe. Cut them into sections as the rind is marked; pare, remove the seeds, scrape out clean; weigh the pieces. To each seven pounds allow four pounds of brown sugar and one pint of best vinegar,

Put the sugar and vinegar in a porcelain lined kettle; put in a bag a half ounce each of whole cloves, green ginger and stick cinnamon. When hot put in the cantaloupe. Watch carefully until each piece is hot, but not soft. Cover the kettle and press the fruit down often. Lift each piece carefully and place in a stone jar. Put one teaspoon each of ground allspice, ground mace and cinnamon into a cup; mix; divide into fourths; tie each closely in a small piece of cheese cloth; put these in the jar, pour the syrup on the fruit and stand away till the next morning; then pour off all the liquor again; boil and strain it again for nine consecutive days. The last day take out the spices and boil the syrup down to the consistency of molasses; have enough syrup to cover well; press down; keep cool.

Green Tomato Pickle.

One peck green tamatoes, three onions, six green peppers; chop fine, squeeze the juice off through a colander; salt to taste; put on enough vinegar to scald up once, then let it cool and drain off the vinegar. Make a dressing of four cups of sugar, two tablespoons of mustard, two teaspoons black pepper, with vinegar enough to cover it well; heat and pour over.

Spiced Peaches.

7 pounds peaches ½ cup whole cloves
4 pounds sugar ½ cup broken cinnamon
1 pint vinegar ½ pint water

Put the sugar into the vinegar and water to dissolve, put spices in thin bag and let soak in hot syrup (after wetting them in hot water) while you rub the peaches hard with a coarse dry cloth to take off the fuzz; stick each peach with six cloves; put into the syrup to cook as many peaches at a time, as the syrup will cover; let simmer till tender, but they must not break, then fill the cans, shake down and fill up with the syrup, let stand ten minutes, shake down again, fill to the brim, put a double cloth on to keep the top covered with syrup and seal.

Sliced Tomato Pickles.

One peck green tomatoes, six large onions. Slice and cook for five minutes in one quart of vinegar and two quarts of water and two tablespoons of salt. Drain well, then tie in a cheese cloth three tablespoons of white mustard seed, two tablespoons each of ground cloves, cinnamon and ginger and three green peppers chopped fine; put the bag in two quarts of vinegar with the pickles and boil all together till well seasoned; then can tight.

Tomato Salad.

Scald and peel as many ripe tomatoes as you need; lay in ice water till very cold, then slice them, pour off the juice. Pare and slice very thin two cucumbers. Put some fresh lettuce leaves in the salad bowl with one small onion sliced fine; put all on the leaves and serve with a salad dressing.

Tomato Sauce.

Eight pounds of tomatoes, one quart of vinegar, three pounds sugar, one teaspoon cinnamon, one of cloves, one of English mustard and one of red pepper. Boil down till quite thick.

Cabbage Salad.

Select a solid head and one that is white after the outside leaves are taken off. Lay on a board and with a sharp knife cut fine; set in ice box till ready to use. Serve with salad dressing.

Gooseberry Catsup—Very Fine.

Pick off the blows of over a peck of gooseberries; wash; boil in granite kettle in just water enough to come to the top, and cook to pieces. Strain through a fine wire sieve. No seeds must rub through. Measure the pulp, and to eight pints of pulp put six pints of sugar, four teaspoons of ground cinnamon, six teaspoons of ground cloves. Boil till stiff enough not to run on the plate. This is very relishable when rightly made. As there is no vinegar in it all stomachs can bear it. For a smaller quantity: To seven coffee cups of pulp put five cups of sugar, two teaspoons of cinnamon and three of cloves. Can or bottle tightly.

Tomato Catsup.

Put over in a porcelain kettle four quarts of peeled ripe tomatoes. Cook for half an hour till all is soft, then rub through a wire sieve. Return the juice to kettle; add two coffee cups of vinegar, four cups of sugar, a salt spoon of cayenne, a teaspoon each of ground cloves, ginger, allspice, pepper and mustard, one teaspoon of salt when first put over. Mix well all these ingredients in an earthen dish with the juice before returning to the fire. Then let slow boiling evaporate the water, stirring often, till thick enough not to run on the plate. Can tightly while hot and it will keep indefinitely.

COLD CATSUP.

To half a peck of ripe tomatoes, three green and three red peppers, and a large bunch of celery, all cut fine, add three pints of vinegar, one tablespoon of salt, one teacup white mustard seed, one teacup grated horseradish and two tablespoons of black pepper. Put these three last ingredients in a sheer cloth bag, let lie in it and soak, or mix them in it if you like, but I think it better not to.

ODDS AND ENDS.

FRYING SALT PORK.

As this was mislaid, I will insert it away from its regular family. It is very fine. Salt pork to be fried or baked should be cut over night and put to soak in cold water. In the morning, if not fresh enough, put it in hot water, drain off, roll each piece well in flour and place in a sheet iron pan in the oven, let it brown on both sides; it cooks much nicer in the oven. Send the pork to the table hot and crisp; if you wish to make a milk gravy of some of the fat, put it in a gravy dish.

VEAL LOAF.

12 pounds veal ½ pound crackers
¾ pound butter 1 coffee cup water

Have lean veal chopped fine (the butcher will chop it for you), but prepare it for chopping yourself, pepper and salt it well. Mix all the ingredients in well,

Cover the sides and bottom of a long four-inch wide pan with buttered paper, press it well together. Bake well done, from three to four hours. Can make one-fourth of it. Two pounds chopped salt pork, three eggs, a littlee hopped parsley, is a fine addition to the veal.

VEAL CROQUETTES.

Cook the veal tender, and make and cook the same as chicken croquettes.

VEAL PATTIES.

Mix the same as for veal loaf, leaving out the pork; prepare the crust the same as for oyster patties. Bake the patties, fill just before using and heat hot.

BREAKFAST PUFFS.

2 eggs   1 cup flour, salt
1 tablespoon butter   1 cup milk
    1 heaping teaspoon baking-powder.

Sift flour and baking-powder together twice; beat the yolks well; stir all together and lastly stir in the stifly beaten whites. Fill the cups half full. Bake twenty-five or thirty minutes.

RUSKS.

2 cups milk   3 tablespoons yeast
½ cup butter   2 eggs, salt
    2 tablespoons sugar.

Put all in a sponge the night before except the eggs. In the morning add the well-beaten eggs; mix as soft as possible; roll out and cut with cutter. When ready to bake rub over the top with the sweetened beaten white of an egg.

German Toast. Over Fifty Years Old.

Cut slices of stale bread of medium thickness, dip each in well beaten egg and milk with salt, sufficient to moisten (not soak) a little, then in cracker crumbs finely rolled. Brown both sides in flat spider as you would potatoes, in half butter and half lard. It is a change for a breakfast dish.

Baking-Powder.

2 pounds cream tartar	1 pound bi carb. soda
6 ounces corn starch

Mix well and put it through a sieve three times.

Caramel Cream.

Boil two coffee cups of best brown sugar, butter the the size of an egg, and two-thirds of a cup of thin sweet cream twelve minutes after it commences to boil. Dissolve one-half a cup of gelatine in as little water as will dissolve it; add this to it, and the rest of pint of cream. Strain and flavor with vanilla; put in a mold and let it stand over night. Serve with cream.

CANDY.

Ice Cream Candy.

3 cups white sugar	¼ teaspoon cream of tartar
½ cup water

Boil without stirring until when tried in cold water it is brittle. Turn into a buttered platter, butter the hands as soon as cool enough to handle and pull it till it is white and glossy. Flavor and color it when ready for pulling. Cut into sticks.

Fig Candy.

Take one pound of sugar, ¾ pint of water, and set over a slow fire; when brittle add a few drops of vinegar, a lump of butter, and pour onto sliced figs.

Cheese Straws.

Mix one cup of grated cheese with one cup of flour, a half teaspoon salt, a pinch of cayenne pepper, the yolks of two eggs and the white of one, butter the size of an egg. No water nor milk must be added as then they will not be crisp. Roll out to less than a fourth of an inch thick. Cut in strips seven or eight inches long and about one-half inch wide; place on buttered paper in long tins; bake in a moderate oven for five or more minutes; pile in a flat high dish laying two one way and two the other in log cabin style and the effect is very pretty. Tie each corner with ribbons. Keep these in a tight tin box. If they gather dampness, dry five minutes in oven.

How to Pull Candy.

As soon as it is boiled brittle, turn it on a buttered platter, as soon as cool enough to possibly handle, butter your hands, take up the candy what you can pull easily, throw it over a buttered hook and pull both ends toward you, then clap it together and pull over the hook again, repeating it till the candy is white and creamy. This prevents blistering the hands.

Molasses Candy.

1 pint N. O. molasses
2 tablespoons vinegar
1 pint best brown sugar
2 tablespoons butter

Warm and mix well together, then just boil without stirring till brittle when dropped in very cold water, then stir in two teaspoons of powdered baking soda. Pull as directed above. When pulled enough cut in sticks.

Cream Chocolates.

Beat the white of an egg on a plate, then beat in two tablespoons of water, then stir enough confectioner's XXX sugar to make a stiff paste, about one and a quarter pounds, one teaspoon vanilla. Work smooth, make into balls. Melt one-half pound of sweet chocolate in basin, stand it in hot water to melt. Set the balls on buttered paper in cool place for two or three hours to harden. Then with a fork dip one at a time into the melted chocolate (keep it hot in water), and place on the buttered paper till all are dipped. Stand in the cold over night.

Chocolate Caramels.

3 pounds sugar, confectioner's A
1½ pints cream
1 teaspoon lemon juice
6 ounces chocolate

Stir and heat slowly till dissolved, then boil till it hardens. Fill pan the thickness desired; when partly cool, mark the squares. For peanut and walnut candy put the nuts into molasses candy.

CARVING.

It is no trifling accomplishment to be able to carve well and skilfully. It occurs at least once a day in every family, and it is better for both men and women to be able to do it with dispatch and elegance. All display of over-exertion is in bad taste. A little attention and experience will soon put one at ease in his seat of honor. It is well to call the attention of younger persons to observe how it is done, that they, too, may serve their turn. A sharp knife is an absolute necessity to exhibit the ability of the carver. We know it is not considered proper to stand while carving for company, though it is much easier, but we will not be fastidious. In roasts such as ribs, forequarters, etc., the butcher should be instructed to separate the joints. Fowls are easily carved. Ducks have strong ligaments and are therefore more difficult to carve. Place the turkey on its back on the platter, as it was roasted (to a good brown), putting the head to the right-hand of the carver. Fix the fork firmly in the lower end of the breast and you need not remove it till the turkey is nearly all cut up. First sever the legs and wings on both sides (if the whole is to be served), cutting neatly through the joint next the body. Then cut slices from the breast lengthwise, beginning on the lower part, and laying the pieces neatly on the side of the platter; then unjoint the legs and wings at the middle joint, which can be struck almost exactly by an expert carver, or after a little practice. Consult the tastes of the guests as to which part is preferred; if no preference is expressed, serve a portion of both light and dark meat, with a spoonful of dressing, and gravy (unless it is not desired). The dressing is more accessible if the bird is placed with the head to the left. A chicken is carved the same way, whether roasted or broiled. A little more dexterity and force are needed to carve a goose than a turkey, though carved in the same way. The breast of a goose is considered the choicest part; all the meat is good and full of juicy flavor.

Roast Duck.

No other dishes require so much skill in carving as game and poultry; as it is necessary to be well acquainted with the anatomy of the bird, or know just the location of the joints, in order to place the knife at exactly the right point. The wing of a flyer and the leg of a swimmer are the most desirable portions of a duck, after the breast.

A tame duck is nice stuffed as a turkey and roasted, also split open on the back and put in the oven in the roasting pan, on the rack, and basted. Wild ducks should be split open on the back, put on the rack in a well heated oven, for twenty minutes or less, they should be rare, but boiling hot through. When wild ducks live on rice their meat is much the richest eating.

To Make Bread Without a Sponge.

For the yeast:
4 quarts boiled water   12 potatoes, pared
2 tablespoons white sugar   2 tablespoons salt
3 tablespoons flour   1 Twin Bros.' yeast cake

Make this the day before baking; the yeast is all the wetting you need; do not sponge it. The yeast will keep two or three weeks. Pare medium sized potatoes and boil just done in two quarts of the boiled water, then mash and put through a colander into a crock, with the water they were boiled in, then add the other two quarts of hot water, making four quarts, then sugar, salt and flour; when it is cool enough to hold the finger in, add the yeast soaked in a cup of warm water. Let stand over night, in a warm place, stirring once an hour till bed time. Next morning let it get warm, give it a good stir, and use one pint of it for one large loaf of bread, an even teaspoon of salt. Knead it twenty minutes. Do not sponge it, but mix it right up as soft as you can knead it, as other bread, and put it in pans. It will be light enough in three hours to bake, while you are getting dinner. Put the rest of the yeast in glass cans, seal tight, keep in cellar. Remember, no other wetting but the yeast. Do not use the bread till next day, as no bread should be eaten the day it is baked.

To Make Butter.

Cream at a temperature of 58° Fahrenheit, will churn in from fifteen to twenty minutes. Do not churn on the gallop but with a quiet steady hand without leaving it. When it comes whirl the dasher some, to gather the particles of butter together. Do not have it soft, as no standing will make it right again. Some prefer to take it up into very cold water to work out the first buttermilk, others think it not well to do so. Put two heaping teaspoons of salt to every pound of butter, working out the buttermilk so as not to mash the grain (this is a knack or quality that few possess), work it ten minutes, then set it away till next morning, taste to see if it is salt enough, if not, add more and work it again till all the buttermilk is out. Make it into rolls and keep it in a cool place, covered tight, as it absorbs everything in the atmosphere. Butter made while the cow can obtain grass, from the first of June to the last of October, has a superior flavor and is esteemed more highly than that made in winter. Winter butter can be improved by feeding the cows silage that is clean and sweet, with plenty of grain or well cured green cut clover or corn stalks cut and gathered green; add to these generous feedings of bran middlings with one quart of corn meal in it, or linseed meal. Put a little salt in her food and do not give her very cold water in the five winter months. One new milch cow will improve the flavor of all the butter from a small herd. Butter gains nothing by being kept over two or three weeks and loses much in delicacy of flavor by such treatment. The flavor of the Jersey milk and butter is going into disrepute. Cows fed upon rich nutritious food, with some corn meal and yellow carrots will make more highly colored butter than if fed on hay. The ripening of the cream decides largely the flavor of the butter in winter. Sour cream makes the best butter, but not aged. About sixty or sixty-five degrees will ripen it in twenty-four hours. Skim each milking when it is twenty-four hours old, whether sour or not, and for the cream from each cow put in the cream crock two cups of sour buttermilk from the last churning as a starter in the winter and keep the cream at a temperature of fifty-eight degrees, which is right for churning, some say sixty-two; try it. A thermometer to test the cream is as necessary as a churn. Irenæus of the New York Observer tells us of a Mr. Starr, a friend of his that lived at Litchfield, Connecticut, who had a splendid dairy. "Mr. Starr's method of setting his milk for cream, is not in shallow pans, as the women of old were wont to do; but in narrow vessels about twenty inches deep, standing in ice water, or a very cold place. Not only does this low temperature reduce the process of change to a minimum, but quite unexpectedly, it also greatly facilitates the rising of the cream, as the cream is nearly all obtained in twelve hours. The butter churned from the product is not only pure in flavor, but has remarkable keeping qualities. The plan is spreading rapidly." This might work in a large dairy.

CELERY.

Earthing up celery is necessary when it is wanted for autumn or early winter use; but for late winter and spring we never had clearer and whiter stalks than from those plants which were not earthed up at all. Just before winter sets in we had the plants carefully lifted out with a spade, the roots with the earth partly shaken off, the plants then neatly and compactly placed upright in a trench, in a hollow where the wind could not blow, and covered with a foot of dead leaves. They were perfectly blanched in this trench, and kept better than when the blanching had been previously done. This is easily taken out when wanted.

AN ICE HOUSE.

Make a bin in the open air fourteen by sixteen feet. of hemlock boards, with four-inch scantling for posts, and roof it over, leaving the gable ends and three feet on the front side open. Fill in with six inches of course chips for drainage; and put on these ten inches of saw dust. Pack the ice in the center, and cover top and sides with eighteen inches of saw dust. The ice will keep perfectly. Build it in the shade if possible.

Gruels for the Sick.

The lightest possible gruel is made by taking two heaping tablespoons of yellow corn meal, pour upon it one teacup cold water and stir well. Let settle a little and pour this water off into a teacup of water at a keen boil and scald for five minutes. A little salt.

Milk Porridge.

One pint of milk, wet one heaping teaspoon of flour with two tablespoons of the cold milk, a little salt, stir this into the boiling milk. Boil three to six minutes. Excellent for diarrhœa.

Oat Meal Gruel.

Into one quart of boiling water or milk as you like, stir in two tablespoons of oat meal and a little salt. Boil forty minutes and strain if you like.

Indian Meal Gruel.

1 quart water or milk   1 tablespoon flour
2 tablespoons corn meal   1 teaspoon salt

Wet the flour and meal and pour into the boiling water. Boil forty minutes.

Cracker Panada.

Put in double boiler one quart of milk or water as the patient can bear, stir in six tablespoons of sifted rolled cracker and one half teaspoon of salt. Let boil three minutes. Add a little nutmeg, sugar and wine if you like.

Arrowroot Gruel.

To one pint of milk or water, one teaspoon of arrowroot, a little salt; wet it with cold milk, stir it in the boiling milk, and boil ten minutes in double boiler.

Ice Cream for the Sick.

1 cup milk   1 pint cream
1 teaspoon arrowroot   ½ cup sugar

Scald it all and freeze as directed.

Veal Sweet Breads.

These are considered a great delicacy by some. There are two in a calf, one from near the heart called the "heart sweet bread," the other from the neck called the "throat sweet bread." The first is most delicate. They spoil very soon and need to be engaged beforehand, that the butcher may send them to you as soon as the animal is dressed. Put it immediately in warm water, to which add a tablespoon of salt, to soak out the blood; soak one hour, then wash it in cold water. Draw strips of salt pork through it and put in good soup stock or water and boil twenty minutes. As soon as cool enough remove the skinny portions and pipes. Cook in granite kettle and use a silver knife and fork, as they contain a peculiar acid that acts upon iron or tin. After it is thus prepared you can fricassee, slice and fry, broil or bake, after rubbing it with butter and seasoning.

Mushrooms.

As we so often see the notice, "Died from toadstool in mistake for mushrooms," I have refrained from giving the different recipes for cooking mushrooms, as

I feel the risk is too great for the pleasure it might give. Any real mushrooms are poisonous if picked over an hour after they are open. If any one will eat them, they can be stewed, baked or broiled, with seasoning of butter and a little salt and pepper. I quote: "The difference between a toadstool and a mushroom is the difference between an eel and a rattlesnake—in effect. There is but one sure way of telling the difference. The stems of the mushrooms are generally shorter, thicker, and invariably solid; the stems of the toadstools are hollow." This author says he has picked and eaten many mushrooms, using this test alone.

MISCELLANEOUS RECIPES.

Making Over Hair Mattresses.

Empty the tick, wash it nicely with hard soap and enough borax to soften the water. Spread the hair on clean boards or sheets, and whip the dust out entirely then pick it up fine. If for any reason it should need washing, wash it in warm suds, rinse and spread to dry. Weigh all the hair, then weigh one-fourth for each corner of tick. Dividing this way will be of great assistance in getting it evenly laid. You need a mattress needle and strong twine. Put the under tuft in first, in a slip, a noose, at the end of the double twine, then put the needle up through the mattress, tie it tight, then tie in the upper tuft with three knots.

To Clean a Teakettle of Lime.

The thick incrustations that form upon the inside of teakettles when hard water is used, can be easily removed by putting in two quarts of ashes and filling up with water, let boil and soak three hours. While hot empty it out and scrape it clean with an iron spoon. It will easily peel off.

To Clean Moldy Jugs.

Wash clean with ashes and soapsuds, rinse well, fill with hot water, put in a teaspoon of carbolic acid, set it away from sight where no one will see it for a few hours, as it is a deadly poison. Then empty it and wash and rinse well and it will be as sweet as if it had not been tainted.

Ropy Milk.

When the milk is ropy there is probably inflammation of the udder. The milk is acid, and becomes clotted; this is a conditional defect arising from diseased blood. An authority writes, give a dose of twelve ounces of Epsom salts, and before milking inject by a syringe, one-fourth of a pint of solution of carbonate of soda into the teat, and after fifteen minutes milk it out. Dissolve one-fourth of a teaspoon of soda in one-half cup of warm water.

Care of Canaries.

Clean the cage thoroughly every morning, and accustom them to plenty of light and company, but not to sudden noises; do not hang the cage in a draft. Give it clean water for its bath every morning. Feed it with mixed canary seed, a piece of bread and occasionally spread it with a little butter and sprinkle a very little red pepper on it, give it a lump of sugar, a cuttle bone, apple, a little sand in bottom of cage, and in the summer chick weed. If at any time the bird is hoarse, give it a piece of fat salt pork and see how he will enjoy it, and listen for the result. If he appears dumpy remember the bread and butter with the sprinkle of red pepper. If kept perfectly clean no vermin will come to them, but if you only clean them twice a week there is danger. If you are so unfortunate as to have these pests clean thoroughly, take the cage to pieces, boil the perches, then put in a lump of sugar; they will bury themselves in it, and also a little bit of cotton on each end of perch to attract those that still remain on the bird. Remove and burn it and the sugar daily and clean the same way and they will be gone soon. Never allow any one to tease a bird.

Pure Unfermented Wine.

Use perfectly ripe grapes, wash, pick out all defective ones; mash with the hands, scald, press out the juice, boil it gently until all the scum rises, skim it repeatedly till clear, and bottle while hot, cork and seal, or put it in tight fruit jars. Keep in a cool, dark place. Sweeten to the taste when used. The above is considered the best for communion purposes.

To Insure Long Life.

Dr. Abernethey, the great Scotch physician's secret of success in the healing art, and rules of living to insure longevity, found among his effects in a sealed envelope, and for which $5,000 was paid, contained these words: "To insure continued health, and a ripe old age, keep the head cool, the feet warm, and the system open. To secure these conditions keep the ten commandments, observe the laws of life and the science of health." If one does not know how, take some good health journal. Eight hours' sleep each day. Open air exercise every day. Air the sleeping room from one to two hours daily. The use of plain food with plenty of fruit. Frequent bathing. Flannel of some kind next the skin the year round.

The Brain.

It is not so much intellectual work that injures the brain, if one takes physical exercise, but undue emotional excitement. Most men can stand the severest thought and study of which their brains are capable, and be none the worse for it, provided they can recuperate with quiet sleep and out-of-door exercise. It is over ambition, anxiety, disappointment, bad habits, the hopes and fears, the loves and hates of our lives, that wear out the nervous system, and endanger the balance of the brain.

Tooth Ache or Neuralgia.

A white flannel bag filled with good hops wet with boiling water and applied hot, is sometimes wonderful in its power to sooth a tooth-ache, a neuralgia headache or a sharp pain anywhere, and send the patient to sleep.

Warts and Corns.

Rub the wart with lemon and bind on a piece three times a day for a week. The wart will diminish till it disappears. Do the same with corns, rubbing night and morning and bind on at night.

Poisoning.

In case of poisoning the simple rule is to get the poison out of the stomach instantly, for it assimilates very soon. Mustard and salt act very promptly and are always at hand. Stir a teaspoonful of each in a glass of water and swallow it quickly. If it does not cause vomiting in five minutes, repeat the dose. After vomiting, give the unbeaten whites of two or three eggs. Send for the doctor the first thing, but go right to work with the emetic.

THE COMPLEXION.

As so many ladies are in the habit of using dry magnesia as a toilet powder, I feel constrained to warn them against it, both from observation and from the pronouncing of chemists that it is very injurious to the skin, as it dries the cuticle and causes the skin to become rough and scaly. If you have used it, we advise you to stop at once, and heal the face with a weak solution of borax, water and a little glycerine. Most toilet powders on the market contain magnesia. The curious prejudice that some people have against using soap on the face, is a great fallacy. Good toilet soap is the best purifier and preventive of the uncomely looking blackheads so often seen. But if you have them, wash daily with a cloth, warm water and soap. Press them out with the open end of a watch key.

TO CURE A STY.

Rub into a small pinch of powdered alum enough of the white of an egg to make a paste. It will become a curd. Put it between two fine pieces of thin goods and bind it on the eye at night. It is said the sty will be gone in the morning.

INSECT BITES AND STINGS.

The bites of mosquitoes, bees, wasps, hornets, scorpions, may be instantly relieved by the immediate and free application of ammonia (hartshorn) as a wash to the part bitten. Then cover it with a cloth dipped in sweet oil.

CURE FOR RATTLESNAKE POISON.

This is a convenient and simple remedy, used by the Indians more than one hundred years ago, and by the early settlers of our country. A small cupful of the juice of the plantain weed, which is to be found along the roadbed and in nearly every country door yard. Inquiry made among farmers and country people generally, elicited the information that plaintain weed is used extensively for poulticing, to heal running sores, and to break up cases of chills and fever. Dr. A. H. Palmer, of Marlborough, N. Y., says that a handful of plantain leaves made into a cup of tea, breaks up severe attacks of certain malarial disorders when other specifics fail. Wood choppers on the Shawangunk Mountains say they have long known that plaintain juice would prevent fatal results from the bite of a rattlesnake. Toads and other animals seem to know the medicinal properties of the plantain weed. When bitten by a snake they invariably hop to where the specific can be found. Also apply ammonia to the wound immediately.

WHAT TO DO IN A THUNDER STORM

In the open air, during violent storms of any kind, the safest situation is to keep aloof from trees, and as far as possible from any and all elevated structures and regard the storm, the torrents of rain, though it may saturate the clothes, as a protection against the lightning's stroke; for wet clothes would supply so good a conductor that a very large amount of electricity would pass over a person's body through them, while the person would be quite unconscious of it. The rain itself, in its usual form, is one of the best conductors known to modern chemists and electricians. Lightning rods are said to be no protection unless they reach water in the earth.

The Laughing Cure.

A shrewd lady who had recovered from a decline, was asked what cured her. " I stopped worrying and began to laugh, that is all," was the reply.

Piano.

Do not always keep the piano closed, if you wish the keys to remain white. If the keys do not respond readily, there is dampness inside; open the top till all right, then open it once a week.

For Hives in Children.

Rub the irritated skin or postules with castor oil applied with the fingers. Baby will soon slumber.

Restoring the Drowned.

[Prepared by Dr. Benjamin Howard, approved by the Academy of Medicine and adopted by the Life Saving Society of New York.]

The first thing to be done is to *arouse* the patient if possible without moving him. Instantly expose the face to a current of fresh air; wipe dry the mouth and nostrils, rip the clothing so as to expose the chest and waist, and give two or three quick smarting slaps on the stomach and chest with the open hand. If the patient does not revive, then proceed as follows:

Rule I. Turn the patient on his face, a large bundle of tightly-rolled clothing being placed beneath his stomach, and press heavily over it for half a minute, or so long as fluids flow freely from the mouth.

Rule II. Turn the patient on his back, the roll of clothing being so placed beneath it as to raise the pit of the stomach above the level of any other part of the body. If there be another person present, let him, with a piece of dry cloth, hold the tip of the tongue out of one corner of the mouth, and with the other hand grasp both wrists and keep the arms forcibly stretched back above the head. The position prevents the tongue from falling back and choking the entrance to the windpipe, and increasing the prominence of the ribs tends to enlarge the chest; it is not, however, essential to success.

Kneel beside, or astride the patient's hips, and with the balls of the thumbs resting on either side the pit of the stomach, let the fingers fall into the grooves between the short ribs, so as to afford the best grasp of the waist. Now, using your knees as a pivot, throw all your weight forward on your hands, and at the same time squeeze the waist between them, as if you wished to force everything in the chest upward out of the mouth; deepen the pressure while you can count slowly, one, two, three; then *suddenly* let go with a final push, which springs you back to your first kneeling position. Remain erect on your knees while you can count one, two; then repeat the same motions as before, at a rate gradually increased from four or five to fifteen times in a minute, and continue thus this bellows movement with the same regularity that is observable in the natural motions of breathing, which you are imitating.

Continue thus for from one to two hours, or until the patient breathes; for awhile after, carefully deepen the first short gasps into full breaths, and continue the drying and rubbing, which should have been unceasingly practiced from the beginning.

AFTER TREATMENT.

As soon as the breathing has been established, strip the patient, wrap him in blankets only, put him in a bed comfortably warm, but with a free circulation of fresh air, and leave him to perfect rest. If necessary give a little hot brandy and water, or other stimulant at hand, for every ten or fifteen minutes for the first hour, and as often thereafter as may seem expedient.

FAMILY REMEDIES.

To inhale turpentine has proved of great service in bronchitis, pneumonia, pleurisy and other throat and lung affections. If you have a cough, sprinkle a little on a cloth and hold it to your mouth and nose for a few minutes, breathing the odor and note the relief.

FOR ALL LUNG TROUBLE.

Mix equal parts of turpentine and olive tar; bathe the spot affected daily and cover with oiled silk. Wear it night and day till well, and for a cough take wild black cherry cough syrup also.

WILD BLACK CHERRY COUGH SYRUP.

¾ pound wild black cherry bark
4 oz. tincture ipecacuanha
4 oz. tincture bloodroot
3 pounds loaf sugar
1 quart water
4 oz. paregoric
4 oz. antimonial wine

Take the inside of the bark, soak it over night in an earthen covered dish. In the morning let it simmer (not boil) till reduced to one pint of the water; keep it covered all the time. The bark will absorb some of the water. Strain it hot on the sugar, then stir in the other four ingredients. Set the pitcher of syrup in hot water to dissolve the sugar; keep it covered. When sugar is dissolved bottle and cork tightly. Dose: one teaspoon every four hours, or pour some in a cup and set beside you and sip one-fourth of a teaspoon whenever you cough, if bad. This has cured the writer of a bad cough some three times, but do not let your cough continue a year or two before taking it, or applying the olive tar and then say " it does no good." I know of three persons who had coughed a long time, whose lives were prolonged many years by the use of it. Obtain fresh bark from the tree.

Cough Syrup.

Mix equal quantities of unboiled linseed oil, Holland gin and strained honey well together. Dose: Take one teaspoon every three hours or sip some every time you cough. This is excellent for a common cough or where one coughs when attempting to speak.

Cough Syrup.

1 ounce gum arabic
1 ounce paregoric
1 ounce liquorice extract
1 ounce tinct. bloodroot.

Mix loaf sugar enough with this for a syrup. Dose: Take one teaspoon every four hours or so.

Rhubarb Syrup for Infants.

One heaping tablespoon of floured Turkey rhubarb, one teaspoon of soda, two gills of the best French brandy, two gills of soft water, lump sugar for a syrup.

Dose: one-half to a teaspoon, according to age. Good for an acid stomach.

BURNS.

The white of an egg is very efficacious for burns. Seven or eight applications will sooth the pain and exclude the burned part from the air. I should try a flour paste, made of egg and flour, just stiff enough not to run; spread it on a cloth and change it as often as it begins to dry. Another good remedy is to moisten saleratus enough to make a paste and spread it on a cloth; if it gets dry dampen and add more.

STAIR RODS.

Clean brass stair rods with kerosene oil and rotten stone. Rub long and hard and polish with chamois skin and they will keep bright a year.

FLAT IRONS.

Clean smoothing irons by rubbing over them a piece of beeswax in a cloth while hot. Salts of lemon will take stains from ivory knife handles.

CORNS.

Apply at night a poultice made of dry bread soaked in vinegar, in the morning the soreness will be gone and the corn can be removed; if not, do it for three times or through the day, if you can. A piece of lemon bound on will sometimes take out the soreness so it can be cut.

Another—

To cure corns, let a small piece of potash remain in the open air until it slakes, then thicken to a paste with pulverized gum arabic. Pare the corn and apply the paste, leaving it on ten minutes; soak the corn in strong hot vinegar for a little while, then leave it alone and it will soon come out. Do not wear too tight shoes. The ring corn plasters are found to be a great relief. Wet it and hold it on till dry. Keep a stocking on all night, that it may not rub off. Wear them continuously, till you can cut the corn off.

Lockjaw.

Let any one who has an attack of lockjaw take a small quantity of turpentine, warm it and pour it on the wound, no matter where the wound is, and relief will follow in less than a minute. Nothing better can be applied to a severe cut or bruise than cold turpentine; it will give certain relief. If too severe mix it with sweet oil, half and half.

Swelled Feet and Ankles.

Take plantain leaves, which can be found in almost any wet grass-plat; wilt them by putting separately between the hands and warming them; cover the swollen parts with them, and keep in place by winding a narrow strip of cloth around in spiral form. Keep them on day and night, renewing as they dry.

For Burns.

Procure a few ounces of palm oil from a tallow chandler, it is like lard; spread it on a cloth and apply. It will cure the worst burns.

Chilblains.

1 oz. Burgundy pitch
2 oz. beeswax
1 oz. sperm oil
½ oz. turpentine

Simmer the first three ingredients well together, and

when nearly cool add the turpentine. Spread on a cloth and put the plaster on the affected spot, after the feet have been well washed in very hot water. If not relieved in three days repeat the process.

Home Messenger.

Another remedy is, take off the boot and hold the foot, with the sock on, as near the fire as one can stand the heat; if it gets too hot to bear withdraw it, and put it near the fire again. Heat it in this way for ten minutes, keeping it as hot as the pain will permit without blistering. Repeat every time it returns, after bathing the parts with a mixture of kerosene oil and salt. This is too severe for children—must use the plaster for children.

ACIDITY OF THE STOMACH.

A sufferer from want of appetite and acid stomach can be greatly benefited by leaving all medicines alone, and for a time existing entirely on milk and lime-water. A tablespoon of lime-water to a tumbler of milk. If this disagrees in any way, increase the quantity of lime-water. This is made by taking a bowl of unslacked lime, and pour on slowly several quarts of boiling water, perhaps three or four; till well, let settle over night and bottle it.

TOOTHACHE.

Go to a dentist and have it cleaned and filled. If not near a dentist, saturate a piece of cotton with camphor or peppermint and put it in the cavity, and bathe the side of the face with it.

Washes for Inflamed Eyes.

Wash frequently in as hot rain water as you can bear, then lay the warm wet cloth on. If that does not cure, wash them in green tea. If neither of these cure, take sulph. zinc, two grains; wine of opium, ten drops; distilled water, one ounce; mix. Lie flat on the back and drop two or three drops in the outer corner of the eye three times a day.

Consumption.

Dr. Marshall Hall, an eminent physician, says, " If I were seriously ill of consumption, I would live out of doors, except in rainy weather or mid-winter." Lift the windows more or less every night according to weather, wearing something over the head, but have plenty of fresh air to breathe every breath. An excellent thing to ease a cough is to drink plentifully of slippery-elm and flaxseed teas, mixed with loaf sugar and lemon juice. Use wild cherry cough syrup.

Indigestion.

It is said that Voltaire was once troubled for nearly a year with decay of the stomach and the difficulty of finding any kind of food it could bear. Voltaire said he was cured by taking no other food than the following prescription recommended by Sir John Sinclair: Beat up an egg and then add six tablespoons of cold water, mixing well together; then add two tablespoons of farina of potatoes; mix it well in the egg; then pour in as much boiling water only as will convert the whole into a jelly, stirring well. It may be taken alone or with the addition of a little milk in case of stomachic debility from consumptive disorders.

Scientific American.

Catarrh.

A twenty-year sufferer was cured of this disease by smoking dried mullen leaves, three times a day, two or three pipes full at a time. Close the mouth and draw the smoke through the nostrils. It is some six or seven years since the cure. Received some benefit after one week; would advise smoking one or two years till cured.

A Catarrh Snuff.

Rad Senika ʒi   Chlorate potass. ʒii
Pulverize very fine; mix. Snuff a pinch at a time.

Dr. Wm. Smith.

Sore Nipples.

Bathe with a strong decoction of best Japan tea; make it fresh every day. Bathe and let dry and put on a plaster of Dalley's pain extractor or ointment. Repeat this every eight hours, after nursing. Do not nurse the child but once in four hours, giving rest to each side eight hours. Wash off before nursing. A sure cure, if rightly used.

A Remedy for Croup.

Let a healthy person fill his lungs with pure air; then slowly breathe upon the patient's throat and chest, commencing at the point of the chin and moving slowly down to the bottom of the windpipe. Repeat for a few minutes and it will give relief in cases where all other means fail. My boy was always subject to croup; came near dying with the rattling noisy kind at about eleven months old. I saved him with fomentations of warm water (as hot as they can bear). When three years old I let him play in the brook one warm, rainy day and he took a severe cold and had the still kind of croup. In spite of all I could do he grew constantly worse until he could only gasp and breathe with his head thrown back.) I applied the breathing remedy for a minute. When I stopped he looked up and said " Do so again, Mother, do," though he could not speak when I began. You may be assured I did so again, and I believe it saved his life.

Home Messenger.

Some affirm that croup may be cured in one minute by simply using floured alum and sugar. Take one teaspoon of floured alum and mix well with two teaspoons of powdered sugar. I do not know how it is administered, but I should carefully place a little each side of the throat, and often, but I think I should moisten it a little, for fear of sucking the dry powder into the windpipe. After using hot cloths, bathe the throat with equal quantities of sweet oil and turpentine. Keep the feet warm.

CROUP OF CHILDREN.

Many a lovely child is destroyed in a single night by this alarming disease. Its nature is described in the first part. It is a disease of the windpipe, which is filled or lined with a phlegm, which becomes more and more tough, almost leathery, thickens, and at length closes up the passage to the lungs and the child dies. It usually comes on in the night. The destinguishing symptom is a wheezing, barking cough. A mother who has ever heard it once needs no description to enable her to recognize it again. The first born are the most likely to perish with it, simply because the parent has no experience of its nature, and hence is not alarmed in time or knows not what to do while the physician is being sent for. In the hope of being instrumental in saving some little sufferer whose life is inexpressibly dear, at least to one or two, I will make some suggestions, not for the cure of the patient, but to save time. The instant you perceive the child has croup, indicated by the cough, uneasy breathing, restlessness, send for a physician, and as instantly wrap a hot flannel around each foot to keep it warm; while the flannels are being heated, dip another flannel of two or more thicknesses in spirits of turpentine, or spirits of hartshorn, or have a large mustard plaster applied, one that will reach from the top of the throat down to some two inches below the collar bones, wide enough at the top to reach half way around the neck on either side, and nearly across the whole breast at bottom. But it will take time to send for a physician, to prepare flannels, and to make the plaster or to obtain the turpentined flannel, and in some cases fifteen minutes is an age—is death, if lost; therefore, while these things are preparing, give the child if one year old or over (and half as much if less), about half a teaspoonful of hive syrup, and double the dose every fifteen minutes until vomiting is produced; and every half hour after vomiting give half as much as caused the vomiting, until the physician comes, or the child ceases to cough, when he breathes free and is safe. If you have no hive syrup, give a teaspoonful or half teaspoon of syrup of ipecac (according to age), and double the dose every fifteen minutes until vomiting is produced. If you have been so thoughtless as to have nothing at all, boil some water, keep it boiling, dip a woolen flannel of several folds into it, squeeze it out moderately with your hand,

and apply it as hot as the child can possibly bear to the throat, and in from one to three minutes, according to the violence of the symptoms, have another to put on the instant the first is removed, and keep this up until the breathing is easy, and the cough is loose and the phlegm is freely discharged, or until the arrival of the physician.

A SMALL-POX REMEDY.

Last April Dr. James Moore, of Ironton, Ohio, published his experience with lemons as a remedy for small-pox. It is as follows:

" I was taken sick April 14th with what I supposed was a severe cold, having had my hair shingled the previous Friday. The 14th I was quite feverish, with a severe pain in the head and back. Saturday, 16th, I was no better; Sunday, fever somewhat reduced, I presume by the aid of aconite, which had been administered to me by Drs. Morris and Dunn; eruption very indistinct underneath the skin.

" Monday morning, 18th, eruption unmistakably that of small-pox. Tuesday morning eruption very abundant, crop increasing rapidly in size and number. Wednesday morning a very dense crop all over the face, forehead, scalp of head, neck, and soles of feet. Upon the arms, hands, legs and body, they were pretty evenly distributed, but not so closely packed as upon the above mentioned parts. By evening I was suffering intensely from those on the scalp. By 10:30 o'clock the pain was almost intolerable. My nurse had retired and was sound asleep in bed. My feet were so tender that I dare not let them touch the foot-board of the bed. My head I could not suffer to lie on the pillow. I lay, raised on my elbow, my neck resting upon my hand. I had by this time become so nervous I dare not shut my eyes from fear of seeing unpleasant visions. Pulse about 90. I had upon the table at the bedside a pitcher of water and a drinking glass, a box of seidlitz powders and an ounce of chlorate of potash in crystals. I had also at my bedside a paper of lemons, also one of oranges. These were all the agents within my reach.

"I recollected that lemon juice in sufficient quantity was a sedative, and would lower the heart's action, and by so doing might relieve me of those unpleasant visions. I therefore squeezed all the juice I possibly could out of one of the lemons into the glass, to which I added about two tablespoonsful of water and drank it. I then opened the rind and sucked the balance of the juice. In about twenty minutes I took another lemon and used it in the same manner. In a short time I felt very cold, as if I were lying in close proximity to a large mass of snow or ice. My pulse had dropped to 60. I shut my eyes to see if the unpleasant visions were gone. I not only found that they were gone, but by placing my hand upon my head I found the pox had gone also. I laid down and slept two hours comfortably. I awoke, I presumed, from cold, although I had plenty of cover over me and the fire was still burning in the grate. I felt so well pleased that I took a little more lemon juice. I kept my pulse at from 60 to 67 for 36 hours, when all eruption and elevations had disappeared from my skin. I then bid good-by to lemon juice and small-pox.

"So strongly am I convinced of the power of lemon juice to abort any and every case of small-pox, if administered as I administered it myself, that I look upon it as a specific of as much certainty and power in small-pox as quinine is in intermittent fever. I therefore publish my experiments, hoping every physician having a case of small-pox will give it a fair trial and report the result to me."

MEASLES AND SCARLET FEVER.

It is important to be able to readily distinguish between these two diseases, which are in some respects similar. Measles presents the appearance of a patchy redness of a circular form, showing white between, with small pimples that feel like little hard points. The mouth and throat are red and inflamed, causing a cough and other symptoms of cold. About the third day the eyes become inflamed and watery. In spite of all remedies the symptoms do not abate. A day or two later the eruption appears upon the neck and head, and then extends over the rest of the body. At last it attacks the bowels, causing diarrhœa, and then the other symptoms quickly disappear. The essential point in the treatment is to avoid taking cold. There are few diseases that so readily and completely recover with perfect nursing, and few that entail such a series of misfortunes without it. Medicine is seldom necessary. A portion of the body at a time may be sponged with warm water and then carefully wiped dry before extending the operation. The room should be well aired, but no current of air should touch the patient. The food should be light and easy of digestion.

Scarlet fever is also red, but it has a smooth feel in the skin, and the redness is suffused like a blush, which deepens till it is very red. There is loss of appetite, pains in the limbs and sore throat; this is the dangerous part. In scarlet fever the rash comes out the second day; in measles the fourth. In scarlet fever, there is sore throat; none in measles. In scarlet fever the patient seems to have no cold, as in measles. But little treatment is needed in mild cases. If the urine is not free, drink flax-seed tea or lemonade. Gargle the throat with red pepper, vinegar and water, or a solution of chlorate of potash. The main thing is to bring out the rash and keep it out. Nothing can compare with frequent warm baths for this purpose; or, if there is much debility, warm sponge baths. Check thirst with lemonade, buttermilk, etc. Keep the room cool and well ventilated. Meat or poultry broth and soups may be given. Scarlet fever is also a disease that must run its course, and the patient is to be protected by careful nursing from death, or some of the unfortunate complications that so frequently follow this disease.

Hall's Journal of Health.

Sulphur for Diphtheria.

Dr. Field, of Victoria, used powdered sulphur and a quill. He put one teaspoon of flour of sulphur into a wine glass of water and stirred it with his finger instead of a spoon; as the sulphur does not readily mix with water. When the sulphur was well mixed he gave it as a gargle. Brimstone kills every species of fungus in man, beast and plant in a very few minutes. Instead of spitting out the gargle, he recommended the swallowing of it. In extreme cases, when the fungus was too nearly closing the throat to allow of the gargle, he blew the sulphur through a quill, each side of the throat, and after the fungus had shrunk to allow of it, then the gargling.

If the patient can not gargle, take a pan of hot coals and sprinkle a teaspoon of sulphur upon them.

Let the sufferer inhale it somewhat, but not too strong. The patient can walk about the room inhaling the fumes. It is an excellent disinfectant of the room. — *Home Messenger.*

SALT IN DIPHTHERIA.

In a paper read at the Medical Society of Victoria, Australia, Dr. Day stated that, " having for many years regarded diphtheria, in its early stage, as a purely local affection, characterized by a marked tendency to take on putrafactive decomposition, he has trusted most to the free and constant application of antiseptics, and when they have been used from the first, and been combined with nourishing food, he has seldom seen blood poisoning ensue. The frequent use of a gargle, made of a teaspoon of salt in a glass of water, giving children who can not gargle one or two teaspoons full to drink occasionally. Adults should use the gargle as a preventive four times a day." I should not cease to use other helps and send for a physician at once. Do not forget to use the sulphur smudge as a disinfectant.

DIPHTHERIA AND SCARLET FEVER.

The following extract from a circular issued by Dr. James Crane of the Brooklyn Health Department, has important suggestions which are equally applicable to city and country, wherever these diseases exist:

Diphtheria and scarlet fever are highly contagious diseases, attacking persons of all ages. They must be contracted from persons that are already affected, from the clothes they have worn and from everything which has been in the room with them. Even the walls of the room may infect persons coming into it after the patient has recovered, unless the poison is destroyed. In order to prevent their spread in a family or house where they exist and to promote the recovery of the persons attacked, the following simple measures should be conscientiously and rigidly carried out, thereby preventing much suffering and saving human life: An upper, sunny room, provided, if possible, with an open fireplace, and with no other children on the same floor, should be arranged for the patient by removing everything from it which can possibly be spared, such as books, clothing and window curtains, remembering that when once the patient has entered the room nothing can with safety be removed until disinfected or fumigated. One or two adults should take entire charge of the patient, under no circumstances coming in contact with other persons, more especially children. Open windows and open fireplaces, with fire in them day and night, avoiding draughts and chilly air, protect the sick and those who nurse them. Nothing should be removed from the room when the patient has once entered it until it has been thoroughly disinfected or fumigated.

Procure from a drug store one pound of sulphate of zinc; the price should not exceed thirty cents. Put into an ordinary water pail eight tablespoonsful of sulphate of zinc and four of common salt, and to this add one gallon of boiling water. This disinfecting solution is to be kept in the room, and into it should be placed and kept for one hour every article of soiled clothing, bedding, handkerchiefs, etc. When they are removed from this they should be put into boiling water before being washed. The dishes and spoons used by the patient should be put into boiling water before they are permitted to leave the room. Remember that every article which is in the room can convey the disease and that nothing should go from it until the poison which it might carry is destroyed.

See that the whole house from cellar to attic is clean. Keep the cellar dry, well ventilated and well whitewashed. Never allow, even for a day, garbage or other filth to be kept in it. Open the windows of sleeping rooms every day for as long a time as possible, fresh air being an excellent disinfectant.

Sulphur in Scarlet Fever.

Thoroughly annoint the patient twice daily with sulphur ointment; give five to ten grains of sulphur stirred in molasses three times a day. Sufficient sulphur was burned twice daily on hot coals to fill the room with the fumes, and of course was thoroughly inhaled by the patient. Under this mode of treatment each case improved immediately, and none were over eight days in making a complete recovery, and I firmly believe in each it was prevented from spreading by the treatment adopted. One case was in a large school. Having had a large experience in scarlet fever last year and this, I feel some confidence in my own judgment, and am of the opinion that the mildest cases I ever saw do not do half so well without as bad cases do with the sulphur treatment; and as far as I can judge, sulphur is as near a specific for scarlet fever as possible.

Dr. Henry Pigeon, in London Lancet.

I have copied these remedies or helps (from good authority) for these contagious diseases, not to take the place of a physician, by no means, but only as helps when a physician is not at hand. Always send for the most experienced one, immediately, that you may know just what the disease is and take it in time.

Disinfectants.

Dr. Doremus, of New York, says that to insure the destruction of germs of contagious diseases that chloride of zinc is the most efficient agent, and must be used freely and constantly, and in direct contact with the water and air which are connected with the sewers either through closets, sinks, or washstands. Saucers of wet chloride of lime should be placed in every room, where a house has a contagious disease, also the sulphur smudge as recommended above.

Typhoid Fever.

Dr. Guillasse, of the French navy, reports that in the early stages of the disease, coffee is almost a specific against typhoid fever. He gives to adults two or three tablespoons of strong coffee every two hours, alternating with one or two teaspoons of claret or Burgundy wine. The beneficient effect is immediate. A little lemonade or citrate of magnesia should be given daily, and after a while quinine.

Sciatic and Neuralgic Pains.

Dr. Ehrard, of Nimes, states " that he has for many years treated all his cases of sciatic and neuralgic pains with a sufficiently hot flat-iron to vaporize the strong vinegar that a woolen cloth has been wet in, and placed over the hot flat-iron, applied at once to the painful spot. The application may be repeated two or three times a day. As a rule, the pain disappears in twenty-four hours, and recovery ensues at once."

A friend of mine found relief in a few days from sciatic pains, by being rubbed freely with " Radway's

Ready Relief," and then with "Stafford's Olive Tar," then pin tightly a large bandage of double flannel (previously put under him), around the hips. Three times daily.

A Simple Remedy for Cholera.

Dr. Henry B. Cooper prescribes this remedy for cholera: " One ounce of camphor should be dissolved in six ounces of spirits of wine, and a small bottle should be given to any intelligent person who will undertake to administer it to his poor neighbors, when they are seized with cholera or any of its symptoms. The following instructions should be carried out at the same time with the utmost care and attention to detail. On the appearance of any cholera symptoms such as vomiting, purging, sudden weakness, coldness, cramps or spasms, instead of administering brandy, whisky or any other kind of medicine, put the patient to bed, after putting feet and hands in hot water, covering him warmly with blankets. Administer (for an adult) at once, two drops (not more) of the camphor mixture on a little powdered sugar in a teaspoon of cold or iced water. Five minutes after let him take a second dose of two drops in the same way, and in five minutes more a third dose. He can then wait ten or fifteen minutes to see whether or not there is a sense of returning warmth, with any signs of perspiration, and manifest decrease of sickness to the stomach, cramps, etc. If the improvement is not satisfactory, take two drops more as before, and repeat every five minutes, until fourteen drops have been taken. In administering the remedy particular caution must be observed, that the patient be not allowed to take anything of any sort or kind while the medicine is operating, or its effect will be destroyed, for the least foreign medicine neutralizes the camphor, which is given to check vomiting and to produce a free, warm perspiration. The use of cold iced water is advisedly recommended, as it promotes free perspiration and the discharge of bile. The patient must not be allowed to rise and become exposed to slightest degree of cold, and should not be tormented with baths, steamings, or rubbings of any kind, but be permitted to lie still, as he will fall asleep when perspiration comes on. After some hours he will awake well, although weak and languid and may be a little feverish, in which case he may take a teaspoon of rhubarb syrup, with a little peppermint sling. Above all, he must be kept perfectly quiet, taking mutton broth and then light nourishing food."

Rev. Arthur T. Pierson, D. D., after visiting Siam, says: "Dr. Samuel R. House, so long in Siam, told me he seldom lost a case of cholera when called before the stage of collapse, and his sole remedy was spirits of camphor." As the main object is to get up a natural action in the system and cause the nausea to cease, it looks reasonable. A mustard plaster on the stomach and bowels is an excellent thing to settle the stomach. It is recommended to burn a sulphur stick on a pan of coals, the size of a hickory nut (break it fine), three or four times a day, with open windows and doors, as a disinfectant. This is good also for tubercular affections of the lungs, for man and beast. Saucers of chloride of lime should stand in the room.

To Extract a Piece of Needle or Glass from the Foot or Hand.

Bind on hand as soon as possible a slice of well salted fat pork (fresh piece) every night and morning, until you find it on the pork. I once had the smallest point of a needle in the ball of my foot. It was twenty-four hours before I could make the application of salt pork wet with the brine. Just twenty-four hours after the first application, as it was removed for the third piece, I found the needle point on the pork. This is equally affective for injury by a nail or a piece of iron, or a sprained ankle or wrist. Bathe the parts first with spirits of turpentine; then bind it on tight. Many a sore and wound has been cured by bathing in strong green tea and a plaster of Dalley's ointment. But with any of these applications you must keep the foot up in a chair.

A Mustard Plaster.

Mix a paste of flour and warm water so stiff it will not run off of cloth, lay the cloth on a plate, spread the paste the size you need, sift the mustard over it very sparingly. Wet a double piece of new sheer muslin and lay carefully over the mustard. Sprinkle it very wet with very hot water, put it on and cover with flannel. Leave it on ten or fifteen minutes as they can bear it. Be careful not to draw a blister.

Mustard Poultice.

A mustard poultice should never make a blister. If a blister is wanted there are other plasters far better than mustard, as it is the sorest kind of blister. Mix the mustard with the whites of eggs, use no water and the result will be a plaster that will "draw" perfectly, but will not produce a blister, even upon the skin of an infant, no matter how long it is allowed to remain.

Home Messenger.

To Make Lime Water.

Put a few lumps of unslacked lime in a jar, slowly slack it with boiling water, stir it well. Let it settle over night, when clear bottle. Use from two to three tablespoons to a goblet of milk.

Chronic Diarrhœa.

A teaspoon of wheat flour mixed into a cup of sweet milk with a little nutmeg grated into it. Take it cold and raw. Pour a little milk on the flour at a time, beat it well so that it foams. To be taken three or four times a day.

Home Messenger.

For Neuralgia and Headache.

1 ounce alcohol	⅛ ounce laudanum
⅝ ounce chloroform	½ ounce gum camphor
½ drachm oil of cloves	1 drachm oil of lavender

¾ drachm sulphuric ether

Rub the part affected and inhale the liniment a little. It is also good for sick headache.

Home Messenger.

I have known of persons being cured of neuralgia by drinking good home-made buttermilk.

In Case of Accident.

A good memory well stored with self possession in emergencies, enables a person to relieve suffering and often to save life. One who faints at the appearance of danger or becomes excited or confused is well nigh useless. A clear brain and strong will can do much toward overcoming physical weakness. It is especially important that mothers should school themselves in self control and learn what should be done in times of sudden sickness or accident, which occur more or less in every home.

For dust or any foreign substance in the eye avoid rubbing; lie on the back with head low, drop sweet milk in the corner of the eye and wink it in, repeat if necessary. If this does not wash it out, whether cinders or eyelashes, take a handglass to the light, and lift the lid, take the point of a lead pencil with a thin, wet cloth over it, and touch it; the substance will cling to it.

EAR.

Remove hardened wax from the ear with warm water: Use a syringe. Use no hard instrument.

A CUT.

If an artery is cut, compress above the wound. If a vein is cut, compress below.

If choked, get down upon all fours and cough.

TO SMOTHER FIRE.

Smother fire with any woolen goods, salt, shovels of earth, or ashes. Water poured on burning oil, will only spread it and increase the danger. Before passing through smoke take a full breath and then stoop low; but if carbonic gas is suspected, walk erect.

For apoplexy, raise the head and body; for fainting, lay the body flat.

If in the water, float on the back, with the nose and mouth projecting. Be careful not to swallow the water.

To Guard Against Fire.

Every person, who sleeps above the first floor, either in hotels, boarding houses, or at home, should be provided with a fire-escape rope, a pair of thick old gloves, and a large cotton bag, a strong cord run in it to tie it up, into which on a moment's notice, you could empty drawers, or trunks, or the most valuable of your wardrobe, or tie up your clothing in a blanket or sheet to throw out of window. Fasten the iron hook around lower bed post or some heavy article of furniture, and drop the other end out of the window, and descend with gloves on or it will tear the flesh off of the hands. If there are two or three persons, the stronger could let down the weaker, and then descend himself.

Corks.

Corks may be made air and water tight by keeping them for five minutes in melted parafine.

Is Alum Poisonous.

Alum is used by many bakers to whiten their bread, enabling them to use an inferior flour. It is more extensively employed as a cheap substitute for cream of tartar in the manufacture of baking-powders. It has not been considered immediately dangerous, although if continued it induces dyspepsia and osbtinate constipation. We are in entire sympathy with the manufacturers of the Royal Baking Powder—who commenced and are vigorously conducting the war against the use of alum in baking-powders. We prefer the Royal Baking Powder.

ADULTERATIONS.

We can not be too strongly warned against the adulterations of food.

WHAT PEOPLE EAT.

BOSTON, Jan. 8.—Mr. Geo. T. Angell read a paper before the American Social Science Association here to-day on "Public Health Associations," in which he made some startling assertions about the adulteration of food. He said:

Cayenne pepper is adulterated with red lead; mustard with chromate of lead; curry powder with red lead, vinegar with sulphuric acid, arsenic and corrosive sublimate. It is stated that probably half the vinegar now sold in our cities is rank poison. One of our Boston chemists analyzed 12 packages of pickles put up by 12 different wholesale dealers, and found copper in 10 of them. Many of our flavoring oils, syrups, jellies and preserved fruits contain poisons. The adulterations of tea are too numerous to mention. Coffee is not only adulterated, but a patent has been taken out for molding chicory into the form of coffee berries, and I am told that clay is now molded, and perhaps flavored with an essence to represent coffee. Cocoa and chocolate are adulterated with various mineral substances.

Several mills in New England, and probably many elsewhere, are now engaged in grinding white stone into a fine powder for purposes of adulteration. At some of these mills they grind three grades—soda grade, sugar grade, and flour grade. It sells for about half a cent a pound. Flour has been adulterated in England, and probably here, with plaster of Paris, bone dust, sand, clay, chalk, and other articles. I am told that large quantities of damaged and unwholesome grain are ground in with flour, particularly with that kind called graham flour. Certainly hundreds, and probably thousands, of bushels of "terra alba," or white earth, are sold in our cities every year to be mixed with sugars in confectionery and other white substances. I am told by an eminent physician that this tends to produce stone, kidney complaints, and various diseases of the stomach. A Boston chemist tells me that he has found 75 per cent. of "terra alba" in what was sold as cream of tartar used for cooking. A large New York house sells three grades of cream of tartar. A Boston chemist recently analyzed a sample of the best grade, and found 50 per cent. of "terra alba" in that. Much of our confectionery contains 33 per cent. or more of "terra alba." The coloring matter of confectionery frequently contains lead, mercury, arsenic and copper. Baking-powders are widely sold which contain a large percentage of "terra alba" and alum.

It is not water alone that is mixed with milk. Thousands of gallons, and probably hundreds of thousands, are sold in our cities which have passed through large tins, or vats, in which it has been mixed with various substances. Receipts for the mixture can be bought by new milkmen from old, on payment of the required sum. I am assured, on what I believe to be reliable authority, that thousands of gallons of so-called milk have been, and probably are, sold in this city which do not contain one drop of the genuine article. Large quantities of the meats of animals more or less diseased are sold in our markets. Cows in the neighborhood of our large cities are fed upon material which produces a large flow of unwholesome milk. Poultry are fed upon material which produces unwholesome eggs. Meats and fish are made unwholesome, frequently poisonous, by careless and cruel methods of killing. A California chemist recently analyzed many samples of whisky, purchased at different places in San Francisco. He found them adulterated with creosote, salts of copper, alum and other injurious substances. He states it, in his published report, as his opinion that there is hardly any pure whisky sold in that city. A gentleman recently purchased from a prominent Boston firm a cask of pure sherry wine for his sick wife. His wife grew worse. He had the wine analyzed, and found there was not a drop of the juice of the grape in it. An eminent medical gentleman of Boston said to me: " The adulterations of drugs and spices in this country are perfectly abominable." I say that laws should be enacted and enforced prohibiting the manufacture and sale of these poisonous and dangerous articles, under severe penalties, and compelling the manufacturers and sellers of adulterated articles to tell buyers the precise character of the adulterations.

Neither can too much be said against the candies known as " rock and rye." Upon being analyzed two pounds of the candy contained enough fusel oil for a fatal dose. A smaller quantity produces dizziness, headache, sense of falling and suffocation. This should be explained to school children and to our own. Will not some honest manufacturer arise and expose the secrets of a business that is doing untold mischief to our children?

HINTS FOR THE HOUSEHOLD.

To purify the room of unpleasant odors, pour vinegar on a hot brick or burn sugar or coffee on coals.

To remove a tight finger-ring hold hand in very cold water a few minutes and rub on soft soap.

When a coal fire gets low throw on some salt. It will help it very much.

When cooking onions set a tin-cup of vinegar on the stove and let boil and no disagreeable odor will be in the room.

Gold jewelry washed in ammonia water with a brush will look nearly equal to new. It is excellent to take grease from carpets and clothes.

To remove stains of ink, fruit, wine, mildew, etc., one tablespoon of lemon juice, one tablespoon of pure cream of tartar, one teaspoon of oxalic acid, half a pint of rain water. Wipe off with clear water any article that can not be washed, after using the mixture, or it will eat the fabric.

Borax water will heal all chapping of hands or lips and remove all stains from the hands. Dissolve the borax in hot water, bottle, keep a bowl of it weakened on the washstand; rinse your hands in it after washing.

If frying fat gets too hot, drop in two or three slices of raw potato or bread.

FELON.

Common rock salt mixed with spirits of turpentine in equal parts placed on a cloth and applied to the affected part, removing the application as often as it dries, for twenty-four hours, it is said will effect a cure.

The quickest way to relieve burns caused by fire or steam is to cover the surface with baking soda till a preparation of equal parts of linseed oil and lime water can be applied with soft cloths. For a slight burn brush over with the white of an egg and cover with a cloth spread with pure lard. To a burn resulting from lime, lye or any alkali, apply vinegar or lemon juice. Burn from an acid, oil of vitriol or aquafortis, apply water instantly and immediately follow with applications of moist earth.

Bruises.

All bruises should be immediately bathed with very hot water to prevent swelling and lessen discoloration.

Convulsions.

Convulsions are not infrequent with young children and while teething. Take off the child's clothing and immerse it to the neck in as warm water as it can bear, apply cold water to the head with a cloth, very cold. The muscles will usually relax soon, when the child should be wiped dry with hot towels, wrapped warm and placed in bed. If produced by undigested food give an emetic, if by constipation give a clyster.

Soft Bed.

Why should soft beds be considered unhealthy? Certainly they afford more comfort than hard ones. Hard beds should never be given to little children, and parents who suppose that such beds contribute to health by hardening and developing the constitutions are surely in error. Eminent physicians both here and in England concur in this opinion, and state that hard beds have often proved injurious to the shape of infants. To a weary one there is nothing restful in a hard bed. Birds and animals cover their offspring with the softest material they can obtain, and also make soft beds for them. Why not take lessons from them.

BRICK WALKS.

If you have brick walks becoming grey and mossy, scrub and scrape them clean, then sprinkle with venetian red and scour it in with a broom.

There are many dangerous household liquids, such as benzine, ether, ammonia, oxalic acid and others, which should be kept under lock and key. These are used for cleaning various articles.

ANTIDOTE FOR POISON.

A poison of any conceivable description and degree of potency which has been swallowed by accident or not, may be rendered almost instantaneously harmless by swallowing two gills of sweet oil. An individual with a very strong constitution should take twice the quantity. The oil will neutralize every form of vegetable or mineral poison with which physicians are acquainted. Follow with emetics of a teaspoon of mustard and one of salt; repeat if necessary.

ANTIDOTES FOR POISON.

If any poison is swallowed, drink immediately a half glass of tepid water with a heaping teaspoon each of salt and ground mustard. This vomits as soon as it reaches the stomach, but for fear that some of the poison may still remain, swallow the white of one or two eggs, or drink a cup of strong coffee—these two being antidotes for a greater number of poisons than any other dozen articles known, with the advantage of their always being at hand. For oil of vitriol or aquafortis, give large doses of magnesia and water. For ammonia, give vinegar freely or lemon juice. For oxalic acid, give magnesia or soda, dissolved in water, administered in large and frequently repeated doses, and some soothing drink. This is good for all acids. Acids cause great heat and sensation of burning pain from the mouth down to the stomach. For poisons of alkalies, best remedy is vinegar. For saltpeter an emetic of salt and mustard, one teaspoon of each in cup of tepid water, if not sufficient, repeat; afterward, gum arabic solution and small doses of laudanum, according to age; this should be directed by the physician: For opium or laudanum, give the mustard emetic freely, then strong coffee and acids, dash cold water on the head. Keep them in constant motion by walking, or if too weak to walk, keep them awake by shaking and slapping. They must not be allowed to sleep for ten or twelve hours; give strong coffee. For arsenic the mustard emetic, then the beaten whites of three eggs, lime water, or magnesia; but the freshly prepared hydrated oxide of iron is best, as soon as it can be procured, with directions. For corrosive sublimate, give whites of eggs freely mixed with water until free vomiting takes place, or give wheat flour and water freely. Creosote, mustard emetic and white of eggs. Belladona (night henbane), give emetics and then plenty of water and vinegar or strong lemonade. Mushrooms, when poisonous, give emetics and then plenty of vinegar and water, with doses of ether. Nitrate of silver (lunar caustic), give a strong solution of common salt and then emetics. Nux vomica, first emetics, then brandy. Tartar emetic, give large doses of tea made of galls, peruvian bark or white oak bark.

Poison Oak, Ivy, etc.

Dilute sweet spirits of nitre with the same quantity of water; apply with a cloth every ten minutes until cured. When applied immediately it seldom needs more than one application. Fine table salt in solution is an excellent remedy, also sweet oil. An excellent antidote is to take a handful of quick lime, dissolve in water, let stand for an hour, then paint the poisoned places with it. Three or four applications will cure. All poisonous stings can be instantly arrested, by the application of equal parts of common salt and bicarbonate of soda, well rubbed in on the places bitten or stung.

The Only Antidote for Whisky and Tobacco.

Look at all its evils, ask God's help; make a firm resolution to use it no more and keep it.

Whitewash That Will Not Rub Off.

To half a pail of lime and water, take half a pint of flour, make a starch of it and stir it in well.

To Mend China.

Take liquid glue and stir into it plaster of paris until the mixture is of proper consistency. Rub the edges well, tie it tightly for three days, or hold it, pressing firmly till dry.

The Best Washing Fluid

2½ pounds sal soda   ½ pound borax
¼ pound lime unslacked   2 ounces salts of tartar
1½ ounces liquid ammonia 4 gallons cold water

Dissolve the soda and borax in two quarts of hot water. Settle and when clear pour it off carefully. Pour the solution together and the cold water.

Keep it in keg. The night before washing, take six tablespoons to four pails warm water; put in clothes, soak over night; next morning add hot water enough to wash the clothes with good soap suds. Boil the clothes ten minutes, and wash as usual. One trial of this fluid will show its good effects.

To Clean Black Kid Gloves.

Put a few drops of black ink to a teaspoon of sweet oil, rub in with small cloth and dry in the sun.

To Clean Gloves.

Gloves slightly soiled can be cleaned by placing glove on hand, wet a piece clean flannel with benzine, and wipe the stained part very lightly and carefully. Do not rub but wipe it gently from the tips of the fingers toward the wrist.

A ripe tomato will remove ink stains from the hands or from paper or linen.

Grass Stains on White Goods.

Wet the fabric in suds and some soda in it, let stand half an hour, and wash.

To Wash Lawn, Muslin or any Color that Fades.

Bring to a boil four quarts of bran-middlings, in two pails of water, strain and mix in water, wash, using no soap, put a little of the bran water in rinsing water, you need no starch. Rip skirt from waist and all gathers.

To Renew Wrinkled Crape.

Cover a board about twelve inches wide with cloth, stretch the crape on it round and round perfectly smooth and tight. Hold it over boiling water, shifting as the steam penetrates it. Lay a heavy weight on it to dry. If a good quality of crape, it will look as good as new.

To Starch Black Dresses.

Add a cup of strong coffee to very weak starch.

To Clean Black Cashmere Goods.

Let soak over night in luke warm strong borax water. Squeeze it through the hands as you would yarn; then take out and hang on line to drip, when nearly dry, press on wrong side. Do not rinse or wring.

Ammonia water is good to renovate a black chip hat. One teaspoon, to one pint cold water.

To Clean Chamois Skins.

Put to soak for two hours in warm water, with a little soda and soft soap suds. Then wash, and rinse it well in a weak solution of soda and hard soap in warm water. It must not be put in clear water as it makes it hard.

Striped or Colored Table Linen.

Wash in borax water, put two tablespoons of salt in rinsing water.

Lace Curtains.

Soak over night in warm soap suds, squeeze through two waters; boil in weak borax water, suds and rinse, handle very carefully, do not wring but only squeeze. Starch, pin sheets on carpet and pin the curtains down or dry them on curtain frames. Wring out of starch with clothes-wringer.

To Wash White Flannels.

A good laundress will wash flannels with warm water and hard soap without shrinking. Use one-fourth of a cake of hard soap (shave it up and dissolve in hot water the night previous) to three pails of hot water. Put some of this suds in rinsing water after dissolving two tablespoons of powdered borax in both waters. Clear water leaves the flannels hard. Wring very dry; shake, pull and stretch well. Press them when dry.

How to Relieve Rheumatism.

Put away sheets and counterpane and sleep in blankets, under and over. The sheets and cotton spread do a great deal of mischief. The cotton keeps the sour heat and perspiration from the body in the bed, and so you breathe poisoned air all night, summer and winter, which makes the rheumatism worse. Blankets do not absorb the perspiration. *Selected.*

Relief for Burning Feet.

First discard tight boots; then take one pint of bran and one ounce of bi-carbonate of soda and put it in the foot-bath with one gallon of hot water. When cool enough, soak your feet in this mixture for fifteen minutes; then rub off well all the dead skin. Repeat this, until cured, every other night for eight or ten times. After the first bath the same water will do for three times. The burning sensation is produced by the pores of the skin being closed so that the feet do not perspire.

Asthma.

Take one-half ounce of hydrate potassa, put it into a pint of water, and take a teaspoon two or three times a day. *Viola.*

Piles. $1,000 Reward

For any case of blind, bleeding or itching piles that DeBing's pile remedy fails to cure. It has cured cases of twenty years standing. Try it, and get rid of the most troublesome disease flesh is heir to. Laboratory 142 Franklin street, Baltimore, Md.

Malady of the Stomach.

The wife of Pere Hyacinthe, in her counsel and encouragement to the women workers in the temperance work says, "The great American malady is the malady of the stomach. Bear in mind this fact, that the appetite for drink is not necessarily made by drinking, but in nine cases out of ten it is created and cultivated at your tables—in the children by the use of strong tea and coffee, or pepper, pickles, mustard, spices, too much salt pork, hot bread and pastry, raw meat and grease, and above all by the use of tobacco. The cry of a depraved appetite, an inflamed stomach, is always for something stronger. In short reform your tables if you would reform your drunkards and save your sons." When people feel the need of an acid, if they would let vinegar alone and use lemonade or apples they would feel as well satisfied and receive no injury.

Earache.

Children frequently suffer greatly with earache. I would not advise dropping anything into the ear, as I have known of one person who lost entirely the hearing of that ear for life. Tobacco smoke will often afford great relief. Fill the bowl of a pipe half full of fine tobacco, place a piece of thin muslin over the bowl, insert the stem or hold it to the ear and blow in the smoke, or if you are where you can obtain it, place a piece of cotton wool saturated with chloroform in the bowl of a pipe and blow gently, holding the stem in the ear; the evaporating chloroform will relieve the pain immediately. Then apply at once a bag of hops wet or moistened with very hot water to the ear; bind it on and cover them warm in bed. Put the hops in sheer muslin, and you will sleep all night. If there are no hops, roast onions, put in thin bag and bind on hot.

How to Take out a Cancer.

A Milwaukee paper states that some eight years ago Mr. T. B. Mason, of that city, ascertained that he had a cancer on his face the size of a pin. It was cut out by Dr. Wolcott, and the wound partially healed. Subsequently it grew again, and while he was in Cincinnati on business, it attained the size of a hickory nut. He remained there under treatment and is now perfectly cured. The process is this: A piece of sticking plaster was put over the cancer, with a circular piece cut out of the center a little larger than the cancer, so that the cancer and a small circular rim of the healthy skin next to it were exposed. Then a plaster made of chloride of zinc, bloodroot, and wheat flour was spread on a piece of muslin, the size of this circular opening, and applied to the cancer for twenty-four hours. On removing it, the cancer will be found burst into and appear of the color and hardness of an old shoe sole, and the circular rim outside of it will appear white and parboiled, as if scalded by hot steam. The wound is now dressed, and the outside rim soon separates, and the cancer comes out in a hard lump, and the place heals up. The plaster kills the cancer, so that it sloughs out like dead flesh, and never grows again. This remedy was discovered by Dr. Fell, of London, and has been used by him many years with unfailing success, and not a case has been known of the reappearance of the cancer when this remedy has been applied. Note:—As the quantities are not given it would be best to consult a good physician and he give you the proportions, and care for it till it is healed. Keep still till healed. See cure for wounds. Perhaps this is painful. Let the doctor take charge.

For Tape Worm.

First be sure you have one, as pieces will pass from you, which is the surest evidence. Fast, and eat nothing for twenty-four hours. Then take a pint of shelled pumpkin seeds, chop fine, and mix in common molasses enough to make it eatable, eat it all at once. Twelve hours after, take one and a half tablespoons of castor oil. Eat nothing till the oil operates, except a little coffee once or twice with two mouthfuls of bread. This will cost a struggle of two days; eat lightly after it, at first. Two cases are positively known to have been cured by this process.

Frozen Hands or Feet.

Put them in very cold water or rub them with snow. Frozen ears also.

Tar Cordial.

Is excellent for a cough.

Water Bugs and Roaches.

Powdered borax sprinkled on the floor or in the chinks which they frequent, is said to clear them out. If it does not, hellebore will; mix it with double the quantity of oat meal, adding a little sugar, strew it where they run, but take it up in the morning, if children or servants are around, and put it down at night again, as it is a deadly poison.

To Rid a House of Punkies.

If two or three little dishes of household ammonia are set in their places of resort, they will soon leave.

Flies.

The only way to keep out flies, is to have window and door screens, darken the room from nine A. M. to five P. M. and have no eatables or smells around.

Moths.

I have for many years used camphor gum as a preventive against moths, and it has never failed, either in furs, woolens or feathers. All goods must be shook and brushed clean from all dust, all spots cleaned. Cover all goods with newspapers, putting in each package a piece of camphor (cutting it in squares) as large as a large hickory nut in each package and one in each end of trunk or box, doing it up tightly in paper. This will last all summer. Everything else has failed.

Buffalo Moths.

The state entomologist recommends benzine for the extirpation of the grub, which usually begins its ravages in the middle of April. It is a hairy worm-like larvae scarcely half an inch long, which easily hides in the fuzz of the carpet, or in any woolen article, or even in trunks. The beetle is never found about the house except during the short period when it is laying its eggs in summer. It feeds on the pollen of the spirea and other plants and never touches carpets. The grub alone feeds on carpets, woolens, furs, etc.

Black Ants.

Crush them as fast as you can just as you find them and let them lie just where you killed them, the next morning you will look in vain for their carcasses, as during the night their brethren have carried them off. They will not return to that city of destruction again for the summer, perhaps never.

Creeping Charlie.

To arrange "creeping Charlie" to grow luxuriantly in a vase, place some broken pieces of charcoal in the bottom of vase, with some beach sand on it to the depth of two inches; place the stems of the plant in this sand and fill the vase with water. Set it in the coolest corner of the room.

Pressing Leaves and Flowers.

Always press flowers between soft papers such as newspapers, as soon as possible after picking. Stiff paper will not absorb the dampness; open them every day to dry and see that they are not shoved any.

PLANTS.

Plants that you desire for the house for the winter, should be slipped in the summer for potting in the middle of September. Small pots are best for blooming. Put in rich soil, with powdered charcoal mixed in the soil will give rich dark green leaves and brilliant coloring to the flowers. Pot the plants in September and bring them in about two weeks before requiring fires. Use liquid manure, very weak, once a week. Stirring the top soil once a week is very good especially for roses. Plants are very much like children, will thrive and reward us according to the loving tender care they receive, or the abuse and neglect. Plants packed away in cellars that are quite dark will require very little water once a week, according to dryness of cellar. Do not allow gas to escape in the cellar, as it is dangerous both to plants and people.

Wall Roses.

Make a two feet deep border of strong loam, four or five feet wide, to be as rich as rotten manure can make it; the border to be thoroughly soaked with soft water twice a week in dry weather, and when the roses are in bloom, to keep them thin in the branches as if they were peach trees and to play the water engine against them as for a house on fire, from the first appearance of insects till no more come. There is a reason for everything under the sun, and the reason for insects attacking roses in general and those on walls more particularly, is from too much dryness at the roots causing the juices to be more palatable through the action of the leaves.

Worms at the Roots of Plants.

Sprinkle soot over the top of the ground around them. For angle worms in house plants insert in the mold a long sharp hair pin or wire, and then pour lime water upon the soil, it will cause the worms to come to the top and crawl off.

For Insects on Rose Bushes and Small Fruits.

To destroy the insects strew the ground around them with air slacked lime under the bushes in early spring.

Currant Worms.

Take one large teacup of powdered white hellebore, at the first appearance of the worms, to a pail of warm water and syringe with it. This will kill the worms all off, but in ten days another lot will be hatched out, which should be dealt with as before. I have used this ever since the worm appeared and it has never failed.

Carbolic Acid for Insects.

Obtain crude carbolic acid, use it in this form because it is stronger and better for the purpose and costs, but very little. Two or three tablespoons of acid to a quart of domestic soft soap may first be tried. Stir well together, and let stand for a few hours. Then test the compound by mixing a little of it with soft water. If too much acid, oily particles of carbolic acid will be floating on the surface. More soap should be added to balance the excess of acid. Some soaps are stronger than others, so no definite rule can be given. Make as strong with acid as the soap will perfectly cut. The refined acid may be used when the crude is not at hand. When prepared as above, make a moderately strong suds and apply with syringe, or turn up the bush and sprinkle with a broom. In using on delicate plants, make it weaker and rinse off after a few minutes.

Grape Mildew and Curculio.

To one part sulphur add two parts lime unslacked with about two thousand times their bulk of boiling water. Let it stand forty-eight hours, draw off the clear liquor and apply with a common garden pump.

The Apple Worm.

After the worm has entered the fruit and accomplished its damage, the time arrives when it has to leave the fruit and hide itself in a quiet secure position to undergo the transition from the larva to the pupa state, which requires, in the early part of the season, eight or ten days; after this time the miller is hatched and is again ready to besiege the fruit with its sting.

The insect being two-brooded at least, if not disturbed, has an increased force to do mischief the second time. The progeny for the succeeding year have alone to depend on the security of this second generation of larvæ. They may often be found under the outside bark of apple trees during winter. This bark should be thoroughly scraped off and washed in strong soft-soap suds. Sprinkle the ground under the tree with wood-ashes and then sprinkle this with water enough to wet the ashes. Last of June, wrap around the trees woolen rags about four inches wide, dip in either of the above preparations, or wet with hellebore fluid, as directed, for currant worms. Every few days examine the trees, and destroy the worms secreted under the woolen cloth and carefully picking up and destroying all dropped apples, for the rest of the summer. This is an effective remedy, but it will require your utmost diligence.

RED ANTS.

Have plenty of swing shelves in pantry and cellar. Place sugar boxes, cereals and every thing eatable or sweet upon them. Wash off the shelves where you find them with strong spirits of camphor. Place lumps of camphor in corners and occasionally on shelf. But to keep them from the floor, put coarse salt two inches deep and three inches wide next to the mop-board. This I have found very effectual. I have found little dishes of chloride of lime set around in addition, good, for sometimes they seem desperate and then we have to be very thorough too. Everything must be very clean; not a crumb dropped around.

Ants Black and Red.

"Having had years of trial with ants, both black and red, we lighted upon the following remedy, which with us has worked like magic. One tablespoon of tartar emetic, one tablespoon sugar, mixed into a thin syrup with water as it evaporates or is carried off, add ingredients as needed. When the water dries up, fill up again; the emetic will last a long time. A sicker lot of pests it would be hard to find. Whether they impart the results to the home firm, or whether all are killed, I trow not; certain it is they do not pay us a second visit."

Another to drive away red ants:—One pint of tar in two quarts of hot water, put in earthen dishes or tin covers and set where their haunts are. Some say powdered borax sprinkled around will drive away all kinds of insects. I find dry sulphur the best. Spread it on shelf.

To Drive off Rats and Mice.

Rats will leave the premises if wet chloride of lime is spread where they run, and around and in their holes. Tar is good.

Another for rats and mice:—Two parts well bruised squills, three parts of finely chopped bacon, corn meal to thicken. Roll thin and bake in small cakes. Place where they run. Sure thing.

Bed Bugs.

The only certain cure for bedbugs is a solution of corrosive sublimate, put into the cracks and crevices, after the bedstead is thoroughly washed and scalded, where you can. If they are in the walls, smoke with brimstone. Examine often and repeat the process every week if necessary. This is a deadly poison, therefore keep it locked up, away from servants and children.

A Useful Cement.

A good cement for mending almost anything, made by mixing together litharge and glycerine to the consistency of fresh putty. This cement is useful for mending stone jars, or any coarse earthenware, stopping leaks in seams of tin pans, washboilers, cracks or holes in iron kettles, to tighten loose boxes in wagon hubs, etc. The article mended should stand a few days to harden.

Suggestions about House Plants and Insects.

The calla lily blooms at three years, in the early spring. Take an ordinary earthen one-gallon, or more, jar, without a hole in the bottom, fill the jar within one inch from top with rich earth, in the fall, taking off all extra bulbs and rootlets, press the soil firmly around. The first of January bring them out of cellar and fill full every other day with quite warm water. A few drops of ammonia in the water will hasten their blooming. Give plenty of water, and as much light and sun as possible. In California they only bloom during the winter months; always outdoors in the coldest rains. The pots should be set in a shady corner during the months of June and July and be given no water except that which falls from the clouds. The English or German ivy will grow nicely if put in a bottle of water.

Bulbs.

Hyacinth bulbs can be planted the last of August, or tulips, after having been up out of ground in a dry place for two months. For house bloom plant in pots, or place in water in hyacinth glasses. Set in dark, dry place for two or three weeks, then give them plenty of light and warm water, and they will soon bloom. Tulips, narcissus, crocus, can be treated in the same way.

Scarlet Amaryllis.

These should be potted the first of March, in quite a small pot; break off about half the rootlets, and all the new bulbs. After flowering the bulb may remain in pot until the following spring, and should be kept pretty cool and not very moist.

Lady Slippers.

Collect seeds from center stalks only of double ladyslippers to make them double next year.

Training of Grape Vine.

As the method or plan of training the vine has much to do with the way it is pruned or trimmed I will say that our style is a modified Fuller process. We, the first year, run up one cane, the second year we run up two, which in the fall we cut back to two or three eyes, each above the surface of the soil. The following season we let only two canes grow, fruiting them this year. We use poles or stakes up to the fall of this year or the early spring following, when we put up our trellis of three wires, the first one eighteen inches from the ground, and the others twelve or fourteen inches apart. The two canes of last year are now made to act as arms, thus ———, they being wound around and tied to the lower wire. We now let all the shoots grow, pinching back every other one to the second wire. In the fall the longest ones, or those permitted to grow unchecked, are cut back to within two eyes of the arm, and the others permitted to grow unchecked the following season as far as the top of the wires. One cane is also permitted to grow from each cane which was cut back, these being for the fruiting canes the following year—the others being cut back in the fall to two eyes, the same as the other canes the preceding fall. If the vine be very short jointed we have found that fruiting canes from every other eye was too much of a drain upon the vine, especially with young vines, and we then use only every third eye; or, to make it still more plain, we try to leave from four to six inches of space between the fruiting canes.

About every fourth or fifth year we have found it to be a good plan to renew the arms, which is readily done by permitting a young shoot to grow near the base of the vine on each side for one or two seasons before it is wanted, when the old arm is cut away and the young one substituted.

Cleaning Silver or Metal.

Camphene oil and rotten stone give a far brighter polish than can be obtained by the use of other powders. Camphene is used in producing the exquisite polish of the photo plates. Nothing has been found to equal it.

A Few Suggestions.

Every good housekeeper knows the advantage of an early start in the morning, after having everything prepared to make a quick fire, and the breakfast planned the day before.

After breakfast always plan for the next three meals.

Monday morning, plan the work for the week as far as is necessary. Usually Monday is wash day.

Tuesday is ironing.

Wednesday for sweeping and dusting.

Thursday, see that everything is washed up and refilled, such as sugar bowl, salt dishes, etc.

Friday, clean pantry, cupboards and kitchen.

Saturday, baking for the week, and prepare, as far as possible, for Sunday dinner.

Of course, many other things will step in and demand the attention, and all has to be done in time and anticipated, thereby avoiding much worry and confusion.

Study your cook book as you would any other lesson, not only just as it is wanted, but at leisure moments.

Keep all the groceries, cereals, etc., in glass or tin cans, covered tight.

Always keep a supply of rolled cracker on hand, rolling the broken ones; keep in covered jar.

It is best to have everything ready for use when wanted; therefore, everything should be perfectly clean when put away.

Always use a wooden spoon to stir all kinds of fruits and tomatoes while cooking.

Never throw water on burning oil (as it spreads it); throw on flour, ashes or earth.

Keep gasoline, kerosene and coal oil cans in the wood-house, and not near any food.

If your clothes take fire do not run about, or out of doors; if you can not slip them off quickly; get the nearest woolen goods, such as a shawl, blanket or carpet, overcoat, or anything to wrap around you, and roll on the floor to extinguish the flames.

Use crash for dish towels or dish cloths.

Always provide yourselves with little conveniences for working, such as holders, brushes, etc. Keep a stick with a strip of cotton cloth tied on the end of it to butter the baking pans. Use salt pork for griddle greasers.

Purchase only the quantity of sweet potatoes you can use in a week, as they do not keep long. Do not purchase more than you can use before it spoils; you will soon learn the bill of fare if you really desire to be a helpmeet.

Keep house on a cash basis and do not purchase unless you can pay down.

When going to housekeeping purchase steel silver-plated knives, as they are sharper than the white metal.

Pieces of bread should be dried in heater, grated, and kept in tight jar ready for puddings or croquettes. With a little care there will not be many.

Clean bottles with shot, soap and ashes; clean the shot for next time.

Use spirits of camphor to take out fresh paint, but if dried on persevere with spirits of turpentine.

To clean steel knives, cut a raw potato in two, and dip in brick-dust, rub hard.

Take one teaspoon of spirits of ammonia to one cup of hot water, to clean coat collars, woolen goods, rusty silk, or spots on carpet. Good to clean silver.

Never put new papering over old. It is very easily taken off by putting two or three pails of boiling hot water in the closed room, as often as it stops steaming, till it will peel off; perhaps two days or more. Where it does not peel off easily take a pail of hot water soak paper with a cloth and scrape the wall clear of paste with a sharp scraper till perfectly smooth.

Every farmer should purchase a reliable recipe book for his wife's next birthday, or for Christmas—which ever comes first—that his table may be furnished with nourishing food, and in such a variety as to satisfy the cravings of nature. What is lacking at the daily table is sometimes made up out of the stimulus of tobacco and whisky. Farmers should provide all kinds of fresh meats, vegetables, fruits, milk, butter, eggs and cereals for their own table and then raise to sell. Do not save them only for company. Man or woman can not work with profit more than ten hours a day. What is needed on the farm, next to plenty of sleep, is plenty of food and a variety on the table at all three of its spreads. Good sweet bread, meat, fruit, unskimmed new milk, should be eaten as appetite desires, and not salt meat and fried potatoes, or boiled with the skins on, three times a day. Under the influence of good food and sleep, and the ten-hour law, our skeleton boys and girls, whose lives are on the farm, would put on flesh and the bloom of youth, and would have some light in their eyes and some happiness in their hearts. Does not the farmer's wife need help in the kitchen, as well as help on the farm? An over wearied body can not keep up a cheerful heart.

Ignorant mistresses make poor servants and receive poor service from what would be good material if properly directed.

While princesses are taught the rules of cooking and dressmaking and to know how long it takes a woman and a broom to sweep and dust a room, there are many daughters in our country who have felt it beneath them to learn the necessary duties of life, and when married have not known whether they were requiring impossibilities of their one servant or otherwise. There are so many helps nowadays that no beginner need be discouraged if she keeps patience and perseverance at her side. A cook, if such a person has any inherent capacity, can be made a good cook only by an intelligent mistress. Good health in our homes is more to be considered than sumptuous upholstery, elegant dinners or expensive table service. A beautiful home is a comfortable one. The condition of the mind has more influence upon the bodily health than is generally supposed. It is no doubt true that diseases of the body cause a depressing and morbid condition of the mind, but it is no less true that sorrowful and disagreeable emotions produce disease in persons who, uninfluenced by them, would be in sound health. Or, if disease is not produced, the functions are disordered. Agreeable emotions set in motion nervous currents which stimulate the blood, brain and every part of the system into healthful activity; while grief, disappointment of feeling and brooding over present sorrows or past mistakes depress all vital forces. To be physically well one must in general be happy. The reverse is not always true. One may be happy and cheerful and yet be a constant sufferer in body. Let us all see that we have the free sunshine of the soul in our homes.

We and our children, as well as all plant life, need the full light of the sun to shine upon us daily, and its subtle tonic has a wonderful curative influence upon both our physical and mental ailments. It pierces into the secret corners, deodorizes the foul places, kills disease germs and brings life, health and joy on its beams. Let us have the lovely dancing sunlight in our homes.

Let fresh air from the outside find access in all the sleeping rooms all the year round (except when down to zero). I believe there are many early graves from breathing foul air at night that has been breathed over and over again. How weak and languid one feels after sleeping in a closed room. Pure air and sunlight go far toward the making of the perfect man, but their action must be supplemented by that of plain, nutritious food to attain the best results. With more simplicity in our homes there would be fewer tired, anxious faces. I will give you a sample of the table for one day of an intelligent lady that did her own work except the washing and scrubbing.

Breakfast—White and graham bread, cold meat, fruit, coffee.

Dinner—Meat, potatoes, one other vegetable, fruit or a very simple baked pudding.

Tea—Bread of both kinds, fruit, cocoa.

The problem of how to " make both ends meet " is a serious one in most of households. Two things are very essential in the management of small resources, either of strength or of means; one should be very careful not to overdraw on either, and it is very necessary to cultivate the faculty of making the best use possible of what one has—to cling to the essential and leave the non-essentials till a convenient time.

Industry and economy are both as essential in housekeeping as in any other department of life. Economy is simply the art of gathering up all the fragments so that nothing be lost, fragments of time as well as of material. Nothing should be thrown away so long as it is possible to make use of it. For example: Save in a box all the twine that comes around the packages for the house. Fold up also all the good wrapping paper and keep in a box or drawer, also all the good paper bags; they will all be found useful.

When about to furnish a home, purchase as few things as possible, as it is only by experience that one can tell what will be the needs of that home. It is wise to keep an account of all one spends; this answers a double purpose, as it enables one to know whether he is living within his income, and it is also good for reference.

No false pride or foolish ambition to appear just like some one else, should ever tempt us to live quite up to our income. To lay up one-sixth or one-tenth for an emergency is a good rule. "Economy is a poor man's revenue; extravagance a rich man's ruin." True economy is not covetousness, or parsimoniousness, which is the ruin of many an otherwise happy family.

A penurious person is not a happy one, and he is always afraid others will be happy; when his children grow up, he may meet with no penurious reward, if brought up without the love of God in their hearts.

Your child is not your child in the sense which it is commonly thought to be. It is not only connected with your life but with an older and wider life back of yours. The child is not only the outgrowth of its father's and mother's life, but is the latest manifestation of a larger and wider life which circles through the arteries of society. A recognition of these facts will lead to the conclusion that your child is not a gift, but a loan to you, to instruct, counsel and polish for the Giver of Life. We are to consider that each child has an individuality of its own, different from any child that ever before existed, and our duty is to bring out its best capacities. "Oh, banish the tears of children! Continual rains upon the blossoms are hurtful." It is a great defect in parents not to be able to govern themselves. Here "let patience have its perfect work." Do not punish children merely because you have the power. Scold never. Do not punish cruelly.

We are glad to see that whipping, both in schools and at home, is being done away with by the most cultivated and enlightened class of people. Do not be impatient with a child because it made a mistake or met with an accident, but encourage them to try again. Mistakes are often our best teachers and developers. Let the child understand this, that it be not discouraged. Is not the average child made to feel that a mistake is the worst thing that could happen to him? This is a great fallacy. Does a mother require an infant to perform the feat of walking alone till he has learned through many failures? Or what teacher would expect his pupil to learn to read or to write without making a mistake? The honest effort should be approved and encouragement given that will surely meet with success.

Children need outdoor plays and work. Give them a little garden of their own to care for and let them help you or think they do, and take an interest in all things that you are interested in; they can lend a helping hand in the dooryard or trimming up the dead or wayward branches of the shrubbery. Let them feel a sense of responsibility and proprietorship, which will add to their enjoyment in their work, as it stimulates their industry, care and self-reliance. Do not crowd the children's minds with too many studies. A daily bath for children at night in hot weather is quite essential to good health. Always brush the children's teeth after supper.

The Medicinal Value of Water.

The human body is constantly undergoing tissue change. Worn-out particles are cast aside and eliminated from the system, while the new are ever being formed, from the inception of life to its close.

Water has the power of increasing these tissue changes, which multiplies the waste products, but at the same time they are renewed by its agency, giving rise to increased appetite, which in turn provides fresh nutriment. Persons but little accustomed to drinking water are liable to have the waste products formed faster than they are removed. Any obstruction to the free working of natural laws at once produces disease, which, if once firmly seated, requires both time and money to cure.

People accustomed to rise in the morning weak and languid will find the cause in the imperfect secretion of wastes, which many times may be remedied by drinking a full tumbler of water before retiring. This very materially assists in the process during the night, and leaves the tissues fresh and strong, ready for the active work of the day.

To drink hot water is one of our best remedial agents.

A hot bath on going to bed, even in the hot nights of summer, is a better reliever of insomnia than many drugs.

Inflamed parts will subside under the continual poulticing of real hot water.

Very hot water, as we all know, is a prompt checker of bleeding, and besides, if it is clean, as it should be, it aids in sterlizing wounds.

Hall's Journal of Health.

There must ever be sympathy of occupation between the united heads of the household. The wife must not feel that the husband has had no struggles at the store, office, or shop; also the husband must realize that the wife has had to endure many disappointments through the day and only half the work is accomplished that she anticipated. Let a note of sympathy or a helping hand be extended to each other, ever observing the small courtesies of life in your daily intercourse. Your gains are one, your interests are one, your losses are one; lay hold of the work of life cheerfully, with two heads to plan, four hands to work, four eyes to watch, four shoulders on which shall rest its joys or trials. Every woman should have a thorough knowledge of the chemistry of foods and cooking, in order to understand the composition of substances, and the changes which they undergo, and also of dietetics to regulate the kind and quantity to be eaten. One who has studied the question for years says: "Not only the age and occupation, but also the individuality of the person play an important part in the regulation of diet, and decide not only the quantity but also the kind of food, and the form in which it is to be taken. For the proper assimilation of the nourishment and its complete effect in the organism, the food must be agreeable; it must relish. A supply of needed nourishment is not enough, man requires yet more. He must find his food pleasing to the taste. The boiling and roasting of food materials are operations which we find only among civilized people, and they have been developed with the advance of civilization. The whole art of cooking amounts to this: So to prepare food that it will best sustain a healthy, vigorous life." *Dr. J. Konig, Berlin.*

"The nutrition of the animal body, that is, the assimilation of the food taken, is dependent upon absorption. This depends upon previous chemical processes. These processes are contingent upon the secretions, the saliva, the gastric juice, etc.; and it is a well known fact that the flow of these liquids is, to a great extent under the control of the nerves. Whatever excites the nerves pleasantly, causes an abundant secretion of the chemical agents of food change. In this fact lies the secret of modern cooking, and the judicious use of condiments or relishes."

The Chemistry of Cooking.

Petterhofer says of condiments: "I may compare them to the right use of lubricants for an engine, which indeed can not replace the steam power, but may help it to a much easier and more regular action, and besides, prevents, quite naturally, the wearing out of the machine. In order to do this, one condition is absolutely necessary: the lubricant must not attack the machine; it must be harmless."

If any are dyspeptic, let them replenish their vital energies with oxygen, by exercise in the open air. Nature will often restore itself, if it is not **clogged by ourselves**.

HINTS FOR THE TABLE.

"Entice all neatly to what they know best,
For so thou dost thyself and him a pleasure."
Geo. Herbert.

Every housekeeper, after making out her bill of fare, will endeavor, as far as is in her power, to serve it acceptably to those who sit at her table, and in a well arranged, dainty and pretty way. If one has the means, there are innumerable articles to be had for the money which beautify the table. Yet, for those whose means are limited, there are also many ways in which the table may be made altogether a delight to those who sit about it. The first requisites are clean white linen table covers and napkins, which may be adorned with a pretty center-piece, embroidered by some member of the family, on which may rest a bowl or vase of fresh garden or wild flowers, or in winter a fernery. A fernery may be made by gathering small ferns with the roots, and planting them in earth, in a metal basin, which can be placed in an outside basket of silver, celluloid, or basket-work. Something we already have on hand may answer the purpose, as a lady I know used the bottom of an old-fashioned silver castor, which made a very handsome receptacle for the basin of ferns. Doylies, platter or tray cloths, and candlesticks with colored shades also add to the completeness and adornment of the modern table. Tasteful, though inexpensive tableware, if china is not within reach, and all the eatables served in a dainty way, and in their proper course—not everything on the table at once—all tend to make a meal acceptable and enjoyable. If one does not have the opportunity of seeing the novelties brought out, or of attending a fashionable dinner or lunch party, there is so much information given in papers, periodicals and books, that one can keep well informed on the modes of the day.

> "A table full of welcome
> Makes scarce one dainty dish.
> *Shakespeare.*

Every one must make out her bill of fare according to circumstances and the season of the year. A few are given which may prove helpful and suggestive.

Breakfast Menus. No. 1.

Fruit.
Cracked Wheat   Cream and Sugar
Broiled Chicken   Potatoes, Hashed and Browned
Rolls   Coffee

Breakfast No. 2.

Peaches and Grapes
Pork Chops   Creamed Potatoes   Graham Muffins
Coffee   Griddle Cakes   Maple Syrup

Breakfast No. 3.

Steamed Hominy   Sugar and Cream
Lamb Chops   Baked Potatoes   Scrambled Eggs
Coffee

Breakfast No. 4.

Fruit.
Oat Meal   Sugar and Cream
Beef Steak   French Fried Potatoes   Boiled Eggs
Coffee   Dry Toast

Breakfast No. 5.

Melons
Cod Fish Balls   Poached Eggs   Corn Meal Muffins
Coffee

Breakfast Menu No. 6.

Canteloupe
Creamed Fish   Potatoes a la Royal   Tomatoes
Rolls   Dry Toast   Coffee

Dinner Menu No. 1.

Oysters on Half Shell
Cream of Chicken with Noodles
Boiled White Fish   Hollandaise Sauce
Small Round Potatoes
Ribs of Beef   Mashed Potatoes
Two vegetables in season
Spiced Pickles   Currant Jelly
Lettuce Salad with French Dressing
Wafers or Thin Bread and Butter
Pineapple Sherbet   Small Cakes
Coffee   Fruit   Nuts

Dinner No. 2.

Cream of Celery   Crackers
Oyster Patties   Small Rolls
Roast Turkey or Duck
Potatoes, Mashed   Two other Vegetables
Spiced Peaches   Olives   Celery
Lettuce Salad with Dressing
Plum Pudding with Foaming Sauce
Ice Cream   Cakes
Coffee

Dinner No. 3.

Mock Turtle Soup   Crackers
Steamed White Fish with Mayonnaise Dressing or Sauce Tartare
Roast Saddle of Venison   Sauce   Grape Jam
Roast Duck
Macaroni, Celery, Pickles and Vegetables
Bread and Butter
Squash or Lemon Pie   Peach Meringue
Cheese   Fruits   Nuts
Coffee

Menu for New Year's Dinner.

Tomato Soup   Crackers
Roast Goose or Duck   Mashed Potatoes
Baked Sweet Potatoes   Creamed Corn
Fried Oysters   Apple Sauce
Jelly   Celery   Pickles
Brown Bread   White Bread
Baked Indian Pudding
Ice Cream
Coffee   Mixed Nuts
Oranges.

Thanksgiving Dinner.

First Course.
Blue Points on the Half Shell   Wafers

Second Course.
Consommé
Celery   Olives   **Almonds**

Third Course.
Fish Soufflé   Puffed Potatoes

Fourth Course.
Roast Turkey   Chicken Pie   Parisienne Potatoes
Baked Sweet Potatoes
Creamed Corn or Succotash   Gooseberry Catsup
Cranberry Jam   Pickles

Fifth Course.
Lettuce Salad   Wafers

Sixth Course.
English Plum Pudding with Foaming Sauce

Seventh Course.
Mince Pie   Orange Jelly
Coffee

Eighth Course.
Fruit   Nuts   Raisins

DINNER NO. 4.

First Course.
Cream Oyster Soup with Wafers and Celery

Second Course.
Roast Beef with Browned Mashed Potatoes
Corn   Tomatoes   Peas

Third Course.
Lettuce salad with thin Bread and Butter

Fourth Course.
Pudding or Pie, or only
Ice Cream   Cakes

Fifth Course.
Coffee   **Fruit**

Lunch Menu No. 1

First Course.

Bouillon Served in Small China Cups

Second Course.

Lamb Chops   Saratoga Chips

Rolls and Bread

Third Course.

Chicken Salad with Mayonnaise Dressing

Wafers   Salted Almonds   Olives

Fourth Course.

Ice Cream   Cakes

Chocolate with Whipped Cream

Fruit

Flowers are Always Appropriate

Lunch No. 2.

First Course.

Escalloped Oysters   Baked Potatoes

Bread   Spiced Pickles   Biscuit

Second Course.

Lettuce and Egg Salad with Dressing

Third Course.

Grape Fruit Served with Chopped Ice

Cake   Coffee

Lunch No. 3.

First Course.
Bouillon Served in Small Cups

Second Course.
Fried Sweet Breads   Escalloped Potatoes
Minced Ham Sandwiches
Rolls   Celery   Olives   Pickles

Third Course.
Chicken Salad   Wafers

Fourth Course.
Peach Sherbet   Mixed Cake
Coffee   Chocolate with Whipped Cream
Fruit and Flowers

Supper Menu.

First Course.
White Fish, a la Creme
Served in individual shells

Second Course.
Sweet Breads   French Peas
Julienne Potatoes   Bread and Rolls
Cheese Straws.   Olives   Pickles

Third Course.
Chocolate Blanc Mange with Whipped Cream
Cake   Coffee   Cocoa

In the season the combination of vanilla blanc mange with fresh raspberries and whipped cream is delicious. Other fruits may be substituted in their season.

Allowance of Supplies for an Evening Entertainment.

It is usually safe to provide for only about two-thirds out of every hundred invited. Allow one quart of oysters for four persons present; six white chickens, a ten or twelve pound turkey, and twenty heads of celery for chicken salad, are enough for fifty guests; one gallon of ice cream to every twenty guests; one hundred sandwiches for sixty guests.

TABLE OF WEIGHTS AND MEASURES.

2 heaping teaspoons = 1 heaping tablespoon.
2 teaspoons of liquid = 1 tablespoon.
5 tablespoons of liquid = 1 gill.
2 tablespoons of liquid = 1 ounce.
4 gills = 1 pint.
1 small coffeecup = ½ pint.
4 cups flour = 1 quart.
1 heaping quart flour = 1 pound.
2 rounded tablespoons flour = 1 ounce.
1½ pints corn meal = 1 pound.
3 cups corn meal = 1 pound.
1 cup butter = ½ pound.
1 pint butter = 1 pound.
Butter the size of an egg = 2 ounces.
1 rounded tablespoon of butter = 1 ounce.
1 pint chopped meat = 1 pound.
10 eggs = 1 pound.
1 pint coffee sugar = 1 pound.
2 cups coffee sugar = 1 pound
2½ cups powdered sugar = 1 pound.
1 heaping pint brown sugar = 1 pound.

Dry Measure.

16 ounces make 1 pound   2 pints make 1 quart
4 gills make 1 pint   4 quarts make 1 gallon.

Long Measure.

12 inches make 1 foot   3 feet 1 yard
5½ yards make 1 rod   4 rods make 1 furlong
320 rods make 1 mile.

To Keep Mold from Jell.

After turning the jell into glasses, and it is cooled, butter the top of the paper placed over the jell.

INDEX.

*The asterisks designate favorite recipes of the author.

Accidents, In Case of	274	Stuffed Roast	54
Adulterations, or What People Eat	277-279	Tea for Invalids, No. 1	57
		Tea for Invalids, No. 2	57
Alum, Is Alum Poisonous.	276	*A Nice Brine to Pickle	58
Amarylis, Scarlet	299	Beets, Baked	119
Ants, Black	292	Boiled	119
Ants, Red	296, 297	For Winter	120
Apple Sauce	130, 221	Biscuit, *Baking powder	16
Apple Worm	295	Bread	21
Asparagus on Toast	123	Cream	17
Asthma	238	Egg	25
Beans, Lima	122	Maryland	24
Pickled	123	Raised Tea	18
*Boston Baked	122	Bread and Biscuit	9, 10
Bed Bugs	297	*Bottled Yeast, for	11
Bed, Soft	281	Baked Graham	13
Beef Balls	58	Boston Brown	13, 14
Cakes—Raw	58	Corn for Breakfast	21
Cold Pressed	58	Corn Bread	22
Cooked Dried	56	Corn	19
Corn Hash	56	Graham without Yeast	14
Croquettes	53	Rye Baked	13
Boiled Soup Bone		Rye and Indian	12
Broiled Steak	52	For the Sea	12
A Flank of	53	Salt Rising	11
Fillet of	50	*Without a Sponge	240
Fresh Hashes	56	Wheat and Indian	21
Loaf	54	Brain	249
Meat Pie	55	Bruises	281
à la Mode	51	Bulbs	299
Roast, With Yorkshire Pudding	49	Burns	257, 258, 280
		Butter, To Make	241
To Fry a Round or Tough Steak	53	Cake, Mixing	189
		*Almond	200
Scalloped Meats	54	Almonds, To Blanch	200
Scraped for Sandwiches	57	Angel's Food	204, 205
		Chocolate	201
Spiced	55	*Cocoanut	201

*Confectionery 193
Cup 198, 203
Delicate 196
*Delicate 196
Delicate 196, 200
Dried Apple 195
One Egg 206
*Fruit 192
Fruit, Plain 193
Fruit, Rich 193
Fruit, Good 194
Fruit, Very Nice 194
Fruit, White 195
Gold 204
Ice Cream 200
Imperial 194
*Loaf 192, 197
Molasses 206
*White Mountain 201
*Pound 198
Queen's 203
Silver 204
Sunshine 206
Sponge 198, 199
*Sponge Cake Cream
    Pie 142, 204
Layer Cakes.
Washington 202
Dark 203
Fig Layer 197
Hickory Nut 196
Lemon or Orange Jelly 202
Light Marble Layer . . 203
*Icing for 207
Icing, Boiled 207
Rule for Frosting 207
*Chocolate and Cocoa-
    nut Jumbles 211
*Ginger Snaps 210
Baker Cookies 212
Ginger Cookies 210
Sugared Cookies 211
New England Cookies 211
Gingerbread, Soft and
    Hard 208, 209
Cream Shortcake 23
*Orange Shortcake . 24, 173
*Strawberry Short-
    cake 24, 174

Fried 28
Crullers 211
Doughnuts, Queen of 28
Raised, Fried 29
*Bread, Griddle 23
Rice, Griddle 23
Buckwheat 22
Flour, Griddle 23
Sweet Corn, Griddle . . 23
Cabbage, Cooking 125
    Dressing 101, 126
    Salad 233
Canaries, Care of 247
Cancer, To Take Out 289
Candy, How to Pull 237
    Chocolate Caramels . . . 238
    Cream Chocolates 238
    Fig 237
    Ice Cream 178, 236
    Molasses 238, 177
    Of Any Flavor 178
    Pea Nut 238
    Walnut 230
Canning Fruits 212
    Apple 214
    Citron, Melon, Pre-
        served 220
    Peaches 215
    Pears 216
    Pineapple 219, 220
    Plums 216, 217
    Quinces 217
    Raspberries 218
    Tomatoes 220
    Strawberries 218
Carving 239
Carrots, Boiled and Fried. 121
Catarrh and Catarrh Snuff 260
Catsup *Gooseberry 233
    Tomato 233
    Cold 234
Cauliflower, Boiled 124
Celery and Radishes 125
Celery Care of 243
Cement, a Useful 298
Cheese Straws 237, 128
    Toasted 128
Chicken, Boiled or
    Steamed 66, 67

Index

Broiled Spring....... 67
Creamed............. 68
Croquettes........... 70
Forcemeat........... 78
Fricassee, White and Brown.............. 68
Fried................. 68
Jellied............... 62
*and Oyster Croquettes............. 71
*Pot Pie.............. 69
*Pie Baked........... 69
Roast................ 67
Salad, No. 1 and Dressing................69, 70
Tender............... 71
Chamois Skin, to Clean... 286
Chilblains, to Cure........ 257
Choked, if.............. 275
China, to Mend.......... 284
Cocoa.................. 31
Coffee................. 32
Coffee, to Make......... 33
Without Boiling...... 34
Chocolate............ 32
Complexion, the......... 250
Cholera, a Simple Remedy for................. 271
Cholera, this is from a Doctor in Siam, by A. T. Pierson, D.D. 272
Consumption............ 259
Convulsions............. 281
Corks.................. 276
Corns, to cure........... 250
*Cough Syrup, Wild Black Cherry Bark........ 254
Cough Syrups........... 255
Cranberry Sauce......... 221
Crape, to Renew......... 286
Curtains, to Wash Lace.. 287
*Corn, Sweet-boiled....... 116
*To Dry.............. 117
*To Cook Dried Sweet 118
Mock Oysters......... 118
Mrs. Rorer's Dried... 118
Roast Green.......... 118
*Succotash............ 116

Creams, *American...166, 171
Blanc Mange......... 172
Blanc Mange Neopolitan................ 225
Caramel 236
Chocolate Blanc Mange............. 172
Chocolate............ 168
Coffee................ 167
Italian............... 166
Whipped and Fresh Made Jelly......... 172
Peach Meringue...... 171
Lemon Snow......... 166
*Spanish............. 168
Strawberry........... 166
Whipped............. 167
Creeping Charley... ... 292
Croup, a Remedy for..... 260
Of Children......... 261
Crumpets.............. 20
Cut A................. 275
Almond Custard.......... 251
Custard, Baked.......... 169
Boiled............... 169
Cocoanut............. 170
Chocolate 170
Fluff................. 168
Floating Island....... 169
Lemon, Keep Three Days............... 171
Moonshine............
Orange............... 170
Curculio............... 295
Currant Worms.......... 294
Dandelions for Greens.... 125
Diarrhœa, Chronic....... 274
Diphtheria, Salt for....... 267
Sulphur.............. 266
and Scarlet Fever.... 267
Disinfectants............ 270
Dresses, to Starch, Black.. 286
Ear, Wax in the......... 275
Earache................ 289
Eels, Stewed or Fried.... 89
Eggs, Boiled..........102, 103
à la Cream........... 107
Gems................ 107

à la Lavallette	107	German Puff	161
Poached	104	Lemon Puff	161
Omelet	105	Lemon Meringue Puff	161
*Omelet, Bob the Sea Cook's	106	Puffs For Tea	237
Point Shirly Style	105	Glass, To Extract from Hand or Foot	273
*Scrambled	104	Gloves, to Clean Black Kid	285
Egg Plant, to Fry	107	Goods, to Clean Cashmere	286
Eye, Dust in the	275	To Clean Light	285
Eyes, Washes for Inflamed	259	Grape, Mildew	295
Feet and Ankles Swelled	257	Vine Training	299
Relief for Burning	280	Grass Stains on White Goods	285
Felon	287	Gruels, For the Sick	244
Fever, Scarlet	267, 269	Arrow Root	245
Fire, to Smother	275	*Cracker Panada	244
To Guard Against	276	Indian Meal	244
Fish, Baked	80	Milk Porridge	244
Boiled	80	Oat Meal	244
Boiled Cod	86	Ham, Baked	74
Broiled	83	Boiled	73
*Cod Fish Balls	85	Boiled Cold	74
*Creamed Cod	85	Forcemeat	77
Creamed	81	Fried, and Eggs	74
A Supper Dish	83	Pickle for Curing	78
Fried	81	Virginia Cured	75
Steamed	80	Halibut Steak with Hollandaise Sauce	84
Potted Shad or Any Fresh	82	Hints for the Household	280
*Soufflé, to Bake in Shells or Scalloped	82	Hints for the Table	311
Sturgeon	88	Hives, in Children	252
*Turbot à la Cream	81	How to Freeze Creams and Ices	180
Flannels, to Wash White	287	Ice Cream, Very Nice, No. 1	183
Flat Irons	256	No. 2 and No. 3	183
Flies	291	Not so Rich	184
Frogs, Fried	86	Biscuit Glacé	186
Frozen Hands, Ears or Feet	291	Chocolate	185
Fritters, Sweet Corn Oyster	27, 119	Cocoanut	186
French	28	Coffee	186
Japanese	27	Custard, Frozen	184
Plain	26	Lemon	185
Galettes	17	Orange	185
*Gems, Oat Meal	20	Peach	185
*Cream Puffs	162	Pineapple	185
*Custard Soufflé with Cream Sauce	162	Strawberry	184

Tutti Frutti	189	Macaroons, Almond	176
For the Sick	245	Hickory Nut	177
Ices, Water	187	Mackerel, Boiled and	
Cherry	188	Broiled Salt	84
Coffee	188	Mattresses, Making Over	
Currants	188	Hair	246
Grape	188	Measure, Dry and Long	319
Lemon	187	Meats, Baked	47, 48
Orange	188	Boiled	49
*Pineapple	187	Boiled with Robert	
Strawberry	184	Sauce	55
Ice House, to Build an	243	Croquettes	71
Indigestion	259	Measles and Scarlet Fever	265
Insects, Bites and Stings	250	Menus	312, 318
On House Plants	298	Meringue	171, 175
On Roses and Small		Meringue, Golden	176
Fruits	294	Milk, Ropy	247
Carbolic Acid for	295	Moths and Buffalo	291, 292
Jellies	222	Muffins and Gems	19
*Calf's Foot	225	*Corn Meal	19
Cranberry Jam and		Flour	19
*Currant	222	*Graham	19
*Lemon	223	*Oat Meal Gems or	
*Grape, Apple, Peach, Plum, Quince and Strawberry, read under Currant Jelly	222	Raised	20
		Mustard Plaster	273
		Mush, Corn Meal	25
		Fried	26
*Orange No. 1 and No. 2	174, 175	Mushrooms	245
		Mutton and Lamb	59
*Wine	223	A Boiled Leg of	59
To Keep Mould From	319	Needle, To Extract from	
Jugs, To Clean Mouldy	247	Foot or Hand	273
Lamb, Baked, Boiled and		Neuralgia and Toothache	274
Broiled	59, 60	Neuralgia and Headache	274
Chops	60	Nipples, Sore	260
Lady Slippers	299	Oat Meal, Cracked Wheat,	
Laughing Cure	252	Hominy, Rice	26
Lime Water, to Make	274	Onions, Boiled	124
Lobsters	86	Oysters, Baked or	
To Boil and Open a	87	Broiled	91, 92
Turbot	88	*Fried	91
Lockjaw, To Cure	257	*Fritters	91
Long Life, To Insure	248	*Patties	92
Lung Trouble, For All	254	Raw	93
Macaroni, Baked	126	Scalloped	93
Creamed	127	*Stewed	89
a l' Italienne	127	*On Toast	90
Oyster	127	Vegetable or Salsify	124

Parsnips, Boiled or Fried. 121
Pastry, *Puff Paste... 132, 133
   *For Tarts or Patties. 134
   A Crust for Tarts... 134
   Pie Crust............. 135
   Plain Crust........135, 136
Pastry, Crust with Lard.. 135
   A good Plain Crust... 136
Peas, *Green............. 121
Piano.................... 252
Pickles, *Cantaloupe,
   .... Spiced.. 230
   Cucumber............ 228
   *Mango.............. 229
   Tomato, Green....... 231
   Tomato, Sliced....... 232
   Watermelon Rinds... 230
   *Spiced Sweet, and
   .... Peaches ..229, 231
Pie, *Apple.............. 136
   Cherry............... 138
   Cocoanut............. 140
   Cream No. 1.......... 139
   Cream No. 2.......... 139
   Custard.............. 140
   *Huckleberry......... 142
   Lemon No. 1 and 2... 141
   *Lemon No. 3........ 140
   Lemon Tarts......... 142
   *Mince No. 1........ 143
   Mince No. 2.......... 144
   Mince No. 3.......... 145
   Orange............... 141
   *Peach............... 139
   Pieplant or Rhubarb 137
   *Pumpkin............ 137
   *Squash, Hubbard... 138
   Washington.......... 142
Pigeons, Baked........... 62
   Glazed 62
*Pigs Head Cheese....... 78
   *Feet or Souse....... 79
Piles..................... 288
Plants, Worms at roots of 294
   Plants 293
Plum Marmalade......... 217
Poisoning 249
Poisons, Antidote for..... 282
Poison, Oak, Ivy, etc...... 284

Pork..................... 71
   Fried Salt.........73, 234
   Roast Leg of Fresh... 72
   Roast Loin of........ 72
   Steaks and Chops.... 73
   Tenderloin........... 73
   Roast Spare Rib..... 72
Potatoes, Baked.......... 110
   Boiled Plain.......... 108
   Browned with a Roast 113
   Croquettes........... 115
   Creamed or Hashed 109 114
   Curled............... 111
   Mashed.............. 110
   New à la Cream...... 114
   Plain Fried........... 110
   French Fried......... 112
   Lyonnaise No. 1...... 113
   Lyonnaise No. 2...... 113
   Puffs Parisienne...... 112
Potato Puffs............. 113
Potatoes à la Royal......, 112
Potato Salad............. 115
   Scalloped............ 111
   Saratoga Chips....... 114
   Baked Sweet......... 115
   Fried Sweet.......... 116
   *Steamed Sweet...... 115
   Cooked over Sweet... 116
Powder, Baking.......... 236
Prunes, Stewed........... 221
Puddings................. 145
   Apple Snow Balls.... 156
   *Apple, Tapioca or
     Sago.............. 155
   *Batter, Baked....146, 153
   Boiled or Steamed
     Batter..........147, 165
   Bread and Sauce..... 151
   Chocolate............ 158
   *Cocoanut and Corn
     Starch............ 160
   Cocoanut and Rice.... 160
   *Cup Cake and
     Sauce..........153, 154
   Custard Soufflé...162, 163
   *Corn Meal, Baked... 155
   Corn, Sweet.......... 150
   Easter............... 158

Frozen—Sauce No. 4	159	Salad, *Cabbage	
Graham, Steamed	150	*Chicken, No. 2	101
Graham, More Simple	150	Crab, Fish or Shrimps	98
*Indian, Baked	152	Boiled Dressing	94
Indian, Boiled	151	Egg and Cream Dressing	102, 132
*Lemon No. 1	151	Fruit	99
Lemon No. 2	152	*Lobster, No. 1	96
Peach Balls	157	Tomato	232
*Plum—English—Genuine	148	Lobster, No. 2	97
English Plum	149	Dressing	96, 97, 99
Poor Man's	160	Salsify, Fried and Parsnips	124
Puff	165	Sandwiches, Chicken	100
Snow, No. 1 and No. 2	155, 156	Ham	101
A Plain Steamed	149	Lamb	100
*Steamed, Delicious	156	Tongue	100
Rice, Plain Boiled	159	Veal	100
*Rice, Ground	153	Sauce, Hollandaise, for Salads	94
Rice	146, 159	Drawn Butter	93
*A Delicate Baked Rice	146	Mayonnaise	94, 95, 98
*Tapioca	154	Tartar	99
Puffs, Breakfast No. 1..22,	235	Sauces, Stock for Sauces and Gravies	129
Breakfast No. 2...161,	162	Anchovy	129
Pressing Leaves and Flowers	293	Apple	130
Punkies, to Rid a House of	291	A Plain	132
Quinces, *Baked	227	Bernaise	130
Rats and Mice	297	Brown	130
Rattlesnake Poison, Cure for	251	Caper	130
Rhubarb Syrup for Infants	255	Celery	131
Rheumatism	287	Cranberry	131
Rods, to Clean Stair	259	Currant Jell	131
Roaches and Water Bugs	291	Lobster	131
Roses, Wall	293	Matre d'Hotel	129
Rolls, French Breakfast	15	Sauces for Puddings	163
Parker House	15	A Plain Pudding	164
Rusks	17, 235	*Bath Lemon	164
Russe, *Charlotte	224	Cream	164
Sally Lunn, Raised	18	*Creamy	163
Sally Lunn, Baking Powder	18	Creamy without Cream	165
Salmon, Canned	82	*Fairy or Nun's Butter	164
Creamed	82	*Foaming	163
Pickled	88	*Lemon	165, 176
		Orange	177
		Strawberry	164

Sauerkraut	126
Sciatic and Neuralgic Pains	270
Sherbets, Cocoanut	179
Orange	179
Lemon	180
*Peach	178
*Pineapple	179
Silver and Metals, Cleaning of	300
Smelts, Fried	89
Small Pox, Remedy for	263
Soups	34 to 37
*Croutons for	37
Browning for	37
Caramel, to Make	37
Asparagus	39
*Bean, Plain	40
Beef, Stock for	34-37
Bouillon	41
Cream of Celery	37
*Chicken	45
*Clam	44
Consommé	41
*Corn, Sweet, Green	39
Dumpling	43
*Haricot (har-a-co)	39
Jenny Lind	44
Julienne	42
*Mutton	43
*Ox Tail	44
*Oyster	45
Pea, Green	38
*Tomato, No. 1, Queen of Soups	38
*Tomato, No. 2, with Stock	38
*Turtle, Perfect Mock	46
Vegetable	43
Vermicelli or Noodle	42
Stomach, Acidity of	258
Stomach Trouble	288
Sty, to Cure	250
Suggestions, a few	301-311
Table Linen, to Wash Colored	286
Tape Worm, to Get Rid of	290
Tar Cordial	291

Tea	29, 30
Tea Kettle, to Clean of Lime	246
Thunder Storm, What to do in a	251
Toast, German	236
Tongue, Boiled and Jellied	61
Toothache or Neuralgia	249, 258
Tomato Sauce	232
Turkey and Chicken, to Dress	63
To Boil or Steam a	66
Dressing, to Make for	64
Giblets, to Prepare	66
*To Roast a	65
Cold Roast	66
Tomatoes, Stewed	120
To Can	121
Raw	121
Turnips, Boiled	120
Typhoid Fever	270
Veal Cutlets	60
Croquettes	235
*Loaf	234
*Patties	235
Roast Leg of	60
Sweet Breads, Baked	245
Sweet Breads, Fried	245
Vegetables, Cooking of	108
Vinegar, Sugar	227
*Waffles	22
Walks, Brick	282
Warts and Corns	249
Wash Lawns or any Color that Fades	285
Washing Fluids, the Best	284
Weights and Measures, Table of	318, 319
Whisky and Tobacco, Only Cure for	284
Wine, Grape — Pure, for the Sick	226
Pure Unfermented	248
Whitewash, Not Rub Off	284
*Yeast, Bottled	11
Old School	14
Potato	15